THE ART OF VERGIL: Image and Symbol in the Aeneid

THE ART OF VERGIL

IMAGE AND SYMBOL IN THE AENEID

BY VIKTOR PÖSCHL

TRANSLATED BY GERDA SELIGSON

ANN ARBOR PAPERBACKS
THE UNIVERSITY OF MICHIGAN PRESS

CONTENTS

INTRODUCTION: THE PROBLEM   1

CHAPTER I: BASIC THEMES

The First Sequence of Scenes (I. 8–296) as Symbolic
Anticipation of the Whole Poem   13

The Storm at Sea and the Allecto Scenes as Initial Symbols of the "Odyssey" and "Iliad" Halves of the *Aeneid*   24

CHAPTER II: THE PRINCIPAL FIGURES

Aeneas   34
Dido   60
Turnus   91

CHAPTER III: ARTISTIC PRINCIPLES

Symbolism of the Sequence of Mood   139
Forms of Sequence of Mood   157

NOTES   175

INDEX   211

THE PROBLEM

In Vergil the symbolic character of poetry is revealed with a clarity previously unknown in the history of Western poetic art. This revelation partly explains the influence he had upon the literature of the Middle Ages and the Renaissance; the European of these periods, inclined instinctively toward symbolic interpretation, was easily attracted by his art.

Just as the *Bucolics* and the *Georgics* are much more significant than the titles might suggest, the *Aeneid* is much more than an epic story. As an interpretation of Roman history and as a portrayal of human life, it is symbolic.

Like all genuine poetry, Vergil's great models, the epics of Homer, are essentially symbolic. Vergil, however, is far more *consciously* symbolic than is Homer. Vergil's word imagery, with its transparent and several deeper levels of reality, and his invention of images in which symbol becomes allegory are alien to Homer. Completely free of symbolism in the sense of an intentional transformation of statement into symbol, Homer is symbolic in spite of himself.

Symbolism and transparency are characteristics of mature artistry, of a late stage in the development of art. They reveal the awareness of form as expression that we identify with "the Classical." This awareness pervades the *Aeneid* to an astonishing extent. Thus, the *Aeneid* and not the *Iliad* is the classical poem *par excellence*. And thus the attempt to illuminate Vergil's art by spotlighting poetic symbolism is justified. Those who are suspicious of the word "symbol" may wish to use another designation. I should be at a loss to find a word better suited to show that artistic forms are not simply vessels for content having separate existence, but are themselves content, indeed, according to Hebbel, the highest content.

Although image *and* sound are the basic poetic symbols, I shall limit myself for the most part to image and shall stress the more hidden manifestations of symbolism. It is not my intention to prepare a complete morphology of the similes and images in the *Aeneid;* rather, I shall investigate to what extent the basic themes of the poem and the fortunes and characters of its leading figures are expressed through imagery, and I shall inquire which artistic principles are involved. Such an inquiry will not only serve to increase our understanding of Vergil, but will clarify several fundamental problems of the art of poetry. The history of the image in poetry at that crucial moment in our cultural development will be outlined, and Vergil's role in the inner history of poetry (a subject which so far has received little if any attention) will perhaps begin to become clear.

There is hardly a sentence in the *Aeneid* without a metaphor, and few scenes are without a simile. And, as the result of the inner law of the epic form created by Homer—of its *Plastik* (to use an often repeated expression of Goethe's)— there is hardly a gesture without concrete significance. The Homeric epic form demands the representation of things, not as they are thought or felt, but as they are heard or seen. The feelings and thoughts of the characters must be deduced from their gestures and utterances. This stylistic tendency of the Ancients, combining productive talent and ease in creating myths and symbols with an ability to look upon the visible as an expression of the invisible, leads to a wealth of forms giving meaning to the externally discernible and shape to the inner experience. Vergil is heir to this tradition; he is also its master. At the same time he is the first representative of an important new development; for with him the internalization of poetry, a process which characterizes the long Greek development, took a considerable step forward. Since then it has never disappeared. The sensation underlying discernible matter shows more clearly through Vergil's poetic language than through that of the Greeks, and the symbolic power of language in its function as metaphor of feeling has gained an entirely new intensity.

In Vergil the realm of the soul is revealed with a tenderness and delicacy of nuance unrivaled either by Homer, the Classical, or the Hellenistic Greeks. It is not that Vergil says more about emotions than the older poets; rather, in his hands, as he follows their stylistic tendency, the inherited form becomes more responsive and meaningful—a more sensitive instrument capable of finer expression. The fullness of Homeric art had been modified but not discarded by subsequent development. In Vergil's poetry it exists, tempered with pictorial and musical elements and suffused with a new sensitivity, giving it the lyricism characteristic of Western poetry ever since. He added depth of feeling and symbolic significance to Homer's direct observations and literal meanings.

In Vergil's poetry everything participates in the inner drama and reflects the poet's awareness of the stirrings within the souls of his characters and of the destiny inherent in the events. Everything—landscape, morning, evening, night, dress and arms, every gesture, movement, and image becomes a symbol of the soul. The cadence of each line radiates an inner light and shimmers with nuances of feeling. Surely, no one with a knowledge of the essentials of poetry can fail to recognize what progress and enlargement of scope this represents. It is easily seen how much of what was inexpressible before is now within the range of expression and how great a debt later poets owe Vergil. In this light it seems more than foolish to doubt Vergil's "originality." Such doubt arises from a profound misunderstanding of Vergil's poetry and of artistic creativity in general. The sovereign indifference to originality of content and theme which had led the Greeks to place emphasis on originality of form and nuance (with a new nuance always meaning a new soul made visible) shows a deep-rooted instinct for the essence of art.

Recent interpreters have recognized what probably has always been felt—sensitization (*Durchseelung*) of form is a basic phenomenon of Vergil's art. Still, exact observation of detail has not yet been undertaken—at least not with the *Aeneid*. Now, exact observation is one of the most important and difficult tasks placed before the critic of Vergil. It calls for the description of artistic facts whose meaning cannot, truly speaking, be intellectually stated, but can be only suggested for intuitive understanding. The one who sets himself the goal of discovering the significance of poetic shapes and forms will always enter a realm where important phenomena defy reason.

Literary interpretation shares this problem with interpretation of all the arts and with those sciences which deal with manifestations of the soul and life. It must rely, therefore, on intuitive as well as rational understanding. Still, it would be a grave mistake to exclude poetry from the subjects open to scientific investigation. We must realize that we can become aware of the peculiar content of poetry only by concentrated observation of its forms. A poem, like any other product of art, is by itself only a fragment, a floating offer, a text without tune to be made whole by a reciprocating receiver. As Goethe says, only he who knows how to "supply" (*supplieren*) may understand it. The critic must possess the ability (described by Walter Pater as the *sine qua non* of art criticism) of being deeply moved by beautiful things. His is the task of attuning the inner ear and the inner eye to the soft voice which poetry gives to the seemingly ineffable. If he cannot do this then he has no access to the essence of poetry.

As for Vergil and the Ancients, the critical observer finds formidable obstacles at every turn in the road to understanding. These obstacles are, to be frank, the "schooldust of the ages," accumulations of error made by a philology blind to everything artistic, the sediment of a rationalism estranged from art and life. This dust has settled on the shining, tender beauty of Vergil's poetry and must be removed before its pure splendor and moving magic can be appreciated.

Unfortunately, rationalism is still with us and indeed may stay forever. After all, it is an integral part of philology and of other disciplines and their representatives—even, as some philosophers believe, of the very nature of the intellect. "Whether," says Bergson, "it is a question of dealing with the life of the body or that of the mind, the intellect proceeds with the sharpness, the rigidity, and the brutality of a tool not designed for such use. . . . Intellect exhibits a congenital lack of comprehension for life" (*L'Évolution créatrice,* 7th ed.; 1911, p. 179).

We are not surprised, then, to find traces of such uncouth behavior everywhere in Vergilian scholarship. Commentators from Servius on have rarely had eyes and ears for poetry, and, stubbornly unaware that an appeal to ancient poetics and rhetoric is not always a recommendation, have dragged up a heavy arsenal of concepts derived from antique methods of interpretation. Ancient theory lagged considerably behind ancient art, so much so that Benedetto Croce categorically denied theoretical understanding of aesthetics in antiquity and began its history with Vico.[1] Both the ancient interpreters and their modern counterparts approach poetry with the cold gaze of reason and not with the love of the heart. These same interpreters explain linguistic fact, material motive, and their rationally accessible content—but not their form.

Yet art is always primarily concerned with form and especially with individual form. Simply to assign a phenomenon to such a type, category, or trope is to say nothing about its intrinsic artistic value. As Goethe has truly said, "Form is a secret hidden from the many." Even when, as during the last half century, the disciplines of aesthetics and history of art and the interpretation of some modern literatures have laid a foundation for a scientific art criticism,[2] traditional philology shows a complete lack of interest, as strange as it is obstinate, in the most elementary results of this science. Worse, it has the temerity to set itself against the mere concept of aesthetics, viewing it as scientifically and almost morally tainted. And even though no one can come anywhere near to an understanding of a poem without a knowledge of the specific "optics" of art,[3] traditional philology continues to ignore the fact, well known elsewhere, that a work of art calls for a kind of treatment different from a factual report or a scientific treatise. This is true even of Richard Heinze's *Virgils epische Technik*. This book in its own period represented a considerable achievement, but pursued a much too rationalistic direction. The same is true of Eduard Norden's famous commentary on the sixth book of the *Aeneid*. This, too, needs to be supplemented from the viewpoint of aesthetic analysis.[4]

The task outlined for Vergilian scholars by Friedrich Klingner,[5] who achieved revolutionary results with the *Eclogues* and the *Georgics*,[6] is still to be done for the *Aeneid*. It, too, after so much successful research on its language, technique, sources, ideas, and motives, must be regarded from the aesthetic point of view.

The circumstances of World War II prevented me from making a complete survey of the latest Vergilian literature outside of the German-speaking countries. This is all the more regrettable because research in the Romance and Anglo-Saxon countries did not fall into the above-cited aberrations

—at least not to the same extent. They achieved important interpretations, especially of Vergil, even though they, too, were affected by overrationalization and failed, to my knowledge, to produce anything comparable to Sainte-Beuve's masterly *Essay on Vergil.*[7]

As for the method: the most excellent way to an understanding of Vergil is by comparison with Homer, an endeavor to which every single line offers a challenge. Juxtaposing related forms is always the best way to an individual appreciation of creative works. Since the *Odyssey* and the *Iliad* are reincarnated in the *Aeneid* (Donatus, *Life of Vergil:* *"quasi amborum Homeri carminum instar"*), comparison becomes the pivot of criticism, the point from which the principles of Vergil's art will be most visible. The older Vergilian research in the wake of ancient criticism, as recorded by Gellius and Macrobius, recognized the value of this procedure more distinctly than did later research. I refer especially to the very worthwhile chapters in the fifth book of Julius Caesar Scaliger's *Poetics*. In this primer of Renaissance art Vergil's poetry is illuminated in detail through comparison with Homer, Apollonius Rhodius, and Theocritus, and a wealth of lasting insights is collected. Even though one cannot accept his verdict *"pro Vergilio contra Homerum,"* one must still ask his question: "How does Vergil relate to Homer?"

This is the central question for both aesthetic criticism and intellectual history because when one compares Vergil with Homer, one compares not only two art forms but two stages in the history of creative imagination. The strange reenactment of Homer's poetry in the *Aeneid* and its preservation in the structure of a new work of art, which, as its author claims, will endure for time to come,[8] are in themselves phenomena worthy of our consideration. Western poetry from Dante to Hofmannsthal has again and again produced comparable metamorphoses of older works. The great model for them has been the incorporation of Homer into the *Aeneid*. This incorporation is very closely connected with Vergil's consciousness of symbolic form (form as symbol). Only a poet who has deep convictions regarding the metaphoric character of expression and the symbolic value of each human and historic event can be so original when he quotes—only he can perceive the expression of another as the expression of his own experience. But to state this is to highlight one side of the creative process. Only a complete history of consciousness of form in Greek poetry—with particular attention to the Alexandrian period—could show the roots of the Greco-Roman synthesis.

One major concern, however, is genuinely Roman. Vergil's attachment to Homer is akin to Roman reverence for the *auctoritas* of traditional forms—a reverence found elsewhere in Roman life. Just as political acts were evaluated on their congruency with *"auctoritas maiorum,"* so a philosophical or poetic work was judged on how it measured up to the great Greek models. According to the Roman point of view it is possible to create something perfect only by building on to something else which has itself grown slowly in the course of history. One must carry on and repeat past achievements in a new form. Here, indeed, the concept of perfection excludes by definition the concept of originality!

Not surprisingly, therefore, the Romans were the first to fashion the "Classical" concept as one of "standard" and to make it bear fruit in their reaction to the Greek masterworks. But this was not the result of the particular conditions of Roman literature as it developed from translations of the Greek. If it were, this whole most peculiar development would have to be considered an accident. Nor did it, as Heinze maintained, result from a national defect such as lack of imagination. Rather, it exemplifies the peculiar Roman trait of not allowing something once found to be great and true to disappear, but to appeal to it again and again and thus to preserve it. The generations of the Roman people in passing on the political organization of the old *res publica* never ceased rejuvenating it and being shaped by it. In their intellectual life they strove to express themselves in the old Greek forms and to add to them their own Roman content. The political and religious attachment of the Romans to the *mos maiorum* had its counterpart in a spiritual tie to the Greek form. The same self-control and disciplined resignation was important to both. It was an attitude conducive to combining the healthy roots of Roman agrarian society and the most sublime fruits of the Greek mind—a most fortunate Roman characteristic to which we owe the existence of our Western culture. But while in the political and religious realm the *exempla maiorum* had shaped Roman life since its beginnings, the creation of Greek form was the result of a long process which led Roman writing from the unsteady experiments of Livius Andronicus to the Augustan heights. Greek form could be borne adequately only when the people had become ready. Only in the era of Augustus was a balance struck between Greek form and Roman content—the balance on which the new Classical art of the Augustans rested. The crowning achievement of the Roman epic was made possible when for the first time, Homer, the representative of Greek art and humanity, was absorbed by an equal. (A similar statement could be made for Roman lyric poetry.) Vergil, besides having a theme of national importance (as did Naevius and Ennius), was Homer's peer in artistic greatness and emotional insight, discrimination, and passion. Without hesitation, therefore, he could meet Homer with complete intimacy in spite of the gap between the ages. Add to this the felicity of the hour; between a century of Roman revolution and the peace of the imperial era, it was the fertile historical moment that Hippolyte Taine so expertly describes in his *Italian Journey* ("Florence and Venice," bk. VI, ch. 1): "Always and everywhere, what inspires works of art is a certain complex and mixed state of things in the soul placed between two orders of sentiments: it is about to forsake a love of the grand for a love of the agreeable; but in passing from one to the other it has something of both. One has to possess a taste for grandeur, that is, for noble forms and vigorous passions, without which works of art would only be pretty. And one must have a taste for the agreeable, that is, a craving for pleasure and an interest in the decorative, without which the mind would concern itself with actions only and never delight in works of art. Hence the transient and precious flower only blooms at the confluence of two epochs, between heroic and epicurean habits, at the moment when man, completing some long and painful war, or foundation, or discovery, begins to rest and look about him, meditating on the pleasure of decorating his great bare tenement for which his own hands have laid the foundations and erected the walls. Before this, it would have been too soon, since absorbed with labor he could not think of enjoyment, and a little while after it would be too late, as, dreaming of enjoyment only, he no longer thinks of exerting himself. Between the two is the unique moment, long or short, according as the transformation is more or less prompt, in which men, still strong, impetuous, and capable of sublime emotion and bold enterprise, suffer the tension of their wills to relax in order to enliven the senses and intellect magnificently."

We see Vergil enabled after a flight of centuries to save not only Homer's form but something too of his spirit, which is inseparable from form. He stood before Homer's poetry and was deeply moved just as Aeneas was when he stood before the reliefs in the temple of Juno in Carthage and saw illustrated there the tragic events of the Trojan War: *mentem mortalia tangunt*. On the other hand, through the might of the Greek form, which he appropriated and fused with elements of old Roman poetry and the great inspiration of his art, Vergil gave a new power to the Latin language—the *anima Vergiliana* that has since been a part of it. He instilled a vigor in the Augustan *humanitas* that is not extinguished even now, and which in fact, holds fresh possibilities of a renewed acquaintance. The continued strength of Vergil's influence and glory (which Dante predicted would last forever) vindicates the fundamental Roman belief that what can last must be based on proven and permanent elements. Thus, the synthesis of Greek and Roman cultures of which the *Aeneid* is both fruit and symbol, the Christian culture which developed therefrom, the continuity of the Western world, and the unity of the "Hellenocentric circle" (Werner Jaeger) all grew from the same roots as the Roman *res publica* and the Roman Empire, namely from the Roman will for duration and the special way in which that will is manifested.

For men imbued with this Roman attitude as it subsequently consolidated into the medieval Christian order and the feeling for tradition and form in the Romance tongues, Vergil was the unsurpassed personification of poetry. On the other hand, to the ever-striving modern—and especially to the German mind—he seemed increasingly strange and empty as did the Roman and Christian ways of life. The Romance scholar, Ernst Robert Curtius, a great pathfinder for a Western culture, to whom we are indebted for one of the most charming contributions to Vergil's second millennial celebration,[9] wrote in 1924: "A young German who loves Vergil is an interesting specimen, an aesthetic individualist, not to say an eccentric. The Faustian yearning of the German mind for things Greek blinds it to this purest manifestation of Latinity. Vergil's sovereignty is unchallenged from the Ionian Sea to the shores of Caledonia, but it is unsteady and doubtful beyond the *limes*." [10] Today the time has come for a change and an attempt to conquer this old prejudice against Vergil. The discussion of whether Homer or Vergil is greater is, of course, idle. Our task is to attain a point of view above that of the Romance scholar, who still holds out the palm of victory to Vergil, and of the German to whom such a decision is utterly incomprehensible and who can only laugh at the *"nescio quid maius nascitur Iliade."*

There is more at stake here than just the question of Vergil; it concerns the foundations of Western civilization. We are seeking ties of communication to bind us together.[11] We must, therefore, re-establish a firm place for the *Aeneid* in our cultural consciousness as one of the bibles of the Western world.

BASIC THEMES

THE FIRST SEQUENCE OF SCENES (I.8–296) AS
SYMBOLIC ANTICIPATION OF THE WHOLE POEM

The first climactic point in the *Aeneid*—the event that sets
the tone, arousing and preparing the reader's mind for the
extraordinary actions about to take place—is the storm which
drives Aeneas to the shores of Carthage. Its introductory
position in the poem indicates that it is more than just another episode in the destiny of the homeless Trojans. The
pulsating breath of tragedy and the atmosphere of wild pathos
embody with the greatest compression the nature of the emotion which permeates the whole poem. It is, as it were, the
"musical" motif that from the start marks the events with
passionate grandeur and the demonic power of fate.[1] Only
the image of the strongest, wildest movement in Nature—
which had, of course, been transmitted through Homer, where
it was first raised to the level of art—seemed to Vergil sufficiently grave and imposing for the opening of his Roman epic.

This kind of beginning was not borrowed from the
Odyssey, certainly, for that epic opens much more peacefully.
If there is any parallel in Homer, it is in the plague which
opens the *Iliad*. Indeed, the entire *Aeneid* in its dramatic
impetus is more to be compared with the *Iliad* than with the
Odyssey. But even in the *Iliad* Homer swiftly progresses to

the quarrel between Achilles and Agamemnon as the starting point of the real action, without utilizing the mood established by the plague motif. As for Apollonius Rhodius of Hellenistic times, who in the casual manner of a storyteller began his epic with an almost comical anecdote—the oracle of the man with one shoe—he achieves nothing of the *Aeneid*'s symbolic power. Contrary to common assumption, he is much farther from Vergil's artistic conception than is Homer.

The scene sequence dominated by the storm at sea (I.8–296) anticipates the whole poem in thought as well as mood. It is the prelude of the work, announcing the basic motifs after the manner of an overture.[2] Let us examine it.

As for the motif of Juno's hatred, the poet, after the proem, expounds upon her counterplan for Carthage's control of the world. The opposition of the two world powers is announced immediately upon the introduction of Rome's historic rival: *Carthago Italiam contra* (I.23), in which *"contra"* is meant much more symbolically than geographically. With a slight change it returns in Dido's curse:

> Let your shores oppose their shores, your waves their waves, your arms their arms. That is my imprecation.

IV.628:
> Litora litoribus contraria, fluctibus undas
> Imprecor, arma armis, pugnent ipsique nepotesque . .

Thus, the contest between Rome and Carthage for world dominion appears as a main theme from the very beginning, and Juno's stubborn fight against the hero's *fata* symbolically anticipates it, as do the battles in the last half of the poem—as stated in Jupiter's speech (X.11).

This historically decisive contest is itself only a representative symbol of all the hard wars in Roman history. The last half of the poem is symbolic also of the Italo-Roman struggle and the civil wars. Moreover, it contains a searching examination of the nature and uncanny duality of politics; the image of the dark demon of passion in Turnus confronts the shining spiritual and moral power in Aeneas. Roman history is presented as a struggle between two principles, and Rome's victory is seen as the victory of the higher one. Thus, the first and the last halves of the *Aeneid* are symbolic in different ways. (Here I remind the reader how important to our subject it is to realize that a symbol by its very nature admits of —and demands—more than one interpretation. The essence of a symbolic relation is that the correspondence between the symbol and the thing symbolized is not precise, but flexible, opening up an infinite perspective.)

In a letter to Schiller (August 17, 1797) Goethe [3] wrote: "Symbolic objects are outstanding cases representing in their variety many others. They are characterized by a certain inclusiveness; they demand a certain sequence. They evoke in my mind pertinent and similar as well as foreign ideas. Consequently, from within as well as from without, they claim a certain oneness and universality." And in *Maximen und Reflexionen:* [3a] "The symbol transforms the visible into an idea and the idea into an image in such manner that the idea in the image stays infinitely potent and unattainable, remaining unutterable even if spoken of in all languages." Similarly, in his *Tagebücher* (ed. Bamberger, I, p. 236), Hebbel says: "Every genuine work of art is a mysterious symbol with many meanings, to a certain degree incomprehensible." Juno, then, is first the mythical personification of the historical power of Carthage, and in this role she causes the storm at sea and the shipwrecked landing on Carthaginian soil. It is most significant that her passionate hatred really stems from love. The *Aeneid* has been called the "epic of grief." It could as well be called the "epic of love," for its deepest tragedy is that its people "loved too much." This is true of Euryalus, of whom the poet says (IX.430): *"Infelicem nimium dilexit amicum";* [4] it is just as true of Juno, Venus, Turnus, Dido, and Latinus (XII.29: *Victus amore tui ... vincla omnia rupi*), and of Amata, Laocoön, and Evander. Love is the motivating force in all that Aeneas does. Even the fall of the monster Mezentius is transfigured by grief over the death of his son Lausus in what is basically a suicide for love.

On the human level Aeneas, as the personification of things Roman, meets this very real blow of fate with the firm resolve to strive on through all dangers (I.204 ff.), while on the divine level Jupiter reveals the solution of the conflict to Venus:

> She (Juno) will change her plans for the better and together with me she will protect the Romans, the masters of the world, the people in the toga ...

I.281:

> Consilia in melius referet mecumque fovebit
> Romanos rerum dominos gentemque togatam.

As the action is in the highest sense carried out between Jupiter and Juno, the first unit of the *Aeneid* is framed by the appearances of the two major divinities. The composition is expression of a fact, the balance of scenes is image and symbol of an equivalence of forces. Human action is embedded in divine action, not only as an artistic means but also as a statement of fact. To understand this is to hold one of the keys to the secret of classical composition. Besides being subject to the autonomous law of beauty, the form is founded on the subject itself, which through its organization in clear antitheses appears in its very essence. "Formal perfection is just another aspect of mental penetration" (Ernst Robert Curtius).

The contrast between Jupiter's quiet serenity (I.255) and Juno's angry passion underscores the inner tension of the poem. The passion-consumed goddess is confronted by Vergil's sublime Jupiter, the majestic master of the world, en-

throned above suffering and passion.[5] This aspect of highest
divinity becomes even more evident in the verses preceding
Jupiter's decision in the quarrel between the two goddesses:

> But then the Father Almighty, who holds first authority over
> the world, began to speak; and as he spoke, the gods' high
> hall fell silent, the earth deep down was set trembling, the
> steep sky was soundless, and then too the west winds sank
> and the ocean hushed its surface.

X.100:
> Tum pater omnipotens, rerum cui prima potestas,
> Infit, eo dicente deum domus alta silescit
> Et tremefacta solo tellus, silet arduus aether,
> Tum Zephyri posuere, premit placida aequora pontus.

Heaven and earth, the winds, and the sea are silent; the wild
forces of nature, all elements bow to him.[6] Compared to the
other gods he represents not only a higher power but a higher
level of existence. And in this he differs from the Homeric
Zeus. Zeus is stronger than the other gods, Jupiter more sublime.[7] We do not see Jupiter shaking the universe with his
scowl as Zeus does, but as imposing reverence on it. (Only
at the close of the scene is the famous verse from the *Iliad*
imitated: X.115; also IX.106.)

In Jupiter is most clearly manifest the divine power that
binds the demonic forces and the basic strength of Latinity,
serenitas—which includes in one untranslatable word, mental
clarity, cheerfulness of soul, and the light of the southern
sky. From the image of the Vergilian Jupiter the concept of
serenitas has remained alive in the intellectual history of the
successor states of the Roman Empire into our own time; for
example, in the words with which Romain Rolland late in
life described the human task: *"la liberté de l'esprit qui
sereine l'anarchie chaotique du coeur."*

Vergil's Jupiter is the symbol of what Rome as an idea

embodied. While Juno as the divine symbol of the demonic forces of violence and destruction does not hesitate to call up the spirits of the nether world: *"Flectere si nequeo superos, Acheronta movebo,"* Jupiter is the organizing power that restrains those forces. Thus, on a deeper level, the contrast between the two highest divinities is symbolic of the ambivalence in history and human nature. It is a symbol, too, of the struggle between light and darkness, mind and emotion, order and chaos, which incessantly pervades the cosmos, the soul, and politics. A spiritual path leads from this level of contrast directly to the historical concepts of the Christian Middle Ages as stated by St. Augustine.

The struggle and final victory of order—this subduing of the demonic which is the basic theme of the poem, appears and reappears in many variations. The demonic appears in history as civil or foreign war, in the soul as passion, and in nature as death and destruction. Jupiter, Aeneas, and Augustus are its conquerors, while Juno, Dido, Turnus, and Antony are its conquered representatives. The contrast between Jupiter's powerful composure and Juno's confused passion reappears in the contrast between Aeneas and Dido and between Aeneas and Turnus. The Roman god, the Roman hero, and the Roman emperor are incarnations of the same idea.

Therefore, as the result of inner necessity, Jupiter, in the concluding speech of the initial sequence of scenes, announces that the idea of Augustus' *pax Romana* rests upon the conquest of *furor impius.* At this strongly emphatic place the basic idea of the whole poem becomes visible in a symbolic picture:

> And the terrible iron-constricted Gates of War shall shut; and safe within them shall stay the godless and ghastly Lust of Blood, propped on his pitiless piled armoury, and still roaring from gory mouth, but held fast by a hundred chains of bronze knotted behind his back.

I.294:

> Claudentur Belli portae. Furor impius intus
> Saeva sedens super arma et centum vinctus aenis
> Post tergum nodis fremet horridus ore cruento.

This is the best example in the *Aeneid* of a symbol which condenses a historic event into a single image.[8] This image, still trembling with the bloody events of the civil wars, climaxes and ends the speech of the god, thus channeling the wild motions of human life into the quiet order of the divine *fata*. After the *"altae moenia Romae"* which significantly concludes the proem and the *"tantae molis erat Romanam condere gentem"* which ends the section beginning with *"musa mihi causas memora,"* a view opens for the third time on the real object of the poem—the destiny of Rome. Moreover, the symbolic meaning of Roman history reveals itself here as a divinely inspired order—the result of hard fighting and bitter suffering.

Jupiter and Juno surround the storm at sea and into this larger frame is fitted the smaller one of Aeolus and Neptune. The contrast between Aeolus' ominous calm and Neptune's buoyant ocean voyage corresponds to that of Juno's uncontrolled temper and Jupiter's serenity. The wind-king reins his wild forces with the hand of a Roman master—a gesture without parallel in Homer:

> But Aeolus, the king who rules them, confines them in their prison, disciplined and curbed. They race from door to bolted door, and all the mountain reverberates with the noise of their resentment. But Aeolus, throned securely above them, sceptre in hand tempers their arrogance and controls their fury.

I.52:

> Hic vasto rex Aeolus antro
> Luctantis ventos tempestatesque sonoras
> Imperio premit ac vinclis et carcere frenat.
> Illi indignantes magno cum murmure montis

> Circum claustra fremunt, celsa sedet Aeolus arce
> Sceptra tenens mollitque animos et temperat iras.

Here, political history may be sensed in the nature myth. The relation of Aeolus' mastery of the winds to Augustus' conquest of *furor impius* is easily seen. And it becomes even clearer in the Neptune scene.

The sea god, great Neptune, both in his actions and appearance of contained power, in allaying the raging storm is like Jupiter, a contradiction of brute force.[9] Moreover, the taming itself, in a simile emphasized by being the first in the poem and not taken from Homer, is compared to a political act:

> It had been like a sudden riot in some great assembly, when, as they will, the meaner folk forget themselves and grow violent, so that firebrands and stones are soon flying, for savage passion quickly finds weapons. But then they may chance to see some man whose character and record command their respect. If so, they will wait in silence, listening keenly. He will speak to them, calming their passions and guiding their energies. So, now, all the uproar of the ocean subsided.

I.148:
> Ac veluti magno in populo cum saepe coorta est
> Seditio saevitque animis ignobile volgus
> Iamque faces et saxa volant, furor arma ministrat,
> Tum pietate gravem ac meritis si forte virum quem
> Conspexere, silent arrectisque auribus adstant,
> Ille regit dictis animos et pectora mulcet:
> Sic cunctus pelagi cecidit fragor.

The above has been interpreted as alluding to a political event of the year 54 B.C., when in a similar manner Cato calmed the raging populace (Plutarch *Cato Minor*).[9a] Such an allusion is not impossible. The republican Cato was the ideal Roman in Vergil's eyes and appears as such on Aeneas' shield in contrast to Catiline, who is shown doing penance for his crime (VIII.670).

Sallust had already idealized Cato by introducing him in his *Coniuratio Catilinae* as the incarnation of the principles of Roman grandeur [10] and probably had conceived of the Cato-Catiline contrast as a simile of the conflict (seen in the *Aeneid*) between Octavian and Antony. There is also an ideal image of Cato in Horace's Roman ode, *Iustum et tenacem propositi virum*. The heralds of the Augustan renaissance, Sallust and Cicero (especially in his lost *Cato*), and the poets of the renaissance, Vergil and Horace, each in his own way pays homage to the most uncompromising representative of the Roman mind and attitude. For the Augustan Age, too, Cato embodied the ideal of a true Roman—which is indicative of the spirit of reconciliation toward Caesar's opponents and of the seriousness of the intent to restore the Republic.

However, for the very reason that I am willing to accept the possibility of a connection between an event in the political career of Cato Uticensis [11] and the first simile of the *Aeneid*, I must emphatically declare that it means very little. Even to Sallust, disciple of Thucydides, Cato was no more than an ideal type of Roman statesman, just as the conspiracy of Catiline was no more than a symptom of Rome's decay. The poet's mind, then, is not intent upon Cato nor on any historical individual, but definitely on the *idea* that the individual personifies—in this case, the idea of the statesman whose authority dominates the crowd. He gives to the idea the form of a poetic symbol—of transfigured reality.

The champions of the allegorical interpretation of the *Aeneid* obscure the fact that equations purporting to balance historic and poetic personalities are not only unverifiable but are a priori false—at least as postulated. The mistake is in confusing symbol and *Allegorie:* a symbol may exist even without reference to what takes shape within it, while the

Allegorie [12] exists only through that reference. The symbol permits, even demands, more than one interpretation, the *Allegorie* allows only one.[13] The nobility and style of the *Aeneid* exclude the *Allegorie* that can be completely unlocked with a political or historical key. To resolve the heroic epic into *Allegorie,* then, is to misunderstand both its validity as an ideal and its artistic character. Its scenes may from time to time recall or point symbolically to real events and persons, as with Cato or the monster Cacus (VIII.185 ff.), whose actions, as Conway believes, perhaps unveil the atrocities of Antony's proscriptions.

The true relation between these scenes and historic fact is more mysterious and less simple. The metamorphosis takes place on a higher plane.[14] Historic events and the poet's inner experience are stripped of everything accidental and actual. They are removed from time and transported into the large and distant land of Myth. There, on a higher plane of life, they are developed in symbolic and poetic shapes having a right to an existence of their own. The fact, therefore, that the subjection of the storm is described in a simile for a moment highlighting a very important sphere of the poem (namely that of the historical world) is more decisive than a possible allusion to the younger Cato. In the *princeps rei publicae,* where Cato calms the riotous populace, we meet political reality in a situation representing the defeated antithesis of Augustan order. Then, the historical background of the mythical events becomes momentarily visible.

The idea of regulation is expressed five times in the first sequences of scenes in the *Aeneid:* where Aeolus holds the winds in subjection, where Neptune calms them, in Aeneas' reaction to fortune's blow, where Augustus chains *Furor impius* in Jupiter's prophecy, and finally in the power of the god himself, who firmly controls the *fata.* To find no more than commonplace Roman metaphors in the Roman gesture of Aeolus and in the simile of Neptune and the *princeps rei publicae* is to destroy the poem's unity of form and content as well as to fail to understand that it has a deeper unity than is commonly assumed. In the Neptune episode, for example, a natural event explained by means of a political event serves to show that nature is a symbol of political organization. The connecting simile becomes an expression of the symbolic relation between nature and politics, myth and history, which is at the heart of the *Aeneid*. As in the *Georgics* the relation between the two orders is not only a matter of poetical metaphors but of ontological realities. Jupiter, the master of the world, controls them both. Their unity finds its most sublime expression in the religious and philosophic revelation in the sixth book.

It is more, then, than hyperbolic expression that Augustus sets the limits of empire with the ocean and those of his glory with the stars. Cosmic infinity is united with the majesty of *imperium Romanum*. The conviction that Roman order is founded in the same divine whole from which it derives its grandeur [15] is important to the Augustan view of the world. It is also basic to the interpretation of the Roman *res publica* in Cicero's *de Republica*. Vergil adheres to Cicero's philosophical views. He accepts the Platonic idea of the unity of Cosmos and Politeia from which came the Ciceronian idea of the unity of world order and true *res Romana*. He combined this with the Homeric belief that the unity of nature is incorporated in the human world. He thus created a new synthesis—the Augustan idea of Rome.

Even where it involves natural phenomena, the myth of Aeneas is a metaphor of Roman history and its Augustan fulfillment. But it does not stop there. The *Aeneid* is a poem of humanity, not a political manifesto. In it, myth and history acquire meaning and grandeur as expression of a higher level, the realization of a divine order, the symbol of the cosmic law of destiny revealed in the existence of the world of man. There are three levels of reality: (1) Cosmos, the sphere of divine order, the world of ideas and law; (2) Myth, the heroic world of poetic persons and destiny; (3) History, the world of historical and political phenomena. These are inlaid, one with another, and at the same time they are stratified. Myth, as the poetic intersymbol, partakes of both the upper and lower strata. In one direction it incorporates Roman history, and in the other, the eternally valid laws of the universe. Likewise, the tragedy in the *Aeneid* is a symbol not only of the tragedy in Roman history, but in human life as well. Indeed, it is a symbol of the tragedy in all nature and is found in its most sublime expression in the *Georgics*.[16] Alone, neither of these interpretations would do justice to the poetic depth of the *Aeneid*. Vergil's epic must always be approached with both references, cosmic and Roman, human and historical, in mind. Each is justified and necessary, but only together do they make possible an understanding of the whole.

Here, then, is our result: the initial sequences of scenes in the *Aeneid* contain in essence all forces which constitute the whole. The opening storm is a wave breaking against Roman destiny. Many waves will follow and Augustus will subdue them all, thus limiting the *Imperium* with the ocean and its glory with the stars. The demand made by Goethe upon the drama, that each scene must symbolically represent the whole, is fulfilled in the exposition of the Vergilian epic in an ideal manner.

THE STORM AT SEA (I.8–296)
AND THE ALLECTO SCENES (VII.286–640)
AS INITIAL SYMBOLS OF THE "ODYSSEY"
AND "ILIAD" HALVES OF THE *AENEID*

In the two parts of the *Aeneid,* the *Odyssey* and the *Iliad* are fused to create a higher unity. As early in the work as the proem, a reference to the recreation of the *Odyssey* is made: *"Multum ille terris iactatus et alto,"* while *"multa quoque et bello passus"* refers to the *Iliad*. Possibly, as Servius believed, *arma* in the very first line refers to the *Iliad* and *virumque* to the *Odyssey*. The storm sequence (I.8–296) is significant, therefore, not only as an introduction to the whole but as the first great trial of Aeneas. It is the frontispiece, as it were, of the "Odyssey" half of the poem. The storm is followed by further trials: the Odysseus-like wanderings of Aeneas (III), his Dido adventure (IV), the *Iliupersis* (II) and the games (V). (The *Iliupersis* probably stems from the Trojan War memoirs in the *Odyssey,* especially as contained in Nestor's and Menelaos' speeches in the *Telemachy* and Demodokos' song of the destruction of Troy.)

The storm at sea, the first motif from the *Odyssey,* and the other Homeric passages in the first book adhere more closely to the model than do those of the following books. This fact has been already recognized by Sainte-Beuve in *Étude sur Virgile* (2d ed., p. 107): "This first eclogue, I mean the first chronologically, is scattered with Theocritus' most graceful images, just as the first book of the Aeneid is decked with Homer's most famous and conspicuous similes. He (Vergil) displays and presents them at the beginning and in the most obvious places. Far from being embarrassed by this, he takes pride in it."

Moreover, in the first book it is not a question of appropriating individual motifs and using them in situations of different character, but rather of transposing situations of vital significance to the story. The following come from the *Odyssey:* the hostile divinity's planning of the catastrophe, the catastrophe itself, the hero's monologue of despair, the "Phorcys harbor," the exhortation *O socii* (I.198), Aeneas' encounter with Venus—transposed from that of Odysseus with Athena in Ithaca, invisible Aeneas' walk through Carthage—Odysseus' unseen arrival in the Phaeacian city, the meeting with Dido—the Nausicaa simile, Aeneas' appearance before Dido in the goddess-given guise of a dazzlingly beautiful godlike stranger, the conversation between Jupiter and Venus—after that of Zeus and Athene in the first book—and the *cantus firmus* of Jupiter's speech—the theme of the poem.

The idea of giving the whole poem a higher meaning at the very beginning of the divine father's speech comes from the *Odyssey,* where Zeus, in referring to Orestes' destiny, points to the murder of the suitors as the climax of the story and establishes punishment of guilty mortals as the primary theme. Although Vergil in Aeneas' first two speeches (I.94 and I.198) consciously emphasizes his debt to Homer through verbatim appropriation of the beginning words (I.94/*Ody.* 5.306; I.198/*Ody.* 12.208), he subsequently develops his theme independently, going beyond Homer. Likewise, the drama of the Carthaginian queen begins with Homer's Nausicaa simile, but develops in the *Aeneid* into the tragedy of Dido—not another Nausicaa episode. The scene sequence at the beginning of the poem is simultaneously an indication of Vergil's deep respect for Homer and an example of his competition with him. The more openly he attests his dependence upon Homer, the more ambitiously he strives to surpass him in the perfection of the form and the interpretation and connection of motifs. For this reason the first book offers the most favorable conditions for comparing the two poets and for understanding Vergil's artistic principles.[17]

In contrast, the Odyssean motifs in the remaining books are handled much more independently. As concerns the *Iliupersis* (II), this is well known. In the Wanderings (III), where a close conformity to Homer might certainly be expected, Vergil is more concerned with the melancholy echoes of the past (Polydorus, Helenus, Andromache) and the gradual revelation of the future than with the adventures themselves. The main interest is not in the physical terrors of the journey, but rather in Aeneas' deepening spiritual sorrow as more and more he realizes the importance and greatness of his mission. Echoes of the *Odyssey* are scarce. The theme of feminine attraction, only hinted at in Homer's Calypso, Circe, and Nausicaa, is elevated into tragedy in the figure of the deserted woman, Dido, and Aeneas' concomitant trial (IV). The games differ widely from those of Homer in the manner of the contests (V). Finally, Aeneas' journey to the underworld is much more than just one adventure among many. Like the encounter with Dido, it has become a trial of the hero, a test of his *pietas,* and a revelation of the symbolic meaning of the whole poem (VI). Surpassing Jupiter's speech in the first book, this contains the most comprehensive interpretation of the poem. Here the connection of the legend with the two spheres of which the poetical partakes—Universal order and the Roman order of the world—is most patently visible. In the mythical form of a visit to the underworld from where it is singularly possible to observe the world and its otherwise mysterious machinations from a distance,[18] Aeneas realizes the connection of mortal life with world order and that of his own destiny with the history of Rome. Again, the existence of a firm relation between divine and Roman order is shown. The former is announced by Phlegyas: *"Discite iustitiam moniti et non temnere divos,"* and the latter is revealed by Anchises at the end of the book: *"Tu regere imperio populos Romane memento."* Justice is the foundation of both and is also the first principle of the Platonic-Ciceronian concept of *res Romana.* It is brought about in the underworld as in ours through the subjugation of demonic forces, great criminals, and lawbreakers.

Violators of world order—those who rebel against the rule of Jupiter (VI.583 ff.)—are confined behind a triple wall in Tartarus to pay forever for their crimes. There, too, are the instigators of ruthless war (*"qui arma secuti impia"*: VI.612 f.). The inner connection of motifs is betrayed in the affinity of the triple wall (VI.548 ff.) with the mountain of winds and that of the gate of Tartarus with the gate of Janus. In the "Roman" Tartarus on Aeneas' shield, Catiline, chained to the rock, represents the enemies of the Roman state (VIII.668 ff.—This was excluded from Book VI for "chronological reasons"). Thus, Dante's idea of having great political criminals do penance in purgatory is founded on Vergil.

Inasmuch as the first book clings comparatively closely to the motifs of the *Odyssey,* and the other books stray farther from this model, it is noteworthy (and I believe it to be the result of conscious intention) that of all the books of the "Iliad" half of the *Aeneid,* the last contains the greatest number of transferred situations. Conversely, the seventh and eighth books are the least *Iliad*-engendered, while the sixth book may be considered the most Vergilian of the first or "Odyssey" half. (Book IV shows the influence of Apollonius rather than of Homer.) Vergil with his wonderful sense of balance permeating the whole poem thus achieves perfection: he rises from the narrowly Homeric to his own zenith and returns again to Homer. Within the Homeric shell lies the Vergilian kernel.

The Allecto scenes symbolizing the tragic mood of the last half of the poem (VII–XII) correspond to the dramatic tempest introducing the disastrously fateful atmosphere of Aeneas' "Odyssey" in the first half (I–VI). Heinze [19] has shown that these two groups of scenes balance each other perfectly, particularly in both beginning with Juno. This correspondence proves that the interpretation of the storm as a beginning symbol represents the poet's intention and is not an arbitrary assumption. As this symbolization is the obvious function of the Allecto scenes which have no Homeric model, the same must be true of the storm (according to the law of strict symmetry for classical composition). Therefore, the parallel function of the scenes as "symbolic" overture to both parts of the epic may be added to the correspondences noted by Heinze.

The demonic force of nature in the first book, then, is paralleled by the demonic force of the historical world in the seventh. And inasmuch as the *Iliad* is more majestic than the *Odyssey,* the "Iliad," or second, half of the *Aeneid* is greater than the first:

> A greater sequence of events opens before me, and I now begin a grander enterprise.

VII.44:

> Maior rerum mihi nascitur ordo,
> Maius opus moveo.

Accordingly, in the last half, the power of the hostile fate that rises against the Trojans has grown considerably: Allecto's acts are incomparably wilder and more demoniac than those of Aeolus' winds. And while the storm at sea develops an Odyssean motif, Vergil has become independent of Homer. He dares, as Homer did not, to introduce the powers of Hell into the action of the story. It appears to me highly improbable that Ennius would have had a comparable sequence of scenes, although (as Norden [20] has shown) he contributed some details and prefashioned some important traits of Allecto in his Discordia. There is, however, a considerable difference between Ennius' war demon, Discordia, and Vergil's fury, Allecto.

Allecto's hellish nature is revealed in three scenes: the increasing delusion of Amata,[21] the dramatic violence of Turnus' dream, and the fast-moving hunt for Silvia's stag. She first appears as a snake to invest Amata with her serpent's spirit (VII.351), then as the torch thrust into Turnus' heart (456), and then as the sudden madness of Ascanius' dogs (479).

The first of these scenes, particularly, serves to translate the demonic character of Allecto into impassioned movement and thus contributes to the heightened action. Heinze, the first to inquire into its meaning, concluded that the motif was not fully utilized owing to a "lack of clarity in the treatment." [22] There is, however, no lack of clarity and the poet is not, as Heinze suggested, primarily interested in finding a new reason for the outbreak of war.[23] Friedrich has noted correctly that the *"impotentia"* of the Trojans' adversaries is symbolically expressed here. The object was to symbolize unleashed passion as well as the insanity of civil war. The war is a "civil war" because the Trojans and Italians, from the very beginning conceived of as belonging together, are destined for peace through assimilation. But the scene has a formal reason too: Vergil found it necessary to prepare the war events with a sequence of wildly moving scenes. High pathos and the spirit of tragedy fills the first of these. The Bacchic ecstasy of the Maenads, treated as tragic motif in several of Euripides' plays, may have seemed especially suitable for this purpose.[24] The Dido tragedy is similarly constructed.[25] In both places the image of furious movement in the form of the nocturnal *thiasos* marks a tragic development. The deeper justification and artistic sense of the scene are to be found, therefore, in the inner emotional sequence of the poem. Here at the start of a tragic development it demands the *élan terrible* of a furiously pressing movement, because the poet wished to create an introductory symbol for the "Iliad" half in the form of an *allegro furioso e appassionato* leading to war.[26] At the same time he wanted to give symbolic expression to his concept of war as a creation of Hell, a godless crime and sinful mania.[27] For such a presentation he could borrow nothing of value from Homer to whom this concept was alien.

The three scenes are composed with a rising pitch, swelling mightily toward tempestuous movement. The first scene spins toward the whirling frenzy of the Maenads in the lonely woods, the second plunges toward Turnus' madness which is

then compared to a cauldron boiling over (an image of growing movement in itself), and the third mounts to the uncontrollable commotion of war—to the tidal wave of the Italian
army as it gathers in response to Allecto's call:

> Now they sought decisions by their two-edged [28] blades.
> War's standing crop stretched afar, iron-gray with the
> shudder of drawn steel. Bronze gleamed under the sun's
> reflection, and flashed light upwards against dark clouds;
> as when at a wind's first breath waves begin to whiten,
> and gradually the sea rises and builds them higher, until
> at last it leaps from all its depths to the sky.

VII.525:

> Sed ferro ancipiti decernunt atraque late
> Horrescit strictis seges ensibus aeraque fulgent
> Sole lacessita et lucem sub nubila iactant,
> Fluctus uti primo coepit cum albescere ponto,
> Paulatim sese tollit mare et altius undas
> Erigit, inde imo consurgit ad aethera fundo.

The above is based on the Homeric simile (*Iliad* 7.63):

> The ranks were set close, and bristled with shields and
> helmets and spears, as the waves of the sea ripple and
> crinkle [29] when the west wind blows it black.

Inspired by other parts of the *Iliad* (2.457 and 13.338;
cf. 4.422 ff.; 13.795 ff.; 14.394 ff.; 15.381 ff.) and perhaps by
Ennius, Vergil added the brilliantly glancing reflection of the
weapons, which, in an intensification based on Homer, he
compares to the white crests on a dark sea (*Iliad* 14.696 ff.).
However, he was so caught up in the accelerating movement
and the crescendo of the outbreak of war that he augmented
the whole effect with the simile of the storm becoming a
hurricane. This simile embodies the strong pressure and ex-
citement of Juno's presence. It is part of the rhythm of the
whole poem. Here, one of the most important principles of
Vergil's art becomes effective—the striving for unity, or as

Woelfflin called it in a lecture entitled "The Classical," "the principle of assimilation" (the forms assimilate each other): "the work of art is organized into self-supporting parts, unified by homogeneous imagery and a moving rhythm common to every detail." [30] The tendency to compose whole scene sequences aimed at one goal serves the same purpose—dramatic development. A goal-directed movement is dramatic, while one seemingly without a goal is epic.[31] Vergil's art would be inconceivable without the Greek drama, for that is where the idea of unity first found a perfect poetic form by bringing all parts under the law of the whole. Although this idea is present in the Homeric epic, as emphasized by Goethe in his letter to Schiller of April 28, 1797 (in contrast to Schlegel and Wolf), [32] it is not completely executed. In the *Aeneid,* the unity is complete. It is symptomatic of the ignorance of Vergil among Germans that he does not play a role in the discussion between Goethe and Schiller concerning the nature of the epic, even though the epic "fulfills its nature" only in the *Aeneid*. Vergil was the first to give the epic that closed form for which, contrary to Schlegel's opinion, it had been destined from the beginning. He was the first to give it its "classic form."

Besides rising independently toward an image of increasing movement, the Allecto scenes combine into a larger unit. If the images climaxing each scene are compared, it is evident that they are suitably attuned to each other. Amata's orgiastic frenzy, the surge of boiling water, the whirling black steam of Turnus' cauldron, and the developing hurricane of the war host are increasingly emphatic symbols of uncontrollable elementary forces. And the last of these—the storm at sea, the most powerful manifestation of Nature in action—is the strongest symbol imaginable. Points of comparable function in the framework of composition are accentuated by related symbols and so we see that such a storm occurs at the beginning of both the "Iliad" and "Odyssey" halves of the *Aeneid*. When Latinus, broken and full of disastrous foreboding, finally yields to fate, and when Juno breaks open the iron gates of the temple of Janus, the feeling of unleashed movement is so vivid, the principle of harmonious forms so efficient, and the rhythm, carrying and sweeping away the events like a swollen torrent, so strong, that Latinus is compared to a rock amid the breakers (VII.586 ff.; cf. *Iliad* 15.618 ff.). He perceives the fatal outbreak as a hurricane, in the face of which human power cannot prevail (VII.594: *"Frangimur heu fatis, inquit, ferimurque procella"*). Once again the image of the storm and shipwreck serves as the symbol of destiny.

As a unit, the Allecto scenes clearly show the poet's artistic skill in creating ascending, accelerating movement. From the measured gesture of the hopeful line, *"Sublimes in equis redeunt pacemque reportant,"* [33] which inaugurates Juno's interference, the story becomes increasingly dark and tense as it heightens for the outbreak of war. Yet to appreciate fully this gradual intensification of plot, it is necessary to return to the book's beginning, for the story grows from the blessed morning peace of the Tiber landscape to the tempestuous movement of the resplendent, armored host. The poet strives for external contrast throughout the book. In order to enhance the power of the movement, he begins with a tranquil and distant scene. Thus, we see that the inner development of the seventh book is the reverse of that of the first; the latter develops out of storm and tension through the quasi-serious meeting with Venus [34] to the pleasantly joyful Dido audience and the solemn banquet at the end. Conversely, as we have seen, the seventh book opens in tranquillity which is subsequently replaced by increasingly turbulent movement rising toward the roaring finale of the Italian war hosts, a pageant crammed with violent *élan* and wild power, like a triumphant glorification of all the tribes of Italy.

CHAPTER II

THE PRINCIPAL FIGURES

AENEAS

The angry crescendo of the tempest directs our attention to Aeneas with that sudden jolt found by Richard Heinze to be a favorite artistic device of Vergil: *"Extemplo Aeneae solvuntur frigore membra"* (I.92). He "enters with almost a fainting fit" (Saint-Beuve) and cries out in mortal fear:

> How fortunate were you, thrice fortunate and more, whose luck it was to die under the high walls of Troy before your parents' eyes! Ah, Diomede, most valiant of Greeks, why did your arm not strike me down and give my spirit freedom in death on the battlefields of Ilium, where lie the mighty Sarpedon, and Hector the manslayer, pierced by Achilles' lance, and where Simois rolls down submerged beneath his stream those countless shields and helms and all those valiant dead!

I.94:

> O terque quaterque beati,
> Quis ante ora patrum Troiae sub moenibus altis
> Contigit oppetere! O Danaum fortissime gentis
> Tydide! Mene Iliacis occumbere campis
> Non potuisse tuaque animam hanc effundere dextra,
> Saevus ubi Aeacidae telo iacet Hector, ubi ingens

Sarpedon, ubi tot Simois correpta sub undis
Scuta virum galeasque et fortia corpora volvit?

This is a transformation of Odysseus' words (*Ody.* 5.306) [1]: "Three times happy are the Danaans and four times who fell on the broad plains of Troy, in loyalty to the house of Atreus. If only I had died and met my destiny on the day when so many Trojans hurled their bronze spears against me over the dead son of Peleus. At least I would have been buried with all honor and the Achaeans would spread my name far and wide. But as it is I seem fated to die a sad death." But is it really no more than a quotation from Homer?

Odysseus grieves because he must forego glory and burial honors; he does not mention love. Aeneas' wish to have died *"ante ora patrum"* expresses not only longing for glory but also for love and warmth of home. The thought that the presence of loved ones blunts the sting of death, is a common motif in the *Aeneid*. Thus, Dido's death agony is eased by her sister's presence and by the gesture of release with which Juno sends Iris to shorten her suffering. The dying Camilla is assisted by her fellow-in-arms, Acca, before Diana carries her off. We hear of Aeneas' compassion for Palinurus and of Nisus sacrificing himself for Euryalus. Likewise, the battle death of Pallas and Lausus is relieved through Aeneas' mourning. Turnus and Mezentius die alone but with thoughts of those they love. Even the dead of Actium and the doomed Cleopatra are lovingly received by the god of the river Nile (VIII.711). That is the kind of death for which Aeneas has wished. Moreover, while Odysseus remembers only his own peril before Troy, Aeneas mentions the end of the great Trojan heroes, Hector and Sarpedon, and all the corpses which Simois turns over and over. Thus his ties with the dead comrades of his old home are clearly seen.

He appears as a man of memory and of inner vision. In the extremity of death and suffering the grief burning in his heart breaks out. His speech not only expresses his mortal fear, but also serves to express his character. It allows one a glimpse of his heart and of a basic motif of the poem. This is Vergil's own experience of what it means to be exiled from home, an experience that he had already expressed so movingly in the first *Eclogue*.[2] The sorrowfully pathetic image which climaxes and ends his speech (Homer has no such climax), although inspired by Homer (*Iliad* 21.301), fits the storm at sea as perfectly as if invented especially for it. Shortly afterward the sad destructiveness of the storm is described with a similar image:

I.119:

> Arma virum tabulaeque et Troia gaza per undas

This is an echo of the *"correpta sub undis scuta virum."* And in it the struggle for a homogeneity of imagery and unity of key is clearly visible. The monologue of despair surpasses Homer both in form and content of feeling. By means of its inner correlation to the tempest imagery, it has become more ingenious and somehow deeper and more gentle, but less "natural" than its simple-ending Odyssean counterpart. "I, however, was destined to die a sad death." [3] This loss of natural simplicity is the price paid for perfection of the classical form. The richer, more significant content and riper artistry could not be reconciled with Homer's simple strength.

The sorrowful memory of Troy, emphasized in Aeneas' first words, is a recurring leitmotif in the first third of the *Aeneid*. It recurs in the hero's speech to Venus (I.372: *"O dea si prima repetens ab origine pergam"*) and in his concentration on the Trojan War reliefs in Juno's temple in Carthage; it expands as the great narrative of the city's fall (II), flares up in the meetings with Polydorus, Helenus, and Andromache (III), and reappears in the scene with Dido when Aeneas speaks once more of his longing for Troy (IV.430). Aeneas' close relationship to Hector, his predecessor as the Trojan leader,[4] is also repeatedly revealed in these books, first in the description of the relief in which the particular importance of Hector's fate is emphasized in being set apart; [5] again when Hector approaches the dreaming Aeneas in a decisive moment during Troy's last night (II.270 ff.); then in the pathetic image of Andromache mourning over Hector's ashes (III.302 ff.). Hector's personality is later conjured up in Aeneas' legacy to Ascanius, just before the decisive duel with Turnus:

> But when in due time your own age ripens to maturity, it will be for you to see to it that you do not forget, but recall in your thought the examples set you by your kindred. Your father is Aeneas and your uncle was Hector. Let that be your inspiration.

XII.438:

> Tu facito mox cum matura adoleverit aetas
> Sis memor et te animo repetentem exempla tuorum
> Et pater Aeneas et avunculus excitet Hector.

Troy has gone, but Aeneas preserves its image and its heroes' glory, just as he saves its gods. His strength for founding a new Troy springs from a loving memory. Aeneas is the symbol of the mood existing between collapse and salvation, the chaos of civil war and the advent of Augustan peace.

The Trojan "Iliad" in the first third of the *Aeneid,* inserted in the Carthaginian events as reminiscent narrative and an "unspeakable," heavy burden upon the hero's soul, is counterpart to the Italian "Iliad" in the last third.[6] This balanced way in which the Greco-Trojan past and the Roman future are incorporated into the poem is another example of the classical feeling for symmetry: the correlated parts are equated in form as well as content. The form is expression of organized thought.

The middle third contains, as it were, the hero's emancipation from the burden of the past. We are told how he leaves the *"animos nil magnae laudis egentis"* in Sicily under the

rule of Acestes and founds a second Ilium for them (V).
Then, after a final irresolution (V.700 ff.) he turns decisively
to his new task. The revelation granted him in the underworld
completely fills him with the consciousness of his new mission.
The thought of Troy, which has occupied his heart so far, is
replaced. Memory becomes hope; retrospective longing for
Troy gives way to a visionary longing for Rome. He turns
from his ancestors to his descendants. The proem rising from
"Troiae ab oris" in the first verse to *"altae moenia Romae"* in
the last verse has clearly emphasized the beginning and the
end of the way. *Rome* is the last word of the proem because
it is the inner goal of the epic and the main theme of the
poem. Even the arrangement of words points out what is important.[7] The "historical" attitude of Aeneas expresses the
moral change in Vergil's world and its difference from that
of Homer's. Unlike Homer's heroes, the figure of Aeneas
simultaneously comprises past, present, and future.[8] Even in
mortal extremity the past is with him: his actions spring from
memory and hope. He is under the responsibility of history:
"Attollitque umero famamque et fata nepotum." We might
add: *"atque maiorum."* In the *Aeneid,* we see for the first
time the tragedy of man suffering from historical fate. The
hero is never allowed to belong completely to the moment.
If and when, as in Carthage, he seems to be caught up in the
moment, a god reminds him of his duty.

In the Homeric man the sensual present is supreme. The
past may appear as memory and paradigm, the future as a
fleeting glimpse, and sometimes—as in Homer's most tragic
figure, Achilles—the knowledge of tragic destiny overwhelms
the present. Sometimes, as in Zeus's speech to Achilles'
horses, words expressing the poet's awareness of human
tragedy are put into a god's mouth. But even though Homer's
heroes feel sorrow as keenly as Aeneas does, they appear to
forget it more easily. Aeneas' sorrow is never forgotten; it is
always ready to break forth from the bottom of his heart.

Homeric heroes are not so constantly overshadowed by their melancholies. It is true that the Odyssean figures are subject to some secret longing which brings the soul to light, for when the soul's light falls on the senses, the present fades. In the *Odyssey* we see a shift in emphasis on the importance of the moment and that of the soul. Still, the soul is *in absentia* for long periods. In contrast to the Aeneas of the book of wanderings, Homer's Odysseus, in relating his adventures, is completely enmeshed by current events, and his longing, when it emerges, is confined to the small area of his individual life. It is easy to imagine what Vergil would have done with the subject matter of the *Odyssey*—how he would have enhanced the inner life of the soul and the impact of history and decreased the importance of the sensual present.

Past and future in Homer never extend to such psychological depths and historical distances. The scope of the Greek epic falls short of the scope of the Roman *Aeneid*. It was the Roman poet, Vergil, who discovered the grievous burden of history and its vital meaning. He was the first to perceive deeply the cost of historical greatness; Jacob Burckhardt much later restated the same insight. Aeneas' attitude comes from a superior historical consciousness, developed by the Romans beyond that of the Greeks, and from the characteristic Roman feeling for time insofar as the present was evaluated as only a part of temporal totality and was always connected with historical past and future. In a deeper sense, past and future are always present inasmuch as they give weight and value to the moment.

Moreover, Aeneas' attitude testifies to the Roman sense of duty which is in sharp contrast to the Greek sense of existence, for whatever the Homeric heroes do, they do in fulfillment of their nature rather than their duty. Aeneas, however, is a hero of duty, while Dido is a tragic heroine because she suffers from the guilty consciousness of her violated duty as does Turnus from the god-inflicted delusion on his.[9] The

Aeneid would not be the ideal expression of *res Romana* that it is, if the fulfillment of duty were not fundamental to its hero. The peculiar content of the modern concept of duty is a consequence of Roman morality. The early structures of family and state rest upon this concept and wherever it appears later, as in the Christian ethics of both Kant and Schiller, the influence of Roman thought is effective.[10] This is one of the reasons Schiller felt so deeply attracted to Vergil.

To the hero, Aeneas, the memory of Troy and the hope for Rome are holy obligations, and in their fulfillment he displays *pietas* which is nothing else but doing his duty to gods, country, ancestors, and descendants. "Duty" here, however, is not a response to the dictates of reason, but a response to love, and is without the harsh associations evoked by the word.

The "Homeric quotation" of Aeneas' first words proves to be a farther-reaching transformation of its model than is immediately evident. The outer and inner structure of the *Aeneid* transforms the simple thought of the *Odyssey* into an integral part of itself. After these words, the storm grows more intense and the description of its ravages rises in two climactic peaks, and in comparison with the Homeric storms in the fifth and twelfth books of the *Odyssey,* the accent shifts decidedly. First there is the sinking of the Lycian ship bearing "faithful Orontes"—an epithet which in itself shows the poet's compassion and some measure of the tragedy of Aeneas.[11] In sharp contrast is the Homeric counterpart where Odysseus, himself and not the poet, describes the death of the pilot, his skull smashed by the mast so that he plunges into the sea "like a diver." He tells of the sad fate of his companions "dancing" like seagulls on the waves. He reports the death of his fellows with vivid accuracy but without visible emotional involvement.[12] Even in a speech Homer is objective in viewpoint. Even in narrative Vergil remains subjective. Another climax comes in the words *"Troiae gaza per undas,"* which signify part of the tragedy within Aeneas—the loss of his keepsakes from Troy. They are important, too, in concluding the description proper of the tempest.

Here, then, are an inner and an outer climax: Aeneas' mortal fear increases and is yet surpassed by the feelings aroused in him at the loss of Orontes and the *gaza Troiae*. Here, too, the final climax is the tragedy of Troy.

If Aeneas' first words show his *pietas* above all, his comforting address to his companions after the rescue (198 ff.) reveals still another fundamental feature of his character—his *magnitudo animi*.

> We have forced our way through adventures of every kind, risking all again; but the way is the way to Latium, where Destiny offers us rest and a home, and where imperial Troy may have the right to live again. Hold hard, therefore. Preserve yourselves for better days.

I.204:

> Per varios casus, per tot discrimina rerum
> Tendimus in Latium, sedes ubi fata quietas
> Ostendunt: illic fas regna resurgere Troiae.
> Durate et vosmet rebus servate secundis.

Vergil intensifies the impression of Aeneas' *magnitudo animi* by showing it against the backdrop of his sorrow and grief:

> He was sick at heart, for the cares which he bore were heavy indeed. Yet he concealed his sorrow deep within him, and his face looked confident and cheerful.

I.208:

> Curisque ingentibus aeger
> Spem voltu simulat, premit altum corde dolorem.

This speech is considerably different from Odysseus' words to his comrades, which it recalls (12.208 ff.). Homer's Odysseus is a brave man, who in a perilous situation (between Scylla and Charybdis) gives intelligent and prudent orders. On the other hand, Vergil's Aeneas is a great soul, pressing toward a magnificent goal. Like the first, the second speech culminates in the thought of Troy and its renascent empire to come.[13] In this we see that Vergil differs from Homer in the monumentalization and transformation of something of specific importance into something of general importance; he removed epic reality from a too intimate contact with objective detail to weave the transparency of a larger scene.

Aeneas' first speeches reveal his basic character; they are inwardly and outwardly integral to the whole work because the poet concentrates completely on the essential and significant from the very beginning. However, this tendency to reveal basic traits of character and destiny upon the first appearance of an individual is also occasionally noticeable in Homer's much more loosely composed epic. It is seen, for example, in the sixth book of the *Iliad,* when Hector, failing to find Andromache at home, hears that she is neither with her family nor in the temple of Athena; on learning that the Trojans are being defeated and that the Achaeans' power is growing stronger, she has gone to the great tower of Ilium. In her gesture of madly rushing to the wall, with the nurse carrying the child, her gentle and passionate soul is given expression. The poet need say nothing of her love, for the gesture expresses it better than words could. This is our introduction to Andromache! The scene simultaneously intimates Hector's destiny, for on a deeper level of understanding, Andromache's concern is revealed as tragic premonition.

The connection is not so obvious with the other characters in the *Iliad,* though their first appearance is characteristic. The manner in which Agamemnon screams at Chryses points up his violent and selfish nature, and Thetis instantly shows herself as a loving mother when in response to Achilles' prayer she rises like mist from the sea to caress her son. In his censure of Paris, Hector proves himself an unyielding defender of his people's honor and their true leader. In this expression of long-suppressed resentment he uncovers his passionate nature. But the connection with the development of the story is not so definite. The strict integration of detail with the whole, of words and gestures with character, of character with destiny, of destiny with the structure of the plot—all essentials in the *Aeneid*—are less well developed in the *Iliad*. So there is less immediacy in the establishment of the principle of classical composition, according to which each part receives its true importance only through its relation to the whole. The introduction of a course of events is more leisurely, so there is more opportunity for involvement with each character.

The situation in the *Odyssey* is somewhat different, and this fact must not be ignored in a criticism of the two epics. There, the initial entrance of the main figures is fashioned with great care and harmonious variation around one idea—the longing for the hero's return and the grief over his absence. In an unforgettable picture, Odysseus appears looking tearfully out on the rushing sea.[14] Unable to bear her grief, Penelope descends from her suite to make the minstrel stop singing of the Achaeans' return. At the approach of Athena in the guise of Mentor, Telemachos looks at the gate because in his mind's eye he sees his father coming to chase away the plague of suitors. Eumaios, after driving off the dogs which threaten the stranger, begins immediately to speak of his grief for his absent master. Each one is occupied by a single great feeling of longing which is the main content of his life.

Let us now return to the trials of Aeneas. The basic forces in Aeneas' soul, respect for duty, firmness of resolution, and human feeling appear in the decisive moment of the Dido crisis. The climax of the fourth book of the *Aeneid* comes after Queen Dido's plea to Aeneas to change his cruel decision to leave her:

> He, remembering Jupiter's warning, held his eyes steady,
> and strained to master the agony within him.

IV.331:

> Ille Iovis monitis immota tenebat
> Lumina et obnixus curam [15] sub corde premebat.

The expression *"obnixus curam,"* etc., is very similar to
"premit altum corde dolorem" (I.209), except that more
emphasis is given to the magnitude of effort. However, it is
not so much the passion of his love that moves Aeneas, as is
assumed by modern interpretation, for Vergil has treated this
feeling with the greatest reserve. Rather, he is moved by compassion for Dido's grief. And this compassion, heightened by
love, is a manifestation of *humanitas,*[16] which, according to
the command of the gods, is suppressed. Aeneas' painful resignation is not a renunciation of love, then, but a response to
the gods' prohibition. He is not permitted to relieve the
grieving queen, but is forced by his religious duty to gods and
progeny to neglect his human duty to Dido. He suffers more
because of the sorrow for others than because of his own misfortune. His concern to protect those near to him from grief
and pain never slackens. This protective feeling finds its most
beautiful expression in the *Iliupersis:*

> And now, though up till then I had remained quite unaf-
> fected by any weapons or even the sight of Greeks charging
> towards me, I myself was now ready to be frightened at a
> breath of wind and started at the slightest sound, so nervous
> was I, and so fearful alike for the load on my back and the
> companion at my side.

II.726:

> Et me quem dudum non ulla iniecta movebant
> Tela neque adverso glomerati ex agmine Grai,
> Nunc omnes terrent aurae, sonus excitat omnis
> Suspensum et pariter comitique onerique timentem.[17]

When Dido, upon being refused, hurls her curse at the hero
and is carried into the marble chamber [18] by her maids, the
same sorrowful determination is found in heightened form:

Meanwhile Aeneas the True longed to allay her grief and dispel her sufferings with kind words. Yet he remained obedient to the divine command, and with many a sigh, for he was shaken to the depths by the strength of his love, returned to his ships.

IV.393:

> At pius Aeneas, quamquam lenire dolentem
> Solando cupit et dictis avertere curas,
> Multa gemens magnoque animum labefactus amore,
> Iussa tamen divom exsequitur.

Even more intensified, the motif returns for the third time following Anna's final attempt to change the departing hero's mind. Here, Aeneas' inner struggle is given mighty expression in the oak simile. This simile, symbol of Aeneas' heroic manner, is closely related to that inner strength so prized by the Stoics. In this connection, it is interesting to note that Seneca compares the wise man to a storm-buffeted tree [19]— perhaps with the *Aeneid* in mind:

> Like a strong oak-tree toughened by the years when northern winds from the Alps vie together to tear it from the soil, with their blasts striking on it now this side and now that; creaking, the trunk shakes, and leaves from on high strew the ground; yet still the tree grips among the rocks below, for its roots stretch as far down towards the abyss [20] as its crest reaches up to the airs of heaven. Like that tree, the hero was battered this side and that by their insistent pleas, and deeply his brave heart grieved,[21] but without effect.

IV.441:

> Ac velut annoso validam cum robore quercum
> Alpini Boreae nunc hinc nunc flatibus illinc
> Eruere inter se certant, it stridor et altae
> Consternunt terram concusso stipite frondes,
> Ipsa haeret scopulis et quantum vertice ad auras
> Aetherias tantum radice in Tartara tendit:

> Haud secus adsiduis hinc atque hinc vocibus heros
> Tunditur et magno persentit pectore curas,
> Mens immota manet, lacrimae volvuntur inanes.

The *lacrimae inanes* are the tears which Aeneas sheds in vain;
they have no effect on his unshakable resolution. In contrast
to all modern commentators,[22] Augustine and Servius have
interpreted this passage correctly.[23] To make these the tears
of Anna or Dido would be to weaken the impact considerably,
for the emphasis is not so much on the contest between
Aeneas and Anna as on the hero's divided heart and his painful resignation. The meaning of this simile, then, can be
understood only as an image of this inner struggle or as an
expression of the bitter contest between hard and fast resolution and his human heart. Once the overpowering nature of
this battle is understood, no other interpretation is accept-
able.[24] The bold inner antithesis is much to be preferred to the
lame outer one.[25] The oak suffers, too, as is indicated by its
groaning [26] and the image *"altae consternunt terram concusso
stipite frondes."* As Servius has observed (*"frondes sicut
lacrimae Aeneae"*), there is a distinct inner relation between
Aeneas' tears and the leaves shed by the tree, for there are
fewer superfluous features in Vergil's similes than in
Homer's.[27] Here, the essence of the simile is "suffering." The
oak is similar to the fallen mountain ash which symbolizes the
fall of Troy in the *Iliupersis*. There too the simile, quite un-
Homerically, does not illustrate an event, but expounds a
destiny. The suffering of the tree—its "tragedy"—is the main
thing:

> Like an ancient rowan tree high up among the mountains,
> which, hacked with stroke after stroke of iron axes by
> farmers vying all round to dislodge it, begins to tremble
> and continues threatening while the crest shakes and the
> high boughs sway, till gradually vanquished it gives a final
> groan, and at last overcome by the wounds and wrenched
> from its place it trails havoc down the mountain-side.

II.626:

> Ac veluti summis antiquam in montibus ornum
> Cum ferro accisam crebrisque bipennibus instant
> Eruere agricolae certatim; illa usque minatur
> Et tremefacta comam concusso vertice nutat,
> Volneribus donec paulatim evicta supremum
> Congemuit traxitque iugis avolsa ruinam.

Hercules, too, conquers his grief at the death of Pallas and yet sheds *lacrimas inanes:*

> Hercules heard the young man's prayer. Deep in his heart
> he repressed a heavy sigh; and his tears streamed helplessly.

X.464:

> Audiit Alcides iuvenem magnumque sub imo
> Corde premit gemitum lacrimasque effundit inanes.[28]

The inner relation of these passages is another proof that it is Aeneas who weeps—not Anna. Thus, the allegory of his sublime grandeur that concludes an important section of the fourth book ends with an antithesis which once more points out the strength of his resolution and the sorrow in his heart. It is worthwhile noting that this scene concludes with tears. The hero's humanity is stressed at a moment when he could easily seem cruel. On the whole, the contrast between Aeneas' coolness and Dido's ardor is the original tragic contrast between man and woman as it has been shaped in modern art, by say, Heine and Boecklin. The relation of the Aeneas-Dido antithesis to that between Jupiter and Juno has been mentioned earlier.

Here, a simile signifies the sorrowful resolution of the hero; at the beginning of the fifth book a symbolic gesture does the same thing:

> Aeneas and his fleet were now far out to sea. He set
> course resolutely and ploughed through waves ruffled
> to black by a northerly wind. As he sailed he looked

back to walled Carthage, now aglow with tragic Dido's flames.

V.1:

Interea medium Aeneas iam classe tenebat
Certus iter fluctusque atros aquilone secabat
Moenia respiciens, quae iam infelicis Elissae
Conlucent flammis.

Steadfastly, he follows his course in spite of storm and the memory of Dido (clearly reflected in the words *"moenia respiciens"*). He does so in spite of the glow of the funeral pyre the flames of which awaken dark premonitions in the hearts of the Trojans. Servius' explanation: *"certus: indubitabiliter pergens, id est itineris sui certus,"* approved by Heyne and rejected by Wagner,[29] is basically correct. Although *certus* refers immediately to the straight course of the fleet, the straight course, itself, symbolizes the hero's firm determination. We are dealing here with an example of the language of symbolic gesture, where a gesture reflects an inner attitude. No doubt the metaphor of the "ship of life" (and "state"), familiar to Greek thought and to Mediterranean eyes, influenced this passage.[30] There is also a metaphorical tie between "wind" and "destiny," a frequent notion in antiquity occurring several times in the *Aeneid*. As it is a characteristic of art to create large transparent complexities behind single details, the poetic symbol is meant to disclose such general "philosophical" perspectives. The disparity among commentators in deciding between the visible route and the inner determination, is the result of the misjudgment of the symbolic character of poetic expression which, of course, encompassed both.[31]

Within the above-mentioned metaphors, however, is the great idea that Aeneas' journey and the whole poem are a simile of the life of man. Even in antiquity the *Odyssey* was so interpreted. Of course, there is no question of applying the simplified form of allegorical-philosophical interpretation exemplified, say, by the well-known epistle of Horace (I.2), but there can be no doubt that Vergil was well acquainted with it and that the *Aeneid* is a simile in this sense, too.

Aeneas' firmness in the midst of trouble and confusion is shown in other symbolic gestures. Recall the words following the death of Palinurus at the end of the fifth book:

> Therefore he steered her himself through the midnight waves with many a sigh, for he was deeply shocked by the disaster to his friend.

V.868:
> Ipse ratem nocturnis rexit in undis,
> Multa gemens casuque animum concussus amici.

Here, again, the symbolic meaning of the sea voyage appears. There is sublime simplicity and transparent beauty in image and expression. Another example is the beginning of the eleventh book, which in composition of the whole corresponds to the beginning of the fifth [32]:

> The morrow's rising dawn had emerged from the ocean. Aeneas, deeply burdened as he was by thoughts of death, would naturally have preferred to devote his time to giving his comrades burial. But instead at first light from the east he started to fulfill his vows to the gods in return for his victory.

XI.1:
> Oceanum interea surgens Aurora reliquit,
> Aeneas, quamquam et sociis dare tempus humandis
> Praecipitant curae turbataque funere mens est,
> Vota deum primo victor solvebat Eoo.

Compare the pathetically determined and restrained gesture *"nec plura effatus"* with which he turns back from the corpse of Pallas to the camp:

After the whole procession had gone on far ahead, Aeneas halted, and with a heavy sigh spoke again: 'We are called hence to other tears by this same grim destiny of war. Pallas, great hero, I bid you forever hail, and forever farewell.' Saying no more he moved off towards his own high defence-works and walked back into his camp.

XI.94:

Postquam omnis longe comitum praecesserat ordo,
Substitit Aeneas gemituque haec edidit alto:
Nos alias hinc ad lacrimas eadem horrida belli
Fata vocant. Salve aeternum mihi, maxume Palla,
Aeternumque vale. Nec plura effatus ad altos
Tendebat muros gressumque in castra ferebat.

Here one senses how deeply the poet is affected by the bitterness of war; beneath Aeneas' grief for Pallas flashes a greater tragedy of which his friend's death is only one instance symbolizing the long procession of dead to follow him—the "other tears . . ." In such moments Aeneas is the personification of the feeling of tragedy which is basic to the poem. It is true that all figures created by the poet represent dialectical possibilities of his own soul, but Aeneas represents the innermost core. Vergil's "psychography" may be drawn from Aeneas' personality. The sensitivity to tragedy which characterizes the hero is the same sensitivity with which the poet himself looks at the world and life. It is the compassionate eye with which the Vergilian gods regard the fighting:

In Jupiter's palace the gods pitied the pointless fury of both sides, sad that men doomed in any case to die, should suffer ordeals so terrible.

X.758 ff.:

Di Iovis in tectis iram miserantur inanem
Amborum et tantos mortalibus esse labores . .

Theirs is the astonished sorrow to which Vergil gives voice at the beginning: *"Tantaene animis caelestibus irae?"* It breaks forth again and again from Aeneas—and from him alone. We hear it in the woeful exclamation: *"Heu quantae miseris caedes Laurentibus instant?"* (VIII.537). Or, most nearly related in content to the first question, in the hero's words to the Latins when they ask for a truce to bury their dead:

> Ah, Latins, how unjustly and unhappily you have been involved in this terrible war which leads you to shrink from friendship with us! ...

XI.108:

> Quaenam vos tanto fortuna indigna, Latini,
> Implicuit bello, qui nos fugiatis amicos ..

It finds its highest form in Aeneas' journey through the underworld, since this journey is a symbol of Vergil's experience of the tragedy of life. The guilt, atonement, and suffering he encounters there awaken in him tragically compassionate sorrow—the same enormous sympathy characteristic of his actions and sufferings elsewhere and explicitly stated in the case of Dido:

> Aeneas was shocked by her unjust fate; and as she went long gazed after her with tearful eyes and pity for her in his heart.

VI.475:

> Nec minus Aeneas *casu concussus iniquo*
> Prosequitur lacrimis longe et *miseratur* euntem.

This compassion is the most pathetic when he sees the souls along the river Lethe "drink the waters which abolish care and give enduring release from memory" in order to return to the world:

> Oh, Father, am I therefore to believe that of those souls some go, soaring hence, up to the world beneath our sky and return once more into dreary matter? Why should the poor souls so perversely desire the light of our day?

VI.719:

> O pater, anne aliquas ad caelum hinc ire putandum est
> Sublimis animas iterumque ad tarda reverti
> Corpora? Quae lucis miseris tam dira cupido?

It seems rather like a palinode on Achilles' lament in the *Odyssey*. Achilles would prefer being a hired hand of the poorest man to being a king in the shadowy world of the dead.[33] This is the same Platonism as that of Cicero in the *Somnium Scipionis*. In both cases the soul acquainted with grief finds comfort in expressing its sorrow. Why these passages spoke so eloquently to the hearts of coming generations, filled as they were with an ever-growing longing for redemption, is plain.

Aeneas, measuring his own fate against the better fortune of others, similarly perceived its tragic quality:

> How fortunate were you, thrice fortunate and more, whose luck it was to die under the high walls of Troy before your parents' eyes!

I.94:

> O terque quaterque beati
> Quis ante ora patrum Troiae sub moenibus altis
> Contigit oppetere.

> Aeneas looked up at the buildings. 'Ah, fortunate people,' he exclaimed, 'for your city-walls are already rising!'

I.437:

> O fortunati, quorum iam moenia surgunt,
> Aeneas ait et fastigia suspicit urbis.

Live, and prosper, for all your adventures are past. We are called ever onward from destiny to destiny. For you, your rest is won. You have no expanse of sea to plough, no land of Italy, seeming always to recede before you, as your quest.

III.493 ff.:

> Vivite felices, quibus est fortuna peracta
> Iam sua, nos alia ex aliis in fata vocamur.
> Vobis parta quies, nullum maris aequor arandum
> Arva neque Ausoniae semper cedentia retro
> Quaerenda.

> 'From me, my son,' he said, 'you may learn what is valour and what is strenuous toil; as for what good fortune is, others must teach you that.'

XII.435:

> Disce puer virtutem ex me verumque laborem,
> Fortunam ex aliis.

No matter how often sorrow overwhelms his sensitive heart, he shows heroism by passing through it, by "leading his life through all extremities" (III.315: *"vivo equidem vitamque extrema per omnia duco"*), mastering inner torment (*premit altum corde dolorem*), and yielding to destiny in noble resignation. Thus, he illustrates what Schopenhauer expected of poetry: the power to save us from sentimentality and to raise us to resignation. The grief that Aeneas bears and conquers is, I repeat, less sorrow for his own lost or denied happiness than sympathy and compassion for others who must suffer bitterly for the sake of the command laid on him by destiny. Homer's heroes suffer through "love of self" in the high Aristotelian sense. And Vergil's other protagonists, Dido and Turnus, suffer in a similar way; but Aeneas suffers for the sake of others. A new humanity announcing the Christian philosophy bursts forth from him. He prefigures the Christian hero, whose heart remains gentle through struggle and sorrow and beats in secret sympathy with all suffering creatures.

Vergil also reshaped the idea of duty, which, always a primary element of Roman ethics, is a decisive factor in Aeneas' behavior. In infusing it with deep humanity, he brought it close to the Christian idea of charity and solidarity. This is one of the main reasons why Vergil became a mediator between the antique Roman world and medieval Christianity.

It follows, therefore, from this line of thought that the "Stoic" interpretation of Aeneas, as proposed by Heinze, cannot be correct—at least not if the concept is accepted in its strict sense. The hero experiences sorrow, especially spiritual sorrow, to the utmost. It is always his moral goal to do what is necessary in spite of his great sensitivity and never to make himself insensitive. It is precisely because of this that he affects us as a tragic hero. It enhances the impression of his will power, for it is necessary that he have heroic spiritual strength in order to conquer the sorrows of which he is acutely aware. Vergil widens the distance between the longing in Aeneas' sensitive heart and the harsh demands of destiny, while the Stoic doctrine, on the contrary, hardens and silences the heart with overpowering reason. Although it is true that Aeneas' is the noble sorrow of compassion, it must be remembered that the Stoa did not allow the wise man even this feeling.

Far from aspiring to ataraxia, Aeneas strives to deny sorrow's influence upon his actions rather than to obliterate it through reason. Here, the affinity to Christianity is unmistakable, for in the depth of his being he turns *toward* his sorrow rather than away from it. True, St. Augustine is right, as pointed out earlier, in claiming that the verse *"mens immota manet: lacrimae volvuntur inanes"* is an example of Ciceronian and Middle Stoic thought, according to which there is no difference between Peripatetic and Stoic attitudes toward suffering. But this applies only to the Middle Stoa of Panaitios which was bent on lessening the contrasts between the schools in favor of a middle way. It does not apply to the strict Stoa; the sorrow of Aeneas could not pass its censure. His "stoic" attitude toward the wound (XII.398), his apparent insensibility in the face both of physical pain and the sympathy of his comrades (characteristically emphasized more) is the result of his indignation at the Latins' breach of contract, as is his impetuous rage to meet Turnus in battle. The violation of the truce changes him into an angry warrior, dead-set upon merciless destruction of his opponent to satisfy the demand of *"debellare superbos."* Outraged justice obliterates any other consideration. Here and only here, he is called *"avidus pugnae"* (XII.430).

Seen in this way, Aeneas' attitude toward pain is by no means "stoic." Rather, perhaps, his perception of destiny as a school of suffering can be interpreted as "stoic." He opposes the wild prophecy of the Cumaean sibyl concerning the bloody battles awaiting the Trojans, with the words:

> Maid, no aspect of tribulation which is new to me or unforeseen can rise before me, for I have traced my way through all that may happen in the anticipation of my inward thought.

VI.103:

> Non ulla laborum,
> O virgo, nova mi facies inopinave surgit;
> Omnia praecepi atque animo mecum ante peregi.

The words and his serene attitude form a wonderful contrast with the furor of the priestess. Norden has noted the parallels in his commentary.[34] Elsewhere, too, Aeneas' attitude toward fate may be considered as related to that of the Stoics, for example:

> Instead, my own valor, holy oracles from gods, my kinship between your father and mine, and your own renown throughout the world have all joined me to you and brought me here in willing obedience to my destiny.

VIII.131:

> Sed mea me virtus et sancta oracula divom
> Cognatique patres, tua terris didita fama
> Coniunxere tibi et *fatis egere volentem.*

But there is not always inner acquiescence to fate in Aeneas.

IV.361:

> Italiam non sponte sequor.

VI.460:

> Invitus regina tuo de litore cessi,
> Sed me iussa deum . . . imperiis egere suis.

When, after the burning of the ships, Aeneas, *"casu concussus iniquo"* (a recurring phrase no less characteristic of his justice than his humanity), is wavering again, the old Nautes reminds him of the claim of the Stoic attitude:

> Son of the Goddess, we should accept the lead which Destiny offers us, whether to go forward or not, and choose our way accordingly. Whatever is to befall, it is always our own power of endurance which must give us control over our fortune.

V.709:

> Nate dea, quo fata trahunt retrahuntque sequamur;
> Quidquid erit, superanda omnis fortuna ferendo est.

And in Aeneas' last words to Ascanius the poet restates, as it were, the hero's testament by foretelling the dark doom which will threaten him after Turnus' death:

> From me, my son, he said, you may learn what is valor and what is strenuous toil; as for what good fortune is, others must teach you that.

XII.435:

> Disce, puer, virtutem ex me verumque laborem,
> Fortunam ex aliis.[35]

There is no trace of the gladiatorial challenge and *"ostentatio"* toward fate, the most impressive form of which can perhaps be found in Seneca's *De Providentia.* That he should hate to have his son inherit his *fortuna*—his grievous destiny—shows not only his love for Ascanius, but also a sorrowful pity for his own and other people's sorrow which is anything but Stoic. And in spite of individual points of resemblance, Aeneas' attitude toward fate cannot be called "stoic" without reservations.

That poetic and philosophic perception of fate can never completely coincide was persuasively pointed out by Grillparzer in his essay on fate—and this should be remembered. These concepts are fundamentally different forms of the understanding of reality. It is true that the poetic world can partake of the philosophic world, but it can never be completely absorbed by it or identical with it. The poetic world obeys other laws. What Goethe wrote to Schiller apropos of his conversation with Schelling is of general significance: (In me) "philosophy destroys poetry." [36] The ideal of a Stoic sage could never appear in a poem in its pure form without destroying its poetic character.[37] For the rest, strict Stoicism cannot be expected of Vergil since it would contradict the spirit of the age. Cicero, the herald of the Augustan consciousness, had followed Panaitios in Hellenizing and humanizing the Stoa.[38] The later Roman Stoa likewise did not adhere to strict doctrine. Seneca, himself, of whose attitude the above-mentioned *De Providentia* is by no means characteristic, is on the whole far removed from old Stoic rigidity and extremism. He is dedicated to a humane, liberal point of view which is continued later in the mild Stoicism of Marcus Aurelius.

The character of Aeneas is determined by an amalgamation of several traits: Homeric heroism, early Roman Stoic *"magnitudo animi,"* and Vergilio-Augustan *"humanitas"* combined into a new whole. Should the "stoic" component prevail, the harmony of this vision of man would disappear. The proud sensitivity as well as the greatness of both Aeneas and Dido rests on the tension between *"magnitudo animi"* and *"humanitas."* Any interpretation that emphasizes either the stoic heroism in Aeneas' character or his sensitivity to

the exclusion of the other, is false. It is also false to see him
as too hard or too soft, too stoically Roman or too much like
a modern Christian. And there is an analogous situation for
Dido. In Vergil there is both the granite of ancient Roman
grandeur and the delicate bloom of humanity opening upon a
new dimension of the soul and destined to have a decisive influence on developing Christianity.

In this connection one more problem deserves discussion:
the hero Aeneas' "character development." Heinze has attempted to state such a development. From the despair at-
tending the tempest and the depression expressed in the
monologue: *"O terque quaterque beati"* and the address *"O
socii . . . ,"* Aeneas grows in steadfastness and stature. In the
beginning, according to Heinze, he fails to personify the
Stoic ideal, but finally reaches it in the course of his inner
development. I do not believe that the modern concept of
character development applies here. It is true that the stature
of the hero grows with the situations according to the law of
the intensification which governs the poem. This is true in
the sense that the hero's character proves itself on an ever-
enlarging level and that his inner strength increases with the
gradual revelation of his mission. It is not true, however, in
the sense of a progressive approximation to the ideal Stoic
sage, nor in the sense of an inner development, the psychology
of which would not have attracted the Homerizing poet. His
character, or that which is the mark of his existence, remains
unchanged; the conflict of heroic fulfillment of duty with human sensitivity that determines the shape of his existence pervades the whole poem. It is evident in the first scenes and can
be followed to the last verses where he hesitates between
killing and pardoning Turnus.

Moreover, the address must not be seen as expressing a
lack of wisdom or incomplete self-discipline or faltering
faith in God. On the contrary, the determination in these
words is all the more admirable when we see that beneath

them lies doubt and even despair. He is even here, as the sibyl will later ask him to be, *"audentior quam eius fortuna sinit."* Still, it is true that he passes through much suffering. Perhaps the formula *"Vivo equidem vitamque extrema per omnia duco"* best describes his condition. His potentiality for experiencing sorrow grows with the realization of the greatness of his task. The difference between the Aeneas of the last third of the poem and that of the first third lies not in his greater courage but in his greater experience and in his being more deeply pervaded by Roman attitudes. The sixth to eighth books contain the essential kernel of the poem in that the hero meets Rome physically and spiritually. In the sixth book he finds the Roman idea; in the seventh and eighth books he meets the Roman soil and landscape, the Roman cult and the λιτοδίαιτον of the Roman style of living. Moreover, these books contain religious and political-historical revelations which give a necessary importance and a significant frame to his actions. In the sixth book Aeneas is not only introduced to the tragic fate of this world and the solution and atonement to come in the world hereafter, but also to the order of this world and the course and meaning of Roman history. The eighth book also contains a lesson in that the straightforward simplicity of the old Roman morality is given to Aeneas as a model to be followed. In introducing the guest into his house, Evander formulates the "moral" of the book:

> Hercules himself in the hour of victory bowed his head to enter this door. This royal dwelling was not too small to contain even him. Guest of mine, be strong to scorn wealth and so mold yourself that you also may be fit for a God's converse. Be not exacting as you enter a poor home.

VIII.362:
> ... haec, inquit, limina victor
> Alcides subiit, haec illum regia cepit.

> Aude, hospes, contemnere opes et te quoque dignum
> Finge deo, rebusque veni non asper egenis.

In the eyes of his enemies, the Trojan king, Aeneas, was a rich Asiatic prince who had yielded to Punic luxury [39] and was tainted with oriental effeminacy. Remember Jarbas' prayer in which Aeneas, the "Paris with a retinue of eunuchs and his perfumed hair," is oriental effeminacy personified; and the anger of Turnus (XII.97) and the harsh words of Numanus that contrasted the old Italian *duritia* with the Phrygian *desidia* (IX.603 ff.). In Evander's house Aeneas is cleansed, as it were, of the odium of his Asiatic origin and imbued with Italo-Roman contempt for *luxuria*. In leaving the Oriental world and entering the Roman world, Aeneas becomes a Roman in his heart. This then is the deeper meaning of the eighth book as it concerns Aeneas' inner pilgrimage. And it follows convincingly that at the end of the book—in a prominent place, where the middle third of the poem [40] ends— he should lift the shield of Vulcan whereon Roman history is shown as culminating in Augustus' victory and triumph: "Lifting the glory and destiny of the grandsons upon his shoulders." The vicarious character of his sufferings and actions could not be expressed more earnestly. At last he has acquired the necessary maturity to bear the destiny of Rome. Symbols of the Roman mission and scenes in which he personifies Roman majesty mark the places in the last books in which his appearance is most powerful.[41]

DIDO

As Aeneas the Dardan looked in wonder at these pictures of Troy, rapt and intent in concentration, for he had eyes only for them, the queen herself, Dido, in all her beauty, walked to the temple in state, closely attended by a numerous, youthful retinue. She was like Diana when she keeps her dancers dancing on the banks of Eurotas or along the slopes of Cynthus, with a thousand mountain nymphs following in bands on this side and on that; she is taller than all other goddesses, as with her quiver slung from her shoulder she steps on her way, and a joy beyond words steals into Latona's heart. Like her was Dido, and like her she walked happily with the throng around her, intent on hastening the work for her future realm. And then facing the Goddess's doorway, under her temple dome, with her armed guards about her, she took her seat in the center on a raised throne.

I.494:

> Haec dum Dardanio Aeneae miranda videntur,
> Dum stupet obtutuque haeret defixus in uno,
> Regina ad templum forma pulcherrima Dido
> Incessit magna iuvenum stipante caterva,
> Qualis in Eurotae ripis aut per iuga Cynthi
> Exercet Diana choros, quam mille secutae
> Hinc atque hinc glomerantur Oreades, illa pharetram
> Fert umero gradiensque deas [1] supereminet omnis,
> Latonae tacitum pertemptant gaudia pectus:
> Talis erat Dido, talem se laeta ferebat
> Per medios instans operi regnisque futuris.
> Tum foribus divae media testudine templi
> Saepta armis solioque alte subnixa resedit.

The dark drama of Dido begins with a happy scene. This contrast according to the rules of classical composition [2] adds emphasis to the tragic aspect of the poem. In the mind of the reader Dido's joy contrasts with her subsequent sorrow, her constant interest in the growth of Carthage with that city's destruction. Her destiny, like that of Sophocles' Oedipus, is accomplished in a tragic reversal.[3] At the same time the brilliant opening scene indicates an important start in the same way a clear full melody would. Vergil knew how to heighten the beginning and end of a sequence of action through imagery and how thereby to increase the inner movement.

He has been criticized, however, for transferring the simile of Artemis' joyous hunt from Homer's dance of Nausicaa with her companions (*Ody.* 6.102 ff.) to Dido's stately entrance. Probus, to whom we owe so much in the transmission of Latin literature, is the first in the circle of critics: "I remember hearing from Valerius Probus' pupils," says Gellius (*N.A.* 9.9.12), "that he used to say how Vergil had nowhere been more infelicitous than when he transferred the charming verses written about Nausicaa by Homer. In the first place, Homer had fittingly and properly compared Nausicaa, playing with friends, to Diana, hunting with rural divinities on mountain ridges. Vergil's treatment simply was not fitting because the simile, conceived from Diana's sporting and hunting, could not be applied to Dido as she proceeded in pomp and festive attire through the middle of the city. Second, Homer had spoken clearly and openly of Diana's sporting pleasures, while Vergil, without mentioning the hunt, placed the quiver on Diana's shoulder as if it were a piece of baggage or a burden. Probus was particularly puzzled that Homer's Leto was both mentally and spiritually genuinely joyful—for this is the meaning of γέγηθε δέ τε φρένα Λητώ. Vergil, on the other hand, in imitating this, represented her joy as sluggish and superficial, and in a way, half-hearted. What else could '*pertemptant*' mean? And worst of all, Vergil had skipped the line, 'It is easy to recognize her though all of them are beautiful,' when there is no greater praise of beauty than to say that among beauties she was more beautiful."

The sensitive art critic, Sainte-Beuve, has adopted the essentials of this evaluation in his *Étude sur Virgile* (p. 292). As qualities of the Vergilian imitation, he praises only the rhythm and the splendor of the language. Heinze, too (p. 120, no. 1), following Ribbeck (*Prolegomena zur Vergilausgabe,* p. 143) and Georgii (*Die antike Äneiskritik aus den Scholien und anderen Quellen,* Stuttgart, 1891, p. 44), approves Probus' criticism. Cartault, who joins Sainte-Beuve, judges even more severely: "Quite certainly there is nothing in common between the dance of Diana and the attitude of Dido as she organizes her empire. In fact the comparison is inappropriate." (A. Cartault, *L'art de Virgile dans l'Enéide,* Paris, 1926, p. 123). Yet Servius had already demurred: "Many who find fault with the simile do so because they are ignorant of the fact that chosen examples, parables, and similes do not always have a one-to-one correlation, but correspond sometimes in all parts, sometimes only in one." The fact is, the poet does not need such a defense. The correspondence is actually much more thorough than Servius and Probus surmised. Even Scaliger, the most explicit and successful of Vergil's apologists missed the point.[4] It is true that the point of stress in Homer's comparison, as well as in Vergil's, is the beauty, not the movement. But this is not decisive, because always in Vergil and often in Homer, the whole simile and not just the so-called *tertium comparationis* serves to elucidate and heighten the action.[5] Moreover, Dido's entrance is filled with lively movement. It is by no means as solemn as Probus and others assume. It is tempo *allegro moderato,* not *andante maestoso.* In stark contrast to Aeneas' melancholy contemplation of the Trojan reliefs, it ripples with joy. Here, Aeneas' mournful quietude is contrasted with Dido's joyous activity and his tears for the past contrast with her happy plans for her dominion's future.[6] Subsequently, this is all reversed. Troy will rise again more gloriously; Carthage will fall. The fatal reversal in Dido's life is balanced by the happy change in Aeneas' life.

Although there is more of a correspondence than has been acknowledged between the lively movement of the Diana simile and that of the queen's entrance, the difference between the two situations is so great that the use of the simile may, indeed, seem dubious. But Vergil has taken this into account and has by no means adopted the simile unchanged. In Homer we read (5.102):

> Artemis the Archeress has come down from the mountain along the high ridge of Taygetos or Erymanthos to chase the wild boar or the nimble deer, and the Nymphs of the countryside join with her in the sport.

Vergil's words *"exercet Diana choros quam mille secutae, . . ."* indicate that Diana leads her companions. Her behavior is comparable, therefore, to the regal dignity of Dido as characterized in the words: *"instans operique regnisque futuris."* Besides, Artemis' and the nymphs' hunting sport [7] has been replaced by composed ritualistic performance.[8] This is made clear in *"mille Oreades"* as well as in the first words of the simile: *"in Eurotae ripis aut per juga Cynthi."* The scene has shifted from the hunting grounds of Taygetos and Erymanthos to Artemis' shrines in Sparta and Delos. Simultaneously, the goddess' occupation has changed, too. With Vergil one can easily imagine Diana before or near the temple, in much the same way that Dido appears before the temple of Juno.

I believe that there would have been less criticism of this passage if the change of locale had not been overlooked. The change constitutes the reference to Dido's movement, the absence of which caused the censure of Probus and the others.[9] It has also been overlooked that Dido not only goes to the temple, but organizes and directs the activity of those engaged in the still unfinished work.[10] This must be the concrete and simple meaning of *"instans operi"*—"constant interest in the construction." It refers, therefore, just as much to the queen's inspection of the progress of the building as to her thoughts. As in the simile the nymphs crowd around her, *"hinc atque hinc glomerantur Oreades,"* where she is surrounded by the men engaged in the building. But, if the phrase is understood to refer only to that part of Dido's activities mentioned later (I.507): *"operumque laborem partibus aequabat justis,"* the later mention would be a somewhat superfluous repetition, excusable, of course, on the ever-ready grounds of incompleteness. One hesitates to resort to this. The proposed interpretation makes it evident that the comparison between the queen inspecting the building performance and the goddess, leading the performance of the Oreads on the banks of the Eurotas and the ridges of Cynthos, is excellent; not only the queen grows thereby in stature, but the activity around the unfinished temple is invested with poetic splendor.

Indeed, Vergil has further transformed his material. In Homer, Odysseus is still far away and the beautiful spectacle is seen by none but the poet and reader. Aeneas, on the other hand, awaits and sees the queen.[11] The germ of love in his heart sprouts from this first deeply stirring impression.[12] In Homer's similes, the action is suspended while the poet pauses to elaborate a point of the story. In Vergil's similes the inner action continues in the emotions of the persons involved. To a much greater degree than Homer's, Vergil's similes are transparent signs for inner events. Although it constitutes only a special case of what Richard Heinze said about the "ethos" of the Vergilian story in general,[13] this fact is of the utmost importance to the interpretation of similes in the *Aeneid* and has been nowhere clearly stated.

What, then, of Eduard Norden's thesis that Vergil added his similes subsequently, *ornatus causa?* In spite of Heinze's attempt at refutation (p. 258, note 1), the possibility cannot be completely ignored. A close examination seems, indeed, to prove that many similes have been interpolated, or as I prefer to say, elaborated later. Norden, however, is wrong in assuming that they were added only *ornatus causa,* in the sense of external ornament (the "rhetorical" perception of "tropes" as mere embellishment is equally inadequate for prose and poetry because it is incompatible with the essence of true art). Vergil connected these similes most intimately with the interior action which accompanies the exterior events. As most of them were probably planned from the outset, they are an integral part of the work. To assign them contemptuously to "subsequent" adornment is to misjudge the slow laborious craftsmanship of Vergil as creator of a literary epic who executed his intention with careful details of depth and refinement.[14] Assuming that the similes *are* interpolated, it is still true that their function is to give the poem depth and to bring it closer to the artistic idea as the poet either conceived of it from the beginning or gradually came to conceive of it. There is no reason to consider the similes less important or less valid because of a later conception. Rather, even as later interpolations they attest to the mature artistry and masterly accomplishment of the poet.

The Diana simile expresses a material event, that is, Dido's appearance. It also expresses an inner event: the spiritual behavior of Aeneas, albeit in a symbolic veil. His behavior is expressed as clearly in melody and rhythm as in imagery and thought. Sight and sound form an indivisible unit. The verses start with simple spondaic hexameters:

> She was like Diana when she keeps her dancers dancing
> on the banks of Eurotas or along the slopes of Cynthus,
> with a thousand mountain-nymphs following in bands on
> this side and on that; she is taller than all other goddesses,
> as with her quiver slung from her shoulder she steps on
> her way.

I.498:

> Qualis in Eurotae ripis aut per iuga Cynthi
> Exercet Diana choros, quam mille secutae ...

The movement grows more vivid:

> Hinc atque hinc glomerantur Oreades, illa pharetram,

and ends in pure dactylic hexameters:

> Fert umero gradiensque deas supereminet omnis.

The scene culminates in this line, for only here is the queen seen in all her divine splendor. The tension is then released and falls in a calm hexameter:

and a joy beyond words steals into Latona's heart.

Latonae tacitum pertemptant gaudia pectus.

The joyous sport in Homer's simile emerges here as a dramatic entrance, and the self-contented circle of the dancers has become an accelerating inner movement with a definite direction. Thus, the difference between the similes becomes a simile itself for the difference between the poets. But the real crux of the Diana simile rests in the joy that fills Latona's silent heart,[15] which explains why Vergil, in contrast to Homer, has put it at the end. The hidden emotion of the still unseen spectator is thus revealed.[16] To use an image of Schiller's: "We detect the bud from which Dido's drama develops in the emotion symbolized by the simile—Aeneas is moved by the queen's charm." Interpreted in this way, the verse is of an exceptional quality. The connection, so delicately hinted at, is underscored by another circumstance. At a later important stage in the drama of Dido, before the fatal hunt, it is Aeneas who appears before the adoring Dido in the simile of an epiphany of Apollo in Delos. Once again there are choirs (IV.145: *instauratque choros = exercetque choros*); again a festive crowd presses around the divinity; and again the god, like Diana, proceeds over the ridges of Cynthos and "arms sound round his shoulders" (as in the *Iliad* 1.46). This is to say that the similes which symbolize the "decisive pantomime of the erotic meeting" (H. v. Hofmannsthal) are plainly related. It is also to say that the change in locale of the Diana simile to the shrines in Sparta and Delos with the addition of the quiver was effected in view of the Apollo simile—inspired by Apollonius Rhodius in content, though not in function (*Arg.* I.307 ff.). Aeneas and Dido, predestined to fatal love, meet in the image of two correlated divinities. The power of love is symbolized in the triumphant force of their divine beauty: Dido is *pulcherrima* (I.496), Aeneas is *pulcherrimus* (IV.141).[17] Co-ordination of the two encounters reveals the first one as having a fatal meaning also. Upon Dido's first entrance, the distant future is shown as already touched with tragedy. Aeneas is present, the trap is set. Dido, unaware, has started on the road to ruin. Moreover, there is a mysterious connection in the fact that Dido appears in the guise of the divine huntress Diana, for this appearance presents not only a parallel to the "arms" of the god in the Aeneas-Apollo simile, it also points to the fateful hunt. The *pharetra,* so severely censured by Probus, is the result of inner necessity. Venus the huntress (I.314 ff.),[18] the simile of Diana as huntress, and Dido the huntress are marks of the destiny that brings Aeneas to Dido; the pictures appear as signs of tragic meaning. We have here a phenomenon which occurs elsewhere in the *Aeneid* and which deserves a separate discussion—the use of related symbols to denote connected events.

The example of the Diana simile plainly shows how Vergil gave a completely new and beautiful meaning to the inspired poetry of older works. Among the Latin and Romance literatures, as much as they neglect the outer in favor of inner originality, Vergil's procedure was unique. His critics and his apologists, influenced by the obvious borrowings, overlooked the decisive changes beneath the surface. This may serve as a warning against the type of interpretation which almost always tacitly assumes that Vergil simply appropriated the content of older works along with the motifs, be it in relation to Homer and Apollonius or Naevius and Ennius. He did not do that! The secret of his originality is hidden in the transformation, connection, and deepening of the motifs to which he gave another meaning and a new beauty.[19] He did this through sensitive changes, through a web of mysterious references, through novel light and sound effects. Such artistry with line and color, composition and combination, is the very nature of his poetry.[20] In a word, it is the *form* through which a new soul emerges as if by magic from the borrowed material. And an inner readiness, a loving, if critical contemplation, is needed to recognize it. "The voice of beauty is a quiet one," Nietzsche said. There is no easy open road to the beauty within the poems of the Roman magician, the chaste Vergilius, who in life retreated quietly from the world and who in his poetry veiled feeling in symbols as every real artist does. In a majestic picture the action caused by Dido's entrance is gentled and smoothed into the *andante maestoso* that Probus missed:

> And then, facing the Goddess's doorway, under her temple-dome, with her armed guards about her, she took her seat in the center on a raised throne. She was already announcing new laws and statutes to her people and deciding by her own balanced judgment, or by lot, a fair division of the toil demanded of them . . .

I.505:

> Tum foribus divae, media testudine templi,[21]
> Saepta armis solioque alte subnixa resedit.
> Iura dabat legesque viris, operumque laborem
> Partibus aequabat iustis aut sorte trahebat . . .

Divine protection and armaments, the foundations of royal power, are named in the first two lines. In the next two lines the contents of that power, the development and realization of justice, are named. All that is essential and important is compressed into a narrow form. This is a basic quality of classical style.

The queen's virtues are revealed in symbolic gestures: in the first verse, *pietas;* in the second, *maiestas* and *dignitas; iustitia,* in the third and fourth. The relation of the queen to the divine powers is expressed in the image of herself as ruler enthroned in Juno's temple before the gates of that goddess. The relation was already implied in the composition of the words which announce her entrance: *"regina ad templum."* This, too, is classical style—the great is co-ordinated with the great. The queen had to make her first appearance in the temple because only there do her person and actions find a worthy frame. At the same time, the inner tie between the queen and her patron goddess is made visible, for enthroned in the temple the queen is a human representative of Juno.

In the further course of the story, the queen's piety and realization of religious duty play a large part. The arrival of Aeneas and Dido's decisions for love and death are accompanied by ritualistic behavior showing the reverence in her soul for the gods. Here, again, she is a match for Aeneas, but her devotion cannot save her from the cruel fate awaiting her. Aeneas' words, spoken in the face of the somber background of her destiny, sound like bitter derision:

> But if Powers of the Beyond take thought for the good, if there exists anywhere any justice at all, or some Intelligence able to know the right, then may your true reward come from them.

I.603:

> Di tibi, si qua pios respectant numina, si quid
> Usquam iustitia est et mens sibi conscia recti,
> Praemia digna ferant.

And so these scenes enhance the tragic effect just as Aeneas' piety intensifies our compassion for his sufferings.[22] The following scenes further enrich and deepen the inner image of the queen. Her humanity, already recognized by Aeneas from the Trojan war reliefs,[23] is at its most beautiful and pure, first in the scenes with Ilioneus and then with the hero himself. It finds expression in the *"voltum demissa"* gesture which delicately shows her embarrassment at the harsh treatment afforded the shipwrecked Trojans.[24] Humanity is the primary tone of her first conversation with Aeneas. After the introductory *"coram quem quaeritis adsum,"* it starts with *"O sola infandos Trojae miserata labores,"* and ends with the classical expression of humanity, *"non ignara mali miseris*

succurrere disco." [25] Her soul is also related to Aeneas' soul
in the gentleness and generosity of her nature and her compassion for others. But at the same time this very atmosphere
of humanity forms an intentional contrast with the irreconcilable hatred to come. And the complete reversal in the final
scenes of the fourth book is possible only when related to
this original warmth and sentiment.

Dido's tragedy develops from her great and noble soul.
This has been contested with the plea that the ending of
the Dido book is the result of the situation and not of the
queen's character.[26] The exact opposite is true. Everything
she does and all that she suffers springs from her innermost
being. She is doomed to die, not because of the situation, but
because of the interaction of her character *with* the situation.
The following considerations make this clear by showing that
the images which illuminate her fate most distinctly, and the
key and the style in which they are couched, have from the
start a higher tragic coloring than the commentators have
realized. This is so, not because the poet wished to "mo-
tivate" the queen's decision for death from the situation, but
because he wished to cover the whole development with a
cloud of foreboding. It is not true that Vergil intends to en-
force the unnoticed necessity of a tragic end upon the reader
only from the moment when Anna's prayers remain un-
heard.[27] In the *Aeneid,* as in most tragedies, everything aims
toward the tragic end from the start, so that nothing else can
be expected. This is quite evident from the way in which the
result of Amor's activity is described at the end of the first
book:

> (Dido), condemned now to sure destruction,
> could not satisfy her longing.

I.712:

> Infelix pesti devota futurae
> Expleri mentem nequit, . . .

And it comes ultimately from Vergil's notion, as expressed in the *Georgics,* that love is a demoniacal, tragic force. In the passage concerning the love of animals, the sinister influence of passion on human fate is represented most directly and with enormous power in the image of the young man mad with love (III.258 ff.). The tragic lights of the final scene in the last book, in which the queen's incipient fascination is intimated, point in the same direction.[28] And finally, the fourth book is bathed in a tragic mood from the very first verse. But the cause of the increase of her passion is concealed, as has been said before, in the very essence of Dido. Aeneas' tale can arouse love in her heart because his heroism touches a responsive chord in herself. Because she is every inch a queen, she cannot but love this regal hero of divine origin.[29] The proddings by Venus and Juno at the decisive moments, the interference of Amor in the shape of Ascanius, the hunt and the convenient thunderstorm are only additional visual aids indicating inner events.

In Vergil's as in Homer's eyes, as shown by Walter F. Otto in his book, *Die Götter Griechenlands,* the divine, to a great extent, coincides with the natural. This does not mean that it is right to explain the interference of the gods in a purely rationalistic manner and to consider them purely as visible symbols of natural phenomena. It is a mistake to assume that Vergil "translated psychological facts and the 'educated' reader retranslates them into psychological terms because he understands, e.g., the appearances of the gods 'allegorically' " (Heinze). Such a game cannot be reconciled with the religious spirit of the poet, nor is it fair to the nature of poetry. The great passions of the heart appear in Vergil's poetry as manifestations of the divine demoniacal just as they do in the poetry of the Greeks. They are quite naturally seen in this manner and are not being made "understandable" nor being given the dignity and ideality of sublime style. In the form of the myth with gods and demons, oracles and dreams, all that is mysterious and sinister in life becomes more tangible, less vague in outline; the higher forces, too, appear closer and more clear. But these forces are found elsewhere, too. The Age of Augustus was not yet blind and had not yet turned its back on the manifestations of the divine. Vergil truly believed in divine power and to this earnest and pious poet the myth was more than a poetic tale—it was a symbol of his religion. As Hugo von Hofmannsthal says in his "Conversation About Poems," which admits so much insight into the nature and symbolic language of poetry: [30] "For the pious, only the symbol is truly real."

Having such reverence for the mystery of fate, having the religiosity of a Roman who believed in visible gods, and the classical man's sensory attitude, which is akin to the demands of poetry, Vergil did not conceive of the soul psychologically, but mythically and religiously. In writing poetry, he was, as Baudelaire said, in a state of *"enfance retrouvée à volonté."* The poet's world is not "more dignified and ideal," but more tangible and primitive. Vergil was not interested in "natural psychology." The gods were visible to him. Any other conception presupposes an idea of art only to be held by a non-artist and an opinion on religion that corresponds to a godless age. In Vergil, moreover, the role of the gods is most intimately connected with his concept of a divine plan controlling and directing universal events. For this reason, too, all that happens must be traced beyond the psychological conditions of individual fate and connected with the divine. Thus, by means of the poetic world of the gods, manifesting the poet's belief in a higher power, the two-fold character of history is expressed. Every historical happening occurs on two planes: one of human purpose, desires, and passions, and another, great and mysterious, held within the hand of the divine manipulator of all events. Understood in this way, Vergil rises to a level of thought common to philosophers of history as varied as Augustine, Hegel, and Jakob Burckhardt.

Dido's experience, also, is truly more than a psychological process. It is destiny willed by divine forces, an event of world history, as it were, and a link in the chain of Roman *fata*. Besides destroying her own existence it produces ruin far beyond her personal fate by putting an end to the existence of Carthage.

That the queen anticipates and represents her city's fate not only derives from the basic idea of the poem—Aeneas and Dido figure as mythical incarnations of the historical powers of Rome and Carthage (as do Jupiter and Juno on a higher plane)—but it is expressly stated in the lines describing the effect of the news of the queen's catastrophe:

> A cry rose to the palace-roof. Carthage was stricken by the shock and Rumor ran riot in the town. Lamentation and sobbing and women's wailing rang through the houses, and high heaven echoed with the loud mourning; as if some enemy had broken through and all Carthage, or ancient Tyre,[31] were falling, with the flames rolling madly up over dwellings of gods and men.

IV.665:

> It clamor ad alta
> Atria; concussam bacchatur Fama per urbem.
> Lamentis gemituque et femineo ululatu
> Tecta fremunt, resonat magnis plangoribus aether,
> Non aliter quam si immissis ruat hostibus omnis
> Karthago aut antiqua Tyros, flammaeque furentes
> Culmina perque hominum volvuntur perque deorum.

This is pathetic intensification and transcendent symbolism as well. The simile is conceived from both the plot situation and from a higher view open to the reader. For a moment a larger context can be seen. Dido's fate has become transparent; it coincides with the fate of the city. Vergil has assumed this effect from a Homeric simile (*Iliad* 22.4081):

> ... and all his people about him were taken with wailing and lamentation all through the city. It was most like what

would have happened, if all towering Ilion had been burning top to bottom in fire.

In this description of the lament for Hector there is also a presentiment of Troy's fate, for in the *Iliad*, Hector's destruction is more than once connected with the final destruction of Troy, which follows: 6.403 ff.; 22.382 ff.; 24.499.[32]

Anna's words also point beyond the poem to the same relation (IV.682):

> Sister, you have destroyed my life with your own, and the lives of our people and Sidon's nobility, and your whole city too.

Within the narrow framework of the story these words are only a hyperbolic expression of a sister's grief. But they are also true in a much deeper sense than is surmised by Anna, for the drama of Dido ends in the destruction of Carthage.

The political and historical symbolism attached to Dido may be disregarded. Her tragedy can be explained in human terms without conflict between the natural and supernatural meanings. After Venus and Juno have instigated the affair, everything develops as a matter of course. Dido, speaking to her sister at the beginning of the fourth book, resists the love she feels for Aeneas because she is not yet willing to break faith with her dead husband. She solemnly exclaims:

> But I could pray that the earth should yawn deep to engulf me, or the Father Almighty blast me to the Shades with a stroke of his thunder, deep down to those pallid Shades in darkest Erebus, before ever I violate my honor or break its laws.

IV.24:

> Sed mihi vel tellus optem prius ima dehiscat
> Vel pater omnipotens adigat me fulmine ad umbras
> Pallentis umbras Erebi noctemque profundam,
> Ante, Pudor, quam te violo aut tua iura resolvo.

This is much more than theatrical pathos. It is a curse on herself that is destined to be cruelly fulfilled. The verses conjure up the descent to the pale shades of Erebus which will become reality. In this way, the end of Book IV is foreseen at its beginning.

Anna is not the lascivious insinuator found in the Attic drama. She is not a Euripidean nurse, no Menandrian confidante. Her first words are those of a tender, loving sister: *"O luce magis dilecta sorori."* She engenders the idea in Dido's already loving heart that the exposed kingdom needs a protector and that only Aeneas can bring about the real greatness of Carthage:

> And, Dido, only imagine, if you make this splendid marriage, what a great future lies in store for your city and our realm! With a Trojan army marching at our side, think what deeds of prowess will exalt the fame of Carthage!

IV.47:
> Quam tu urbem, soror, hanc cernes, quae surgere regna
> Coniugio tali! Teucrum comitantibus armis
> Punica se quantis attollet gloria rebus!

Anna, in the above climactic words, appeals to the Queen's obligations to duty and glory, to the love she holds for the city she has founded and to which she has given all of her time and energy. In this way she kindles the flame from the embers and "loosens the modesty." It is not through the power of passion alone that Dido falls in love. Love comes to her just as much because of her inner inclination toward heroism, greatness, and glory, and through her devotion to her royal work. In fact, all of the nobility of her nature is appealed to: her talent for great love (proven to Sychaeus in life and death [33]), her compassion for the Trojans (so easily converted to love), her feminine nature (also awakened by Anna in IV.33: *"Nec dulcis natos Veneris nec praemia noris"*), and her longing for fulfillment as shown in the tenderness with which she takes Ascanius upon her lap and cries sweetly from her heart, *"si quis mihi parvulus aula luderet Aeneas."*

Dido's love for Aeneas is closely interwoven with the great and noble characteristics of her nature—that is her tragedy. The innate grandeur of her royal soul—and, as a consequence, the depth of her fall—distinguish her from the Greek models to whom she is compared. She is not an intemperate barbarian, a bloodthirsty "lioness" like Euripides' Medea, nor the loving maiden of Apollonius, although she has some traits of both. For example, the sublime passion and antique grandeur of Dido connect her with Euripides, while her tenderness recalls Apollonius. Still, she is more human than Medea, and greater, though less tender, than the maiden. The pendulum of her fate makes a wider arc as it swings from the faith and honor that she holds for her dead husband as *univira* to the shame of free love, from the proud dignity and royal splendor of her first entrance to the worst humiliation (IV.412 ff.), from joy to deepest sadness, from warm humanity to cruel hatred, from royal work to neglect of her duty (IV.86 ff.), from the near-completion of the task of making a great kingdom to its utter destruction. The immensity of Dido's tragedy is in the size of the contrast—in the shattering reversal. This is the important reason why the book of Dido can be compared with the Greek tragedy, as (in the words of Friedrich Leo) no other Roman tragedy can.

The conversation with Anna releases the full force of feeling in Dido's heart. The destruction that advances through passion reaches its first climax in the mad dash through the city and in the simile of the deer. This simile develops in contrast to the preceding image of a Dido who sacrifices and prays for the peace of the gods:

> Lovely Dido herself would take the bowl in her right hand and pour the wine between the horns of a pure white cow, or she would pace in the ritual dance near the gods' reeking altars before the eyes of their statues.

IV.60:

> Ipsa tenens dextra pateram pulcherrima Dido
> Candentis vaccae media inter cornua fundit,
> Aut ante ora deum pinguis spatiatur ad aras.

Lying between the noble composure of this ritual and the wild frenzy of the simile, between the bright sacrificial scene and the dark feverish heat, is the divination scene which in its tragic coloring foreshadows the raging passion and the merciless obsession to which the queen falls prey:

> She would peer with parted lips into the open breasts
> of sheep for the message of their still breathing vitals.

II.63:

> Pecudumque reclusis
> Pectoribus inhians spirantia consulit exta.

This is followed by the poet's painful outcry:

> O why can man's mind not grasp the seer's
> meaning! [34]

> Heu vatum ignarae mentes, . . .

And the next verses, which lead directly to the wild wanderings of the queen, point to the fire that smoulders beneath ostensible calm:

> There lay no help for her infatuation in temples or
> prayers; for all the time the flame ate into her melting
> marrow, and deep in her heart the wound was silently
> alive.

IV.65:

> Quid delubra iuvant? Est mollis flamma medullas
> Interea et tacitum vivit sub pectore volnus.

This echoes the book's beginning. The same images—the wound, the flame, the arrow (IV.4: *"haerent infixi pectore voltus verbaque"*), the restlessness and delusion; these signal her sufferings. If the storm at sea represents the demoniacal power of nature (and by implication, history) and if Allecto's actions represent war, then Dido's wanderings and the deer simile represent the power of Eros:

> There lay no help for her infatuation in temples or in prayers, for all the time the flame ate into her melting marrow, and deep in her heart the wound was silently alive. Poor Dido was afire, and roamed distraught all over her city; like a doe caught off her guard and pierced by an arrow from some armed shepherd, who from the distance had chased her amid Cretan woods and without knowing it has left in her his winged barb; so that she traverses in her flight forests and mountain tracks on Dicte, with the deadly reed fast in her flesh.

IV.66:

> Quid delubra iuvant? est mollis flamma medullas
> Interea et tacitum vivit sub pectore volnus.
> Uritur infelix Dido totaque vagatur
> Urbe furens, qualis coniecta cerva sagitta,
> Quam procul incautam nemora inter Cresia fixit
> Pastor agens telis liquitque volatile ferrum
> Nescius; illa fuga silvas saltusque peragrat
> Dictaeos; haeret lateri letalis harundo.

The scene above cannot be completely understood on a naively realistic basis. It represents a particular point in the story and at the same time is a symbol of a psychophysical event. Passion, according to the ancients, is a sickness of the whole person. Moreover, psychological facts are consistently made apparent through gods and demons (where we speak of symbolization) and especially through gestures, images, and similes. The ancients saw the body as expression of the soul and the outer life as expression of the inner. We miss the point if we speak of a "transformation into the symbolic" as if the symbolic-poetic life is secondary to the psychological. An insoluble unit is composed of both. The understanding of ancient man demands sensory contemplation of inner facts rather than abstract analysis. Ancient man's mind was still filled with images and not yet with concepts, as is the modern mind. Goethe expressed an antique axiom when he said in *Propyläeneinleitung,* "He who cannot speak clearly to the senses, cannot speak directly to the mind either." [35] Something of this attitude has always been inherent in poetry. The poet always inclines toward a symbolic perception of sensory fact as the inborn, original mode of human feeling. Just as an opera does not transpose inner events into music, but experiences them as such, so poetry presents them as sensory events. "Nothing could be more wrong," says Gundolf of Shakespeare, "than to assume that the poet thinks abstractly first and looks for an image afterward, that he feels first and looks for sensory aid afterward. No, he lives, thinks, feels, suffers, and rejoices in images. This, next to the compulsion to react to the world as to rhythm, is the main characteristic of the poet's true state." [36]

The beauty and depth of the famous, often imitated deer simile rests on several circumstances. The flight of the loving woman exhibits a psychological truth as deep as the thought that she is unprotected and exposed (*incauta*) to the danger of falling in love. At the same time, Dido's inner restlessness, the *dubia mens* (IV.55), her shame, and the subjective feeling of guilt are reflected in the image of flight. It is like a last desperate attempt to escape from an inexorable fate. The tragedy of her objective innocence is shown in the word *incautam,* just as *pastor nescius* shows that Aeneas also is guiltless. Moreover, the image of the noble, suffering animal moves us to compassion. But the flight, like the prayer for *pax deorum,* is in vain: *"haeret lateri letalis harundo."*

The final words expose the inner meaning of this simile just as the secret meaning of the Diana simile was made clear in its last verse. The simile partakes of two spheres of meaning; it illuminates a present state and reveals a destiny. In this function, it adds a new dimension to the event.

Homer is different. He aims at illumination of visible relations while Vergil aims to establish moods, interpret states of mind, and to intimate impending fate. Accordingly, the Homeric similes are more severely outlined, often surprisingly rational, and often strangely cold and seemingly insensitive. On the other hand, the Vergilian similes have fluid, flexible contours which allow them to be more felt than observed. Homer strives to make an event explicit. Vergil strives to explain and interpret it.

His similes are complicated structures. If it is possible to analyze what is inseparable, it can be said that the deer simile has a threefold function: (1) It makes the queen's roaming more explicit (this is the original function of a simile in Homer —clarification of an exterior event); (2) it reveals Dido's state of mind (clarification of an inner event); (3) it foreshadows her tragic end (symbolic prediction) through content, key, and pathos of the movement. It is the prologue that sets the mood for a tragic development. To enlarge upon the last point: the wild movement of the deer simile functions within the Dido drama in the same way in which the storm at sea functions within the framework of the whole, or the Allecto episode functions in the second half of the poem. In both cases, tragic action is introduced by a pathetic and dramatic scene and is thereby symbolically anticipated.

Just as in a Greek temple where the proportion and form determining the whole are repeated in the sections, or in a symphony where the parts mirror the whole, the *Aeneid* is in part and whole subject to the same principle of form. This type of scene is repeated a second time in a narrower sense in the course of the Dido drama, when the tragedy begins with the description of the wild action of Fama whose appearance leads in strict succession from Iarbas' prayer to Jupiter's interference with the departure of Aeneas. We meet it for a third time in the description of Dido's rage after she learns of Aeneas' decision to leave. All of these scenes, including that of the sea storm, the Allecto episode, the Sibyl's frenzy (at the beginning of Book VI), Laocoön's death (at the beginning of Book II), Metabus' and the child's flight over the swollen river in the Camilla episode (XI.547 ff.), are variations of the same theme and their function is to accentuate the beginning of a tragic development.

In the next climactic scene, the tragic mood characteristic of this book is expressed in the sublimely terrifying cosmic events which echo the action—the thunderstorm accompanying the love union of the protagonists. Nature had already appeared as the sounding board of action in Homer as a reflection of the original Greek concept of the unity of man and *physis,* that is, the affairs of man are conceived of as being as one with the natural phenomena in which they take place. To this Vergil added the formative principle of classical art, which seeks for unification and refuses anything superfluous or unrelated. The lightning flashes are the marriage torches and the crying of the nymphs on the mountaintop mingling with and embodying the thunder is the hymeneal or marriage song. The love-marriage is expressed symbolically and need not be described. But the signs, multiplied by earth tremor (*"Prima et Tellus et pronuba Juno dant signum"*) [37] are not those of a gay wedding feast, but are rather related to the epiphanies of the gods of the nether world.[38] They are omens of what is coming and bear an explicit comment in the Homeric manner: *"Ille dies primus leti primusque malorum causa fuit."*

Here begins the activity of Fama, which as an inescapable, growing demoniacal power, somewhat like another Allecto, announces and sets off the tragic development.[39] The catastrophe is prepared through the atmosphere created by these images and scenes. This catastrophe, just like the queen's love for Aeneas, is the necessary result of her nature. Her tremendous self-respect is her decisive trait. It is the core of her existence. Love of self in the high Aristotelian sense is perhaps the ultimate value in Roman and ancient ethics. And "glory" connoting so much splendor to the ancients, is most intimately connected with it. "Glory" is the visible brilliance of the inner fire of "self-love." Because Dido is so full of self-respect, she is convinced that she owes her dead husband eternal faithfulness and curses herself should she ever be un-faithful.[40] Therefore, when her love for Aeneas, for which she has paid the price of self-respect, is betrayed, she has no choice but to die. She speaks of death upon first meeting Aeneas (IV.308): *"Nec moritura tenet crudeli funere Dido? Cui me moribundam deseris?"* (323). And again in the first threat of casting a curse upon him:

> I shall be near, haunting you with flames of blackest pitch. And when death's chill has parted my body from its breath, wherever you go my spectre will be there.

IV.384:

> Sequar atris ignibus absens,
> Et cum frigida mors anima seduxerit artus
> Omnibus umbra locis adero.

The words *"sequar atris ignibus absens"* hint darkly at the blazing omen of the funeral pyre to follow the departing Trojan fleet. As the following verses show, the torches of the Eumenides are immediately brought to mind (IV.385 ff.).[41] But the reader, knowing the end, is capable of hearing the double meaning. It is an example of amphibology, a very frequent device in Greek tragedy.[42] The commentators choose one of Servius' interpretations:

> alii 'furiarum facibus' dicunt, hoc est 'invocatas tibi immit-tam diras,' alii 'sociorum' ut paulo post (594) 'ferte citi flammas.' Melius tamen est, ut secundum Urbanum ac-cipiamus 'atris ignibus rogalibus,' qui visi tempestates significant, ut Aeneae sicut in quinto legimus, contigit.

But, for the very reason that the double meaning is intentional, there is no need to make a decision between the explanations. This fact is, of course, incomprehensible to the rationalism of Servius and his modern successors. The reference to the torches of the Eumenides can least of all be excluded (as proposed by Servius Danielis). Servius' reference to the *ignes sociorum* is utterly artificial if (as Thilo assumes with some justification) he was thinking of IV.594. If, on the other hand, he was thinking of the flames of war with which Carthage will pursue Rome (*"exoriare aliquis nostris ex ossibus ultor, qui face Dardanios ferroque sequare colonos"*) there might be some truth in it. Again for a moment, the transcendental symbolism would be visible, as in the simile of the mourning for Dido.

Amphibology as a means of creating tragic tension can be found elsewhere in the Dido drama, for example:

> I have found the way which will either give him back to me or release me from loving him.

IV.478:

> Inveni, germana, viam, gratare sorori,
> Quae mihi reddat eum vel eo me solvat amantem,

> It is my intention to complete certain rites to Stygian Jupiter, which I have formally prepared and begun, and to put an end to my sorrow.

IV.638:

> Sacra Iovi Stygio, quae rite incepta paravi,
> Perficere est animus finemque imponere curis,

> This is my last plea for indulgence, and you must bear with me as sister. And when he has granted it to me, I shall repay the debt with the interest, in death.

IV.435:

> Extremam hanc oro veniam, miserere sororis,
> Quam mihi cum dederit, cumulatam morte remittam.

In the above passage, Heinze, too, missed the double meaning (p. 134, note 2). The words *"cumulatam morte remittam"* are: (1) a hyperbolic expression of gratitude (as understood by Anna), (2) a forecast of death (to the reader and, secretly, to Dido herself).[43] A little earlier in the same speech there is a similar double meaning (IV.429): *"Extremum hoc miserae det munus amanti,"* and (IV.435): *"Extremam hanc veniam."* As Anna understands this, it is the last favor Dido asks Aeneas to grant. And it is also the last favor Dido is ever going to ask in this life. Heinze is wrong in denying that Dido thinks of her death here. This fact is clearly shown (Book IV.308, 323, 385, and 415). A delay in sailing would mean only a delay in death. Without any consideration or reflection on the situation, she is quite sure that Aeneas' departure seals her death. Although her reaction may conceivably be understood as a consequence of her absolute passion, it is also a necessary result of her violated pride. She, alone, who involved herself in this unworthy situation,[44] can find an escape from it.

The words of the nocturnal monologue in which she turns the situation over and over in a last attempt to find an alternative solution have been quoted to prove that Vergil wanted to "force the necessity of a tragic end upon the reader." On the contrary, they show most clearly that the situation will allow another solution, but her character will not. She *could* approach her former suitors, but since she has been scorned by Aeneas, she is too proud to do so (534 ff.). She *could* follow the fleet of Trojans, but this would be an unbearable humiliation (543: *"Sola fuga nautas comitabor ovantis"*). She *could* order the Tyrians to pursue the Trojans' fleet, but she is too humane to push them back into the sea from where they have only just come (544 ff). Death is the only answer as nothing else can save her own ego, her self-respect, and her glory. Death is not only escape from the exterior emergency and a deliverance from unbearable pain, but also a self-imposed atonement (IV.577: *"Quin morere* ut merita es"), and the restitution of the "great image" which she wants to leave to posterity. In the curse that she casts upon Aeneas and the Romans and in the grand manner of her death, her soul restores itself in greatness and liberty. The curse, besides being an expression of love become hate, restores her lost dignity. To the ancient man, revenge meant restoration of his spiritual existence.[45] Thus, Dido in her "epitaph" glories in having avenged Sychaeus' death and, thus, Evander stays alive in order to bring the news of revenge to his son in the realm of the dead (XI.177 ff.). Aeneas' last gesture in the poem is revenge for Pallas just as revenge for Caesar marked the start of Augustus' career.

The queen's pride, her self-respect, her sense of dignity, and her thirst for revenge, all demand her death. Heinze realized this, but argued that Vergil did not allow the grief for her lost love to be the dominant reason "because he followed tradition closely" and "renounced individual characterization" (p. 139). The very character of Dido demands that she not seek death because of lost love, but because of the consciousness of her deep fall. That Queen Dido should commit suicide because of frustrated passion would seem far from great to Vergil. Such a motivation might be sentimental and touching, but Vergil's aim here was to inspire.

The poet did not have to search for a "motivation" for Dido's death, for it is the only solution. Rather, he had to show why the queen delays so long in seeking death. The best reason was that she had not yet abandoned all hope of changing the hero's mind. The real alternative is shown in both of her speeches in the decisive talk with Aeneas. She does not waver, as Heinze assumes, between the possibilities of keeping Aeneas and destroying either him or herself. This vacillation between love and hate, union and destruction, dominates the whole story. She tries three times to alter fate: once when imploring Aeneas to stay, once in the message carried to him by Anna, and then in the monologue of the last tortured night before his departure when she considers the possibility of following her beloved. Every check she encounters leads her unconditionally back to the death decision. The threat of self-destruction and revenge comes after her imploring words. The preparation of the funeral pyre follows the rebuff of Anna's entreaties. The resolution "to die as you deserve" replaces her thought of accompanying the hero.

The poet is at pains to retain a glimmer of hope to the end. Without it the drama would be far less tragic.[46] Dido's hesitation to die is solely the result of this deceptive hope, of her inability to abandon her love. At the moment when Aeneas cuts the ship's painter, her fate is decided.[47]

But before the inexorable judgment following her self-scrutiny, this very hesitation is an additional guilt. This is to say that the more Dido follows the dictates of passion in the face of the impending departure, the further she sinks from proud regality. Vergil is thus enabled to let us feel both the depth of her love and the vileness of her infamy and inner fall. For instance, though her wish to conceive a child of Aeneas' before parting may be touching, it is still undignified. The messages which Anna bears to Aeneas entreat only empty delay: *"Improbe Amor quid non mortalia pectora cogis?"* In the night monologue she even considers following Aeneas in the event he will not take her on board his ship. She, the infinitely proud queen, slides into ever-deepening degradation. Her real tragedy lies in her knowledge of this and not in her obvious fate. In view of this inner disaster she chooses death as the means to liberty and atonement and thus tears herself free from the sinister labyrinth of passion in which she has been lost since the fatal night story of the fall of Troy. Her dignity is restored. The transformation of the ritual wine into blood, the calls of Sychaeus, the mourning of the bird of death, the magic of the priestess,[48] the signs and dreams that pursue her, the feelings of guilt and humiliation that torment her, all considered by Heinze to be the motives of her decision, are really only symptoms, secondary in nature, symbols of her inner movement toward death.

An immense effect of tragic elevation results from the story as we see how her great soul rises again—out of its deformation of sickness and grief and passionate delirium—to the majesty of the words in which she pronounces her own epitaph:

> I have lived my life and finished the course which Fortune allotted me. Now my wraith shall pass in state to the world below.

IV.653:

> Vixi et quem dederat cursum fortuna peregi
> Et nunc magna mei sub terras ibit imago.

Once again she is a queen as in the beginning—and greater and more Roman than ever. If passion obscured her true self, death confirms and maintains it on a higher and purer plane. Through the dignity of death she becomes the "great image," as which she descends into the underworld. "For a man walks among the shades in the form in which he leaves the earth." [49]

This return to greatness is symbolically expressed four times: (1) in the scene (IV.450–521) in which she rises from the dark feeling of doom to the nearly cheerful composure of her speech to Anna (IV.478 ff.) and the magnificently solemn preparation of the funeral pyre; (2) in the nocturnal monologue (534 ff.) when she makes her decision to die and leave the torture of renewed passion behind; (3) in the marvelous monologue in which, as she again controls her emotions, the rending questions and exclamations at the beginning pass into the compressed and inexorable ferocity of the curse (IV.607): *"Sol, qui terrarum flammis opera omnia lustras,"* and she changes from a sublime fury into the proud Queen of Carthage, who, filled with the pathos of holy revenge, vows eternal enmity; and (4) in the final monologue with which she withdraws from existence in this world to eternity as the "great image" whose glory will shine throughout the ages as an illustrious lover and the immortal founder of Carthage.

The sweetly intimate sounds of love are not lacking in her last words, but in genuine Vergilian manner soften the heroic severity of *Exoriare aliquis* and modify the character of Dido's end.

As, in the preparation of the pyre and the prayer to Sol and Juno, Hecate, and the Dirae for revenge, the strict ritual form is the symbol of Dido's restored grandeur, so it is here the lapidary pathos of the Roman inscription style. Her final words are concerned with revenge (IV.661): *"Hauriat hunc oculis ignem crudelis ab alto Dardanus et nostrae secum ferat omina mortis"*), in spite of a last gesture of harmonious loving tenderness (*"paulum lacrimis et mente morata ... dulces exuviae"*). Just so, her parting gesture in the underworld, after a brief hesitation, expresses proud implacability (VI.469 ff.). Thus dies Dido, on her love-bed placed on the pyre, with the sword of Aeneas in her heart [50]—a majestic queen, acknowledging the unbreakable bond of love even in the act of dying. The intensity of her quest for light is expressed once more in the actual moment of death:

> Three times she rose, supporting herself on her elbows, but each time she rolled back onto the bed. With roaming eyes she looked to high heaven for the daylight, and found it, and gave a sigh.

IV.690:

> Ter sese attollens cubitoque adnixa levavit;
> Ter revoluta toro est oculisque errantibus alto
> Quaesivit caelo lucem ingemuitque reperta.

Her prayer begins with an invocation to the sun. Her last glance searches for its light. Her life and her book end with the soothing proximity of her sister Anna, who catches the black blood, and of Juno, who with a benevolent gesture sends Iris down from heaven to release her from life:

> So therefore Iris, saffron-winged, sparkling like dew and trailing a thousand colours as she caught the light of the sun (flew down) across the sky.

IV.700:

> Ergo Iris croceis per caelum roscida pennis
> Mille trahens varios adverso sole colores.

If her death at first seemed to be the result of her passion and grief, it is now seen as the transfiguration and defeat of that passion and grief. Her vacillation between love and hate was apparently also a vacillation between humiliation and grandeur, with grandeur evident even in humiliation. Even though the queen's passion appears to be delusion and ignominy from the point of view of her dignity, we see it also—and this is an essential element of the tragedy of Dido—as the fulfillment of the human potentiality of her great and sensitive soul. In reality she wavers between the demands of her heart and her dignity—between her happiness and her glory.

The battle raging within Dido is related to the conflict which flares up again and again in Aeneas' heart and marks his destiny with tragedy. She, like the hero, suffers from the unrelenting tension between heart's desire and the harsh demands of self-respect and glory. In this inner relationship of personalities, Vergil meets Goethe's demand that the figures, while definitely separate and different from each other, should be of one kind.[51] And the poet's soul is revealed in that which binds them together. Their conflicts are the very conflicts in his soul.

Goethe's second requirement that every part of the drama must represent the whole, is met in the book of Dido. The eruption and conquest of passion is a variation on the basic theme of the conquest of demoniacal forces. Because, in the narrowest sense, this battle is fought in Dido's own soul, the condition mentioned is most tragically expressed in her. Aeneas has to face these forces of passion (God, nature, loving, fighting) outside of himself and must conquer them like a hero and suffer them in open compassion. But his heroism, as well as his suffering, is kept almost free of guilt. In fact, anything that might be interpreted as a sign of guilt is weakened and pushed into the background.[52] On the other hand, Dido (and less majestically, Turnus) falls deeply into sin. Through fate, grief, and sorrow, Aeneas takes part in the world's unhappy turbulence, but he never sinks into it. Like the poet, he is suffering yet elevated—he stands apart from the world. Dido is a more tense, more tragic figure. As *Gestalt,* she is the greater symbol of the tragedy of the poem because she is the embodiment of what the *Aeneid* as a whole separates into different forces. In this sense, the book of Dido can be considered the climax of the whole poem.

TURNUS

That Turnus appears for the first time at midnight (VII.414) is an indication that his destiny belongs to the powers of darkness. When the war-fury, Allecto, "daughter of night," comes to him in the shape of Juno's priestess, Calybe, wearing an olive branch in her hair, he, fully confident of his goddess' help,[1] and with superior sarcasm, refuses her attempt to push him into attacking the anchored Trojan fleet. Thereupon, the enraged Fury drops her mask and shows her true face [2]: "Look here, I am come from the place of the sisters of horror and I bear war and death in my hands." She throws a torch at him and thrusts "the pine-brands in a murky glare" into his chest. Shaking with fear he wakes from his sleep and calls for arms. The "anger," the "passion for iron, the criminal madness of war" begin to rage in him:

> as when a loudly crackling fire of brushwood is piled up high below the ribs of a seething cauldron, where water leaps as it boils, until it can no longer contain itself, but the flood within riots in vapor, dark steam soars into the air, ...

VII.462:

> Magno veluti cum flamma sonore
> Virgea suggeritur costis undantis aëni
> Exsultantque aestu latices, furit intus aquai
> Fumidus atque alte spumis exuberat amnis,
> Nec iam se capit unda, volat vapor ater ad auras.

Homer's image of the burning Scamander [3] (of which *amnis*
reminds us) has become a simile utilizing the metaphor of
boiling, seething rage [4] which is as genuine to Latin as it is
to Greek. It emphasizes the dark, demonic force of Turnus'
fighting passion. The opening of tragic perspective is expressed
by the rhythmical and melodious movement of the verses,
especially the last: *"Nec iam se capit unda, volat vapor ater
ad auras."* As in most of Vergil's similes, the emotional content dominates the perceptible content, and the symbolic content dominates the concrete. Although it is true that the raging
anger is concrete, the love for "iron" and the "criminal madness of war," the eruption of which is pointed out by the simile, border on the abstract. These concepts, even if interpreted as demonic forces transmigrating from Allecto into the
heart of Turnus, produce a vague picture. The simile represents an interpretation of the demonic powers' invasion of the
hero. It does not represent a physical event and the image
is a symbol. Through immediate visualization of an inner
event [5] symbolizing doom, the boiling water simile differs from
Homer's similes in the depth of perspective—just as the deer
simile in the Dido book does. It betrays the poet's intention
of expressing something of the demonic tragedy connected
with the figure of Turnus. This impression is emphasized by
other points.

In the course of the scene, a change takes place in Turnus
that increases our compassion for him. There is manly prudence and faith in his first words, and it is clear that there
is heroic nobility at the core of his nature. It is through Allecto's gesture that he falls prey to the powers of Hell. He

is caught in the flames of passion and pulled from his path.
His original resistance makes possible a contrast between the
priestess and the Hell-fury. This contrast provides a dramatic
effect [6] and at the same time demonstrates the inner fall of
Turnus and the *innocence* [7] of his guilt. The end of the scene
also serves to arouse admiration and sympathy for him. He
possesses the best qualities of a hero: beauty, youth, nobility,
and courage (VII.473). His beauty and noble origin have
already been mentioned (VII.55). He is the most handsome
of the Italians; this means that he is a noble youth (VII.650),
because physical and spiritual beauty are inseparable in the
Aeneid. According to the ancient idea that beauty is the flower
of *arete,* the youthful figures singled out by the poet's eye for
special favor are all distinguished by it—Pallas, Euryalus,
Lausus, and, of course, Aeneas himself. Turnus is no exception.

Although the scene contains the important premises for
the tragic interpretation of Turnus' fate, this has been energetically contested. For example, Friedrich (*Philologus*
1940), following an article by Ehlers in the *Realenzy-
klopädie* [8] and the authority of Heinze,[9] says that Vergil characterizes Turnus as an enemy of the State rather than as a
tragic figure. But the one does not exclude the other. Indeed,
if not depicted as "the enemy of the State," he *is* shown as
the embodiment of *furor impius*. Nevertheless, he is simultaneously a victim of tragic delusion. The main emphasis is
on the latter because Vergil, like any true poet, primarily
portrays human fate, not political evaluations. Nothing could
be more erroneous than the not so new contention that "compared to Homer, Vergil is a 'party poet.' " [10]

The interpretation which Heinze gives to the figure of
Turnus by quoting Cicero (*De officiis* I.62) is also completely
false. "The inner strength visible in danger and battle is a
fault when it lacks justice and strives not for the common
salvation, but for personal advantage. This is not a proof of

virtue but of inhuman violence." Turnus strives in no way for "his own advantage" (*pro suis commodis*). Rather, he strives to protect Italy (VII.468 ff.), to protect his right to Lavinia (VII.423), which he acquired as defender of Latinus' dominion against the Etruscan threat (VII.425 ff., VIII.493) by "his blood spilled in battle," and last but not least, he strives for his glory: "*ut virtus enitescere possit,*" as Sallust says about Caesar. This, according to Roman thinking, is praise, not blame.[11] It is true that the enormous self-respect which forms the basis of the struggle for glory in the man of antiquity,[12] absorbs Turnus completely. But this is the very hallmark of his distinction, and he shares it with the other Vergilian figures. As concerns Dido, this has been shown above. The same is true of Ascanius (VII.496), Nisus and Euryalus (IX.197 ff.; 205 ff.), Pallas,[13] and especially of Aeneas himself. The "*letum pro laude pacisci*" of Turnus (XII.49) has nothing whatever to do with "*pro suis commodis pugnare*" of Cicero. Turnus is one of the great heroes in Italian history and Dante saw him as such when he placed him with Nisus, Euryalus, and Camilla among those who "died for Italy":

> Di quell'umile Italia fia salute,
> Per cui morì la vergine Cammilla,
> Eurialo e Turno e Niso di ferute.
>
> —*Div. Comm. Inf.* I, 106.

There is something of the small and narrow outlook of nineteenth-century scholarship at the bottom of this downgrading of Turnus. There is also something of the political delusion of the twentieth century which is always choosing ideological sides without the slightest realization of the immense disdain which the great geniuses of mankind have for such considerations. The words of Dehmel, "To be a poet means to embrace the world in love and to lift it up to God," apply to Vergil more than to anyone else. The enemies of Aeneas are people, too. Turnus is demoniacal, but not evil, and in his destruction even the monster Mezentius reveals a loving heart.

That Turnus hesitates on the brink of the abyss focuses and enhances his tragedy. The "moment of retardation"—the stop before catastrophe when the reader hopes again that the unavoidable may be avoided—is not only a means to external tension, an exciting moment in the development of tragedy, but also an integral element of tragedy, for through the contrast the abyss is seen in all its horror in contrast with the other "nontragical" possibility.[14] The impending doom appears all the more horrible.

Turnus' destiny, then, is touched with the breath of tragedy from the beginning, and tragic signs and premonitions accompany it to the end.[15] On the other hand, it is characterized as the work of the demons of Hell. And this distinguishes Turnus from the other figures in the poem and from all Homeric models. Through the spell of Allecto he becomes the incarnation of the frenzy of War. His is the flesh of the demonic in history. His battle is ungodly and sinful because it drives the nations destined for "eternal peace" into war (*"aeterna gentes in pace futuras"*). Because of this, Jupiter becomes his enemy (XII.895: *"Juppiter hostis"*). It is civil war, a symbol of the terrible internal strife of the dying republic which Augustus terminated. There is an intimate connection between the figure of Turnus and the *"furor impius"* of the Jupiter speech as it is overcome by the emperor. Turnus' defeat at the hands of Aeneas is the strongest expression of the poem's basic idea as it is manifest at the end of the Jupiter speech, but instead of diminishing Turnus' tragedy this fact serves to heighten it. The moving power of this tragedy springs precisely from the contrast of his noble nature with the demoniacal passion which robs him of insight and sanity [16] and the contrast of his heroism with the devilish deceit which deflects his strength toward a sinful goal.

How is the tragic and demoniacal character of his personality and destiny expressed in the last books? In the catalogue of the Italians, where Turnus takes the last place but one before Camilla, his armament is described as follows:

> His tall helmet was crowned by a triple plume and supported a Chimaera breathing Etna's fires from its jaws; and ever louder it roared, and madder grew the menace of its flames as grimmer grew the battle amid streaming blood.

VII.785:

> Cui triplici crinita iuba galea alta Chimaeram
> Sustinet Aetnaeos efflantem faucibus ignis;
> Tam magis illa fremens et tristibus effera flammis
> Quam magis effuso crudescunt sanguine pugnae.

There is no Homeric model for the fire-breathing Chimaera on Turnus' helmet, just as there is nothing in Homer comparable to his demoniacal nature.[17] Nevertheless, it may be stated that this invention reflects the spirit of the *Iliad,* where the fighting heroes are transformed to battle-demons or seem to change into the elementary force of fire (15.605; 12.465; 13.53; 8.348; 20.490).

Yet Homer stays within the limits of the natural even though his heroes' deeds border on the miraculous. Vergil exceeds that limit.[18] The Chimaera on Turnus' helmet is more than a symbolic expression of the hero's rage and fighting power (Heinze). As the Chimaera, breathing fire and thundering like Etna, comes to life during the battle, she is a real demon from Hell.[19]

The tragic and demonic in Turnus' nature loom large in the ninth book, too, which is entirely devoted to his heroism, except for the Euryalus episode. The book begins with a gesture of *pietas* which demonstrates Turnus' faithful reverence for the ancestors. In a beautiful scene at the beginning, Turnus is shown in relation to his ancestor Pilumnus, whose glory, as it were, he renews:

XII.649:

> Magnorum haud umquam indignus avorum

Thus, the beginning elevates what follows. The scene closes on ritual ceremonies after Iris has called the hero to battle:

> Having spoken his thought he walked forward to the water, scooped a handful from an eddy's surface, and prayed long to the gods, loading high heaven with his vows.

IX.22:

> sic effatus ad undam
> Processit summoque hausit de gurgite lymphas
> Multa deos orans, oneravitque aethera votis.[20]

Like Dido he starts upon the road to destruction with religious rites and prayers. I emphasize this fact because it contradicts the idea of Turnus as an "enemy of the state" and fighter *"pro suis commodis."*

Against this quiet background the wild scenes of battle take place. It is not the devoutly concentrated hero who triumphs, but the ferociously passionate fighter. Impatient for battle to begin, he gallops with a group of horsemen ahead of the troops and burns with lust for blood when the Trojans retreat behind the walls of their camp:

> Like a wolf lying in wait outside a crowded sheepfold, howling right up to the enclosure and facing any force of wind and rain at darkest midnight while the lambs continue incessantly bleating, safe underneath their mothers; he, fierce and persistent in his rage, vents his fury against a prey which is out of reach, for his dry, bloodless jaws and long-mounting, ravenous hunger will not let him rest; such were the Rutulian's spasms of fury, rising to a blaze as he glared at those walls and that camp, and indignation heated his hard bones.

IX.59:

> Ac veluti pleno lupus insidiatus ovili
> Cum fremit ad caulas, ventos perpessus et imbris

> Nocte super media: tuti sub matribus agni
> Balatum exercent, ille asper et improbus ira
> Saevit in absentis, collecta fatigat edendi
> Ex longo rabies et siccae sanguine fauces:
> Haud aliter Rutulo muros et castra tuenti
> Ignescunt irae; duris dolor ossibus ardet.

Here we have a descriptive simile of a battle situation which corresponds to the simile in the *Iliad* (11.548 ff.) and to the essence of Turnus' character. This simile forms the introduction to the bloody and senseless combats of the following scenes. Turnus' fury in battle is repeatedly illustrated by reference to wild animals, while Aeneas is compared to a beast of prey only once. This exception is characteristic:

> Like wolves out for prey in a thick mist, forced blindly onward by hunger's incessant torment and the thought of their cubs left behind and waiting with parched throats for their return, we drove on amid the spears to certain death.

II.355:

> inde, lupi ceu
> Raptores atra in nebula, quos improba ventris
> Exegit caecos rabies catulique relicti
> Faucibus exspectant siccis, per tela, per hostis
> Vadimus haud dubiam in mortem.

The subject matter of the simile is not so much the beasts' bloodthirstiness as their expectation of death, their desperate hunger pangs and instinctive drive to care for the young they left behind. "Despair out of love" is an accurate definition of the mood which possesses Aeneas and his companions as they live through the destruction of their city, Troy. Comparison of the similes used for Turnus and Aeneas may show the difference:

Turnus: wolf IX.59, eagle or wolf IX.563, tiger IX.730, lion IX.792, lion X.454, stallion IX.492, lion XII.4, bull

XII.103, Mars XII.331, Boreas XII.365, stone avalanche XII.684, men in nightmare XII.908.

Aeneas: ivory, silver, and marble surrounded by gold I.592, wolves (Aeneas and his companions) II.355, Apollo IV.143, oak IV.441, the giant Aegaeon X.565, torrent or whirlwind X.603, wanderer in a hailstorm X.803, whirlpool XII.451, Athos, Eryx, and the Apennines XII.701, hunter XII.749.

Aeneas and Turnus: two firebrands or mountain streams XII.521, two bulls XII.715.

Here the poet is striving to characterize Turnus as the personification of demonic forces [21] in contrast to Aeneas whose glory as a fighter is made to shine even more brightly against that dark foil. The passion-filled figures of Dido and Turnus serve to enhance Aeneas' controlled poise and the strength and majesty of his mind. The divine brilliance of Aeneas' heroic nature shines all the more gloriously against the somber background of their dark demoniacal existence. He is, as it were, a being of higher nature.

Moreover, this proves conclusively that Vergil's similes are much more closely connected with the character of the one to whom they apply than are those of Homer.[22] Homer aims to illuminate a particular feature of an event or to represent a sensual impression. Everything else is of secondary importance, which explains why it has been maintained that he is only interested in the *tertium comparationis*. In Vergil's hands the simile is a deeply integrated whole, highlight and focal point for unfolding events. It is a bold and beautiful picture of the idea and destiny of the epic heroes.[23] The poet cannot, therefore, compare Aeneas to a beast of prey. He avoids the harsh discrepancies of some of the Homeric similes, where, for instance, Ajax is compared to an ass, Menelaos to a fly, Odysseus to a *"haggis"* and his chiton to an onionskin, the fight for Patroclos' corpse to the tugging at a bullskin, and

Patroclos' funeral procession to mules dragging a treetrunk. The relation of the objects compared is so important to Vergil that only relatable things and figures admit of a comparison.

The descriptions of the bloody battles of the last third of the poem raise a question of how Vergil could manage a task seemingly so foreign to his artistic sensibilities and, for that matter, to his whole personality. The unsentimental, hard realism of the killing and fighting in the *Iliad* is the sphere in which Homer diverges the most from the concept of "Classical" art as directed toward a goal of harmonious beauty.[24] The so-called classicists of Goethe's period observed and noted this deviation from their idealized image of the Greeks. Schiller in a letter to Goethe (July 7, 1797) remarks: "How much labor has been and is still being spent trying to reconcile the often rough, low, and ugly reality in Homer and the tragedians with the traditional concepts of Greek beauty. If only someone would dare to discard the concept and even the word, identical as it has become with all those false concepts, and to put truth in its place, as is only fair!" Rather than banishing Homer's realism from his work, Vergil has toned it down and transfigured it through his art. After all, realism is necessary as *materia gloriae* for Aeneas and as symbol of the bloody history of Rome. The horrors of war had to be shown; the extent of the suffering and the power of the passions in this dimension of life had to be shown also so that the strength and glory of Rome might shine all the more brightly in the juxtaposition. Nor should it be overlooked that the poet's nature admitted of such a procedure. Over and above his delicacy and tenderness, Vergil *was* a Roman. In Aeneas' hard heroism and humanity, unbending firmness is balanced with mildness; Dido alternates between harsh pride and glowing abandon; hard and soft traits are evenly distributed throughout the whole poem. The poet is as far removed from any effeminacy as he is from the baroque cruelty of Lucan and Seneca. I believe that he is more tough-minded and more "Roman" than his modern interpreters, uninterested in the last books, give him credit for being.

These passionately moving scenes are artistically necessary. With the same fairmindedness with which he looked at all manifestations of life, Homer let his eyes encompass the horrors of war. These, too, he saw as natural and noble—clothed in beauty. Something of his attitude passed into Vergil's presentation, for like Homer, Vergil ennobles and includes horror in the celebration of life and historic grandeur which constitutes his epic. The symbol of the temple in the proem of *Georgics* III that points to the planned Roman epic must be interpreted to mean that Vergil's song is a sacred work in praise of the divinity.

Besides the black aspect of the murder of war, there is in Vergil, as in Homer, the bright heroic flower of strength and the majestic action of battle. Indeed, both aspects are so thoroughly merged that they can never be completely separated. As in Homer, the bloody deeds of war serve to expose the heroes' power and splendor in images of splendid movement.[25] But "beauty" in the sense of something measured, balanced, and harmonious, in spite of wildness, is considerably enhanced in Vergil. On the other hand, Vergil's scenes lack the powerful vitality and primitive strength of the Greek epic. The elemental cruelty and frightening actuality of the *Iliad* have given way to a more remote ideality. Homer, with all the round suppleness and charm which is characteristic of him also—with all his tender, glowing humanity—is harder and rawer. His eyes can stand a closer proximity to reality. The hot breath of life is stronger in him than is the severe and refined beauty of art.

In Turnus' scenes the cruel aspect of war is especially emphasized, while the bright aspect is revealed in the heroism

of Aeneas and of Camilla. The "Roman" fighting style of
Aeneas is contrasted with the barbaric style of Turnus. Camilla's *aristeia* in the eleventh book is also less cruel. The fast,
almost joyous action of the cavalry charge which Camilla's
personality dominates, passes over, as it were, the terror of
death and is all splendor and beauty. Homer's gruesome details have almost disappeared.[26] Here, Vergil has produced
his best description of battle—and one that is entirely his
own. But even Turnus' battle style corresponds to the differing character of the books. A calculated climax can be observed in the last third of the *Aeneid:* the events rise from the
skirmishes in the ninth book (including the slaughter wrought
by Nisus and Euryalus among the sleeping enemy) to the
more "tragic" single combats in the tenth, to reach a climax
of battles in the eleventh and of single combats in the twelfth.
Accordingly, the similes that characterize Turnus are also
graded and fit both the prevailing atmosphere and the spirit
of the whole. In the ninth book Turnus is the brutal battle
demon, the "wolf" outside the sheepfold and the *"lupus
Martius";* in the tenth, which tells of his victory over Pallas,
he is the lion looking for a fight with the bull (X.454). In the
eleventh, the least somber of the battle books, the picture of
the powerful stallion amplifies the impression of his courage.
This simile suits the bright character of the Camilla episode
by preparing for the subsequent cavalry battle in image and
mood. The movement begins here and continues into the battle. Finally, in the twelfth book Turnus is again the lion as in
the beginning—now fatally wounded.

Turnus' demonic ferocity and superhuman strength are
most clearly shown in the ninth book, where they are developed unhindered by the presence of Aeneas. His aggressive
blood-lust unfolds in three ascending scenes: in the attempt
to fire the Trojan ships, in the assault on the camp, and in the
aristeia which lets him break through the walls.

An example of Vergil's art in creating images of deep applicability is the flaming crescendo in which the inner fire of the hero kindles the outer fire. From where he picks up the burning pine torch, the power of the flame mounts to the torches of the men, to the action of the fire-god, to the eruption of fire as a cosmic force which "reaches up to the stars":

IX.66:

> Ignescunt irae; duris dolor ossibus ardet...

> Finally, he attacked the fleet which lay hidden close under the flank of the encampment, fenced on one side by an earth-pier built round it, but elsewhere by nothing but the river-waves. Turnus called to his exultant comrades for fire. In hot passion he held tight in his grasp a blazing pine-brand. Urged by his own powerful presence among them, his men set to work in earnest. Every soldier at once stole any fire near at hand and armed himself with a black-reeking torch. Smoking pine-boughs threw their pitchy glare, and Vulcan sent upwards to the stars a mixture of ashes and sparks.

IX.71:

> Classem...
> Invadit sociosque incendia poscit ovantis
> Atque manum pinu flagranti fervidus implet.
> Tum vero incumbunt (urget praesentia Turni),
> Atque omnis facibus pubes accingitur atris.
> Diripuere focos; piceum fert fumida lumen
> Taeda et commixtam Volcanus ad astra favillam.

Homer's description of Hector hurling flames into the Achaeans' ships (15.596, 716; 16.122) lacks the intensity of Vergil's description of the growing tumult of the fire. Homer mentions fire only briefly, and no use is made of the dramatic possibilities and no connection with Hector's character is implied. Vergil, on the other hand, presents the destructive element as emanating from Turnus' character. The motif is not only heightened, it has acquired a new meaning. Again, the image has become a symbol.

The last part of the book begins with trumpeting in the manner of Ennius:

> But now afar off the trumpet crashed out its dreadful note with the music of its bronze. Shouting followed, and the sky roared back the echo.

IX.503:

> At tuba terribilem sonitum procul aere canoro
> Increpuit, sequitur clamor caelumque remugit.

The following is marked as a climax through the invocation of Calliope (IX.525). The *aristeia* of Turnus is introduced by the collapse of the tower into which he was the first to throw the torch. It is continued in the scene where the hero drags Lycus down together with a portion of the wall,[27] as an eagle attacks a hare or swan or as the Martian wolf attacks a lamb. Then a general fight develops, and the *aristeia* is interrupted by the Ascanius episode, which was obviously inserted after the Calliope proem and the plan of which it is a part had already been designed, for this proem announces something which does not immediately develop. This lack of consistency perhaps results from the unfinished state of the poem. It is true that the odd-numbered books are all less unified than the even-numbered ones which are related to Aeneas. The even-numbered books exhibit a tight composition which approaches dramatic form, while the odd-numbered books come closer to the style of the Homeric epic. This may explain why a digression, inadmissable there, was tolerable here. But it cannot very well be argued that the effectiveness of the story is diminished by such interruptions, especially where the composition demands more room.[28]

The reason for the insertion can be found in Numanus' speech (IX.598 ff.). It can hardly be justified from the context, but owes its existence to Vergil's desire to glorify the Italians. The speech recalls the *laudes Italiae* in the *Georgics* and serves, like the catalogue at the end of the seventh book, to praise the healthy vitality of the Italian peoples. In the light of Numanus' speech, Turnus' subsequent *aristeia* appears as a glorification of *virtus* in the old Italian style and Turnus himself appears as the personification of the *populi feroces* of old Italy. Vergil's positive attitude toward the Italians (clearly seen in the description) is most explicitly pronounced in Juno's prayer to which Jupiter grants fulfillment (XII.827: "Let the Roman race draw power from Italian strength"). This is obviously not in accord with the idea of Vergil taking issue with the chief of the Italian party. To maintain that Vergil puts Turnus in an unfavorable light is to forget completely the symbolic meaning of the second half of the *Aeneid* in which the poet's judgment concerning several centuries of Roman history is revealed. The tragic conception [29] of this and his intention of duly emphasizing Italy's share in Rome's grandeur (a goal corresponding equally to Vergil's origin and Augustus' Italian politics) exclude a negative judgment of Turnus. The poet's heart beats for both parties.

After this episode, the essential *aristeia* begins with the death of Antiphates. It is cruel and bloody as befits Turnus' style:

> The shaft of Italian cornel flew through the unresisting air, cut into his belly, and penetrated upwards into his chest. The wound's black cavern gave forth a foaming flood; the blade warmed inside a pierced lung.

IX.698:

> Volat Itala cornus
> Aera per tenerum stomachoque infixa sub altum
> Pectus abit, reddit specus atri volneris undam
> Spumantem et fixo ferrum in pulmone tepescit.

The words "Italian wood", in emphasizing at the very beginning that an Italian is fighting, serve the purpose outlined above. There follows the liquidation of the Trojan giant Bitias by means of the *phalarica* and of his brother Pandarus in an even bloodier manner. Turnus then enters the walls alone and begins murdering blindly:

> At once the vision of Turnus became a thing of unearthly terror as it blazed on Trojan eyes. Horrifying to them was the clashing of his arms; blood-red quivered his shield.

IX.731:

> Continuo nova lux oculis effulsit et arma
> Horrendum sonuere, tremunt in vertice cristae
> Sanguineae clipeoque micantia fulmina mittit.

The lines are composed of Homeric elements, yet neither Aeneas nor any other Trojan hero is characterized in this fashion.

Driven by his thirst for blood, Turnus neglects to let his companions inside the gate and thereby to end the war (IX.757 ff.), a fact that illuminates his immense strength no less than his tragic delusion. This becomes clearer in the tenth book. In fact, the deepening of his tragedy is part of the general tendency of the whole book. The presence of Aeneas in the even-numbered books always corresponds to a deeper and more tragic interpretation of the events.[30] Although there is much fighting and murdering in the ninth book, the only real tragedy is the death of the two friends, Nisus and Euryalus. The tenth book begins right away with the tragic decision of the assembly of gods that the war intended by Jupiter must be fought. Pallas and especially Lausus and Mezentius are tragic figures because they fall not only through the fatality of war, but because they attract their destinies through the grandeur of their souls. (The latter is a principal mark of the tragic.) Pallas, prepared for "glorious death," faces Turnus (X.450). Lausus sacrifices his life for his father and Mezentius seeks death because life without his son is meaningless. Aeneas' sympathy reaches a shattering climax at the deaths of Pallas and Lausus. When Pallas is killed, it is expressed in the bitterness with which he mows down crowds of his opponents and destines the four sons of Ufens to the sacrifice. At the death of Lausus it is expressed in his words to the dead enemy and in one of those eternal gestures of Vergilian humanity—the lifting of the young hero's corpse with his own hands:

> And it was he who lifted Lausus from the ground where he lay defiling with blood his well-trimmed hair.

X.831:

> Terra sublevat ipsum
> Sanguine turpantem comptos de more capillos.[31]

Accordingly, the tragedy of Turnus gains a greater depth in this book. If his inner ruin had become apparent with the symbol of the Allecto dream in the seventh book and his tragic blindness in the ninth book, here his end is openly predicted with the death of Pallas (X.501—in imitation of Homer's words concerning Patroclos, 16.46, and in the conversation between Jupiter and Juno, X.606 ff.).

Robbing the dead Pallas of his sword belt is Turnus' destruction. His tragedy is more profound in that he shows mercy by this very act. Hector was not so temperate when he stripped Patroclos of his entire harness and did not surrender the body. Turnus, on the contrary, declares:

> I return to him such a Pallas as he deserves. I freely grant what honor a tomb may afford, what solace burial may bring.

X.492:

> Qualem meruit, Pallanta remitto.
> Quisquis honos tumuli, quidquid solamen humandi est,
> Largior.

And above all—here, for the first time, he is in a situation that he himself considers tragic. He follows the phantom of Aeneas aboard the ship (X.636 ff.) [32] while in his absence

the real Aeneas challenges him to combat. The whirlwind that
drives him over the water is a suggestive symbol of his help-
lessness in the face of blind forces. When the tide carries him
to Ardea and he realizes his delusion, he is overwhelmed by
despair. The feeling that he has lost his honor by flight and has
abandoned his followers to the enemy crushes him:

> What of that host of men who followed my standard? The
> horror of it! I have forsaken them, with death unspeakable
> all around them; am I now to see them scattered, and hear
> their groaning as they fall?

X.672:

> Quid manus illa virum, qui me meaque arma secuti?
> Quosne, nefas, omnis infanda in morte reliqui,
> Et nunc palantis video gemitumque cadentum
> Accipio?

He acknowledges his guilt for the first time, and his sorrow is
so profound and piercing that like the Sophoclean Ajax he
calls for death in order not to survive the loss of his honor
and to escape from the *conscia fama* which pursues him:

> Winds, better that you take pity! Drive this ship onto
> reefs or against cliffs. I, Turnus, freely entreat it of you.
> Let her run upon Syrte's cruel quicksands where no
> Rutulian, nor any rumor acquainted with my shame, can
> follow me.

X.676:

> Vos o potius miserescite, venti,
> In rupes in saxa, volens vos Turnus adoro,
> Ferte ratem saevisque vadis immittite Syrtis,
> Quo neque me Rutuli nec conscia fama sequatur.

He tries three times to make an end of himself but Juno restrains him. In spite of being seized with a demoniacal power,
he still has a sense of honor. The nobility of his soul is still
intact. Obviously, this is another scene which is not to be
reconciled with the idea of Turnus as a criminal.

In the council after the serious defeat (XI.225–444) he replies with manly and courageous words to the speeches of Venulus who announces Diomedes' refusal, of Latinus, who as a wise counselor, urges moderation, and of Drances, who attacks him personally. He states his concepts of honor and heroic behavior and his intention of risking his life. He will fight to the end:

> Him I count as beyond all other men happy in his success and of peerless temper, who, rather than see such shame, has fallen and once for all bitten the dust in death.

XI.416:

> Ille mihi ante alios fortunatusque laborum
> Egregiusque animi, qui, ne quid tale videret,
> Procubuit moriens et humum semel ore momordit.

His is the attitude for which Livy praises the Samnites.[33]

The twelfth book belongs to Turnus in the same way that the fourth belongs to Dido. The essential tragedy is heightened and compressed. Here, just as in the fourth book, everything from the very beginning is intended to arouse tragic apprehension. It starts with a simile:

> As some strong lion of the African desert, gravely wounded in the breast by huntsmen, gives battle at last; and, joyously tossing his luxuriant mane from his neck, snaps off, undaunted, the spear which some stalker has planted in him, opens a blood-smeared mouth, and roars. Such was the hot-headed ardor of Turnus, and his obdurate passion mounted.

XII.4:

> Poenorum qualis in arvis
> Saucius ille gravi venantum volnere pectus
> Tum demum movet arma leo gaudetque comantis
> Excutiens cervice toros fixumque latronis
> Impavidus frangit telum et fremit ore cruento:
> Haud secus accenso gliscit violentia Turno.

The excellent Homeric simile of the lion (*Iliad* 20.164) is far surpassed by Vergil's art. Starting from the wounding, the movement climbs over the dark threats expressed in the massed dull *m* and *u* sounds (*"tum demum movet arma leo"*) to the shaking of the mane,[34] to the splintering of the lance, and the roar "from bloody mouth." The end coincides meaningfully with the end of Jupiter's speech as Turnus significantly personifies *furor impius:*

> And safe within them shall stay the godless and ghastly lust of blood, propped on his pitiless piled armory, and still roaring from gory mouth, but held fast by a hundred chains of bronze knotted behind his back.

I.294:

> Furor impius intus
> Saeva sedens super arma et centum vinctus aenis
> Post tergum nodis *fremet horridus ore cruento.*

The beginning of the fourth book is recalled in the deep wound which symbolized the hero's corrosive grief over his army's defeat:

> But the queen gnawed by love's invisible fire =

IV.1:

> At regina gravi iamdudum saucia cura =

> Gravely wounded in the breast by huntsmen.

XII.5:

> Saucius ille gravi venantum volnere pectus.

The Dido book and the Turnus book are linked by a common introductory symbol. The warrior's passion is similar to the queen's, appearing as a festering wound which tragically destroys the victim. It will be shown that other significant compositional similarities between the tragedies of Aeneas' two great antagonists exist elsewhere.

The lion's courage is connected with his wound in the

Iliad simile, too, but Achilles, to whom the simile refers, is not wounded. As he stands at the start of his victory [35] only the eagerness for battle seems to apply to him. Because in reality, Turnus, marked for destruction, is fatally injured, Vergil's comparison seems the more suitable.[36] The lion's wound is mysteriously his, too, just as the deer's wound is Dido's. The fatal outcome is announced symbolically in both similes. Simultaneously, the development of the twelfth book is suggested. The closer Turnus is to the end, the more he grows in inner stature. The more he realizes that the gods are abandoning him, the stronger his resolution becomes to uphold his obligation to his glory to the end: *"Increscunt animi, virescit volnere virtus.*[37] Throughout the whole story his attitude develops in the direction opposite to that of Aeneas.[38] Aeneas comes from despair to the conviction that he is sought out by the will of fate, while Turnus, like Oedipus, is sure of divine protection from the beginning—*"nec regia Juno immemor est nostri"* (VII.438)—and believes himself to be in communication with the gods through signs, sacrifices, and prayers.[39] He cannot recognize the visible proofs of divine help given to the Trojans. He interprets the miracle of the ships becoming sea nymphs in his own favor (IX.128). He usurps the *Fata* to himself (IX.136 ff.). Even the sight of Aeneas and his gleaming shield cannot destroy his confidence in victory (X.276). But in the course of events he becomes less and less certain. In the phantom scene, he feels for the first time that the gods are deceiving and punishing him. In spite of his first serious defeat, Diomedes' refusal, and the many graves which reveal the gods' anger at the Latins [40] (XI.232 ff.), he does not abandon hope (XI.419 f.). But he does begin to consider the possibility of a defeat [41] which he will not survive. He is prepared to sacrifice his life:

> I, Turnus, in valor second to none of the heroes of old, have vowed this my life as my offering to you all, and to Latinus, father of my bride.

XI.440:

> Vobis animam hanc soceroque Latino
> Turnus ego haud ulli veterum virtute secundus
> Devovi.

Again his youthful strength, abundant courage, and unrestrained passion are reflected in the simile of the stallion
escaping from the stable to race away in powerful arrogance.[42]

The lion simile in the twelfth book has already marked
the point of turning toward despair and acceptance of a
tragic death. In Turnus' reply to the king is found the indication of what is to come: *"Letumque sinas pro laude pacisci."*
His confidence is finally shaken by Amata's and Lavinia's [43]
tears:

> Do not, I beg you, Mother, send me forth on my way to
> the pitiless conflict of Mars with so ominous a presage as
> these tears. Not for Turnus is the freedom to postpone
> his death.

XII.72:

> Ne quaeso ne me lacrimis neve omine tanto
> Prosequere in duri certamina Martis euntem,
> O mater, neque enim Turno mora libera mortis.

Although the end of Latinus' speech touched again upon the
thought of victory, there is now only one certainty—the resolve to fight, his readiness to face single combat. This attitude recalls something of the grandeur of Aeschylus' Eteocles:

> By his blood and mine alone are we to settle this war.
> On that field must Lavinia's hand be won.

XII.79:

> Nostro dirimamus sanguine bellum.
> Illo quaeratur coniunx Lavinia campo.

Like Achilles in his conversation with Thetis, he decides on
a glorious death of his own free will. He repeats what has
been called Achilles' "tragic *prohairesis.*"

In the following arming scene his fighting passion amounts almost to madness. Heinze (p. 229, note 1) has correctly asked why the arming did not occur immediately before the battle, as in Homer and Apollonius. In answer, he suggests that the poet was concerned with the character of Turnus rather than with the arming: "On the preceding evening, immediately after the decision, there is the most furious eagerness which cannot wait to attack the hated adversary, in the morning, the collapse in the face of the fight; while Aeneas remains himself and the same." But it is doubtful that this answer is correct. The arrogant words of the javelin-swinging hero as he indulges in cruelty, and the subsequent description of his fury which anticipates the fight, serve more to express the delusion and deception which possess him than his character. "By such furies is he driven and sparks leap from his whole face and fire flashes from his wild eyes." These verses recall the *"stant lumina flamma"* (VI.300) said about Hades' ferryman, Charon, and fit the hellish and demoniacal side of Turnus' being.[44]

The comparison with the love-mad bull not only describes his mad rage for battle, but his delusion and the futility of his efforts. It has the same tragic coloring as the passage from the *Georgics* from which it was taken: *"Ventosque lacessit ictibus."* [45] The verse is related to *"nec ferre videt sua gaudia ventos"* in the delusion scene. It is a continuation of the stallion simile, an enhancement of the motif intimated by the unrestrained passion of love.

The formal reason for this scene's position, however, is that the first scene sequence of the twelfth book, which ends here, demands a rising finale. Turnus' *furor,* appearing as cause and symptom of approaching fate in the lion simile of the beginning, had to appear also at the end. The arming presented an opportunity for this.

Here, again, there is a striking relation to the first scene in the Dido book (IV.1–89). That sequence begins with a description of the queen's suffering. Madness comes after her conversation with Anna as she reviews the repugnant alternatives and decides upon the only "other" possibility. This movement reaches its climax in the deer simile, which enhances the delusion motif of the beginning. The twelfth book begins, too, with Turnus' delusion and suffering, which increase through Latinus' futile warnings and explode with insane fury in the simile of the bull fighting the winds in the arming scene. There is an even closer parallel. Just as the development of Dido's madness starts at the gleaming sacrificial scene and proceeds through the dark inspection of the entrails to its actual outbreak, so the arming scene begins in the shimmering splendor and pageantry of the white horses of Oreithyia only to end in black rage. Conversely, the arming of Achilles, which is correctly accepted as Vergil's model, closes with the entrance of the horses.

These scene sequences are of equal length and serve the same purpose—the exposition of tragedy. They symbolically announce and begin the development of the catastrophe. The functional affinity of this type of exposition with that of the tempest and the Allecto scenes was pointed out in the discussion of the deer simile. The tragedies of Dido and Turnus, and, as it were, the two tragedies of Aeneas in the first and second halves of the poem ("Odyssey" and "Iliad") are developed analogically. The beginning of the twelfth book is in accordance with the type of composition characteristic of Vergil and which is his own creation.[46]

The special inner movement becomes even clearer when it is compared with scenes in the *Iliad,* including Hector, Priam, and Hecuba at the beginning of Book 22 and the parting from Andromache in Book 6, because these, and the conversation between Achilles and Thetis, are Vergil's models here. There is nothing in Hector analogous to Turnus' anger,[47] however. In the Andromache scene Hector's sole motive is glory. In the scene with his parents, the only thing that determines him to face single combat with Achilles is the sober consideration of his honor. There is no sign of a dramatic climax. There is something *like* it to be found in the exposition of the *Iliad*. The manner in which the anger of Achilles is developed has a certain similarity to Vergil's dramatic compositions. Turnus is the center of tragic interest, just as is Achilles in the *Iliad*.

Turnus' solitary grandeur, his divine origin (VI.90: *"natus et ipse dea"*), his unfailing willingness to face death, his loyalty to his comrades, his contrasting gentleness and cruelty, the inner tensions arising from "inhumanity alongside humanity, simultaneous wrath and resignation in the face of destiny" (Karl Reinhardt), are all Achillean characteristics. As the Sibyl introduces him, he is the Achilles of the *Aeneid:*

> A new Achilles, again a goddess's son, already breathes in Latium.

VI.89:

> Alius Latio iam partus Achilles
> Natus et ipse dea.

All that is significant about him comes from Achilles. From Hector comes only the delusion and the exterior points of his career such as his break through the walls, the burning of the ships, the leave-taking, and the defeat in single combat. Even in the leave-taking and before the single combat, Achillean characteristics can be seen. Turnus personifies a hero on the Homeric scale against which Aeneas' personality is drawn with quiet brilliance. After the first scenes of the twelfth book, it becomes clear that Turnus has lost his faith in victory but not his determination to fight to the death. His confidence is even further depleted when the pact with Aeneas is made (XII.161–221).[48] His lack of confidence is apparent upon his entrance:

> Turnus rode behind a pair of white horses, with two broad-headed spear-shafts quivering in his grip.

XII.164 f.:

> Bigis it Turnus in albis
> Bina manu lato crispans hastilia ferro.

Here, *crispans* connotes anxiety.[49] Through the contrast of Aeneas and Ascanius in the following scene, this impression is given more force:

> Then from the Trojan camp came the chieftain Aeneas, the founder of the Roman breed, shining in a blaze of light, with his shield like a star, and arms of Heaven's making; and close by him came forth Ascanius, the second hope of Roman greatness.

XII.166:

> Hinc pater Aeneas, Romanae stirpis origo,
> Sidereo flagrans clipeo et caelestibus armis
> Et iuxta Ascanius, magnae spes altera Romae,
> Procedunt castris.

Foretelling future victory, Aeneas' arms gleam with divine brilliance. These spare, unredundant verses shine with the simple grandeur and with the sacred dignity of Rome. It is no accident that the name of Rome is mentioned twice. The verses are models of Classical style and of fundamental Augustan thought. Here is the spirit of the *Ara Pacis*. The effect of Roman simplicity is further increased by the contrast of Turnus' two white horses and the splendid four-in-hand of Latinus, who approaches wearing the golden crown of the Sun.

Confronted with such grandeur, Turnus loses all hope. He is already marked for death:

> He stepped out in front without a word, and in humble piety paid reverence at the altar with downcast eyes and the down of young manhood showing on his cheeks, where the youthful color had paled.

XII.219:

> Incessu tacito progressus et aram
> Suppliciter venerans demisso lumine Turnus
> Pubentesque genae et iuvenali in corpore pallor.

This is not "characterization" in the sense that Turnus becomes a coward in the face of the present decision [50] while he was brave and boisterous when the fight was far off. Rather, apart from Vergil's technical intention of motivating Juturna's interference and breaking the armistice, he makes the coming catastrophe visible in the ever-decreasing strength of the hero. Turnus begins to understand divine will with a faint feeling of shame,[51] if not of guilt. When Aeneas is wounded, Turnus' hope revives (XII.325): *"Subita spe fervidus ardet."*

Fortune smiles once again on Turnus before the climax, just as it did on Dido when she was permitted the joy of love during the hunt. Destiny is once more suspended, but, because of the contrast with Aeneas, becomes all the more obvious to the understanding spectator. We see Aeneas, unarmed and bareheaded, restraining his clamoring warriors from battle in obedience to a treaty which forbids all contests excepting single combat. When struck by the arrow he becomes a martyr for justice. Turnus, however, appears to have forgotten the very existence of the agreement and acts from blind impulse. In his eyes, Aeneas' disability is nothing but an opportunity for attack. His final *aristeia* is completely different from that of the ninth book. In its passionate sweep and splendor it resembles the *aristeia* of Camilla, although it is consistent with the tragic character of the book in being darker and more cruel. It evolves with a powerful movement. Turnus, at the beginning, is compared to the god of war:

> He was like blood-red Mars himself when, aroused near
> the cold streams of Hebrus, he clashes his shield and gives

rein to his battle-mad horses to herald war; they fly over the open plain outstripping the winds of south and west till farthest Thrace groans under their hoof-beats; and all about him the figures of black Dread, Wrath, and Treachery, the god's own retinue, drive trampling on. Like Mars, and as vital as he, Turnus lashed his horses, steaming, sweating, through the battle's throng. They pranced on enemies pitiably slain, flying hooves sprinkled a bloody dew, and the sand which they kicked up was blended with gore.

XII.331:

Qualis apud gelidi cum flumina concitus Hebri
Sanguineus Mavors clipeo increpat atque furentis
Bella movens immittit equos, illi aequore aperto
Ante notos Zephyrumque volant, gemit ultima pulsu
Thraca pedum circumque atrae Formidinis ora
Iraeque Insidiaeque, dei comitatus, aguntur,
Talis equos alacer media inter proelia Turnus
Fumantis sudore quatit miserabile caesis
Hostibus insultans, spargit rapida ungula rores
Sanguineos mixtaque cruor calcatur harena.

The hero's symbol is no longer the noble beast of prey, but Mars himself. At his height before death, Turnus appears as the bloody demon of war,[52] just as Allecto has fashioned him. The wild beauty of the galloping horses recalls the cavalry battle which surrounded the "Amazon on horseback," Camilla's single combat. It also recalls the image of the stallion to which Turnus was compared (XI.492). It is apparent that as in the *aristeia* of Camilla (where the baroque pathos of the onrushing horses is singularly representative of Vergil's artistic ideals[53]) the full magnificence of the Italian strength is shown. This display leaves Homer far behind.

The movement, beginning with the stormy progress of Mars-Turnus, gathers a momentum that even affects the description of fallen heroes such as Glaucus and Lades:

Imbrasus himself reared them in Lycia, training them both
to fight in close combat and to ride their horses faster than
the wind, and had fitted them out with matching arms.

XII.343:

Imbrasidas Glaucum atque Laden, quos Imbrasus ipse
Nutrierat Lycia paribusque ornaverat armis
Vel conferre manum vel *equo praevertere ventos*.[54]

The image of the wind-swift horses is used for the third time
as the moment rises to the simile of Boreas. The strength,
width, and scope of "Thracian atmosphere" are more highly
intensified:

And as when the blast of north winds from Edonia roars
across the dark Aegean driving the rollers to the shore,
and the storm-clouds flee from the sky before the winds'
assault, so did the ranks retreat before Turnus wherever
he carved his way; their lines turned about, and ran.
Turnus came on, swept forward by the force of his
charge, and as he drove his chariot into the wind it tossed
his flying plume.

XII.365:

Ac velut Edoni Boreae cum spiritus alto
Insonat Aegaeo sequiturque ad litora fluctus,
Qua venti incubuere, fugam dant nubila caelo,
Sic Turno, quacumque viam secat, agmina cedunt
Conversaeque ruunt acies, fert impetus ipsum
Et cristam adverso curru quatit aura volantem.

Homer's simile (*Iliad* 11.305 ff.) is enlarged. Homer compares the number of fallen heads with the number of clouds
and wind-driven waves. Vergil's point of comparison is the
motion of flight. While Homer concludes with the foaming
spray of the waves, Vergil concludes with the flying clouds
as they open a grandiose battle horizon in the skies.

The *aristeia* ends immediately after this simile with the
killing of Phegeus. His death (without Homeric model)
concludes the forward sweep of Turnus' triumphal drive:

But Phegeus could not brook his onset nor his proud battle cry. He thrust himself full in the path of the chariot, and with his strong right arm caught the galloping horses and swung to one side their mouths, foaming on the bits. Phegeus was dragged, clinging to the yoke, with flank exposed. Turnus' broad-headed lance drove home and burst through his two-leashed cuirass, but barely tasted his flesh in a surface-wound. Even so Phegeus turned to face his foe; he held up his shield before him, and attempting self-defense drew his pointed sword. But before he could attack, the chariot-wheel, spinning on its axle in its violent on-rush, drove him headlong down and stretched him on the earth. Instantly Turnus followed up with a slash of his blade between the lower rim of his helmet and his corslet's upper edge, severed his head, and left the trunk on the sand.

XII.371:

Non tulit instantem Phegeus animisque frementem,
Obiecit sese ad currum et spumantia frenis
Ora citatorum dextra detorsit equorum.
Dum trahitur pendetque iugis, hunc lata retectum
Lancea consequitur rumpitque infixa bilicem
Loricam et summum degustat volnere corpus.
Ille tamen clipeo obiecto conversus in hostem
Ibat et auxilium ducto mucrone petebat:
Cum rota praecipitem et procursu concitus axis
Impulit effuditque solo Turnusque secutus
Imam inter galeam summi thoracis et oras
Abstulit ense caput truncumque reliquit harenae.

The point of reversal is in the contrastingly quiet scene of the healing of Aeneas. The "black army" of Aeneas comes like a disastrous thunderstorm from the sea:

Soon all the plain was a confusion of blinding dust, and the earth quaked and shuddered under their tramping feet. From the earthwork opposite, Turnus saw them coming; so did his Ausonians, and the chill tremor ran through the very marrow of their bones. But first, before any of the Latins, Juturna heard the noise and recognized its meaning; she trembled, and recoiled. Aeneas came swiftly on, and hastened the march of his army, a streak of dark menace moving across the open plain. Like some storm-cloud he came, which, at the sky's discharge, travels landwards over mid-sea, while far inland hearts of poor farming-folk shudder in foreboding, for the storm will bring down their trees, flatten their crops, and spread general ruin over wide lands; the winds fly ahead, and carry the sound to the shores.

XII.444:

Tum caeco pulvere campus
Miscetur pulsuque pedum tremit excita tellus.
Vidit ab adverso venientis aggere Turnus,
Videre Ausonii gelidusque per ima cucurrit
Ossa tremor; prima ante omnis Iuturna Latinos
Audiit adgnovitque sonum et tremefacta refugit.
Ille volat campoque atrum rapit agmen aperto.
Qualis ubi ad terras abrupto sidere nimbus
It mare per medium, miseris heu praescia longe
Horrescunt corda agricolis, dabit ille ruinas
Arboribus stragemque satis, ruet omnia late;
Ante volant sonitumque ferunt ad litora venti.

The simile is inspired by Homer (*Iliad* 4.275): "Like some heavy cloud blown over the deep by the west wind; the goatherd sees it afar from his watching place, blacker than pitch over the deep as the whirlwind drives, and he shudders and guides his herd into a cave. So thick black clumps of sturdy younkers moved toward the battle, bristling with spears and shields . . ."

Vergil has four points: (1) the "black" army, or the optical effect, (2) the destruction, or the physical effect, (3) the paralyzing fear, or the psychological effect, (4) the approach of doom, or the symbolic meaning.

The first is the only one of real importance in Homer. Here, the black cloud as a sensory impression is dominant. In Vergil the psychological effect is the main thing. The grief of the farmers at the threatened destruction of their labor parallels Turnus' feelings when he fails at the task to which he has given his whole heart. This is much stronger than the fright of Homer's shepherd who, after all, could still save his sheep. Part of the tragedy of Turnus can now be seen. The destructiveness of the storm and the breathtaking violence of coming doom have been significantly strengthened.[55] Vergil's simile does not end as simply as Homer's "he guides his herd into a cave." It ends, rather, with a grand image of the rushing wind with the message of misfortune. Destiny comes on with an ever-increasing speed—an acceleration shown in the dactylic hexameter at the end: *"Ante volant sonitumque ferunt ad litora venti."* In a context that is more epical than dramatic, Homer's simile is only a minor episode in Agamemnon's path. Vergil makes it an important link in a total chain of development.[56] It has become a symbol of the impending end.

After this prelude, Aeneas and Turnus meet—at first, at a distance. The basic difference between them is mirrored in the kind of death which they inflict upon their adversaries (XII.500). Aeneas kills *"qua fata celerrima."* [57] Turnus stacks the severed dripping heads on his chariot and has the heads of Nisus and Euryalus impaled.[58] In Homer, Hector is not more cruel than Achilles. Homer would not dream of toning down the horror surrounding the Greek hero to clothe him with the splendor of higher humanity as Vergil has done for Aeneas. For Achilles, fighting is the greatest satisfaction and the greatest pleasure. For Aeneas,[59] it is the bitter fulfillment of duty.

It might be objected here that Vergil, at least in this respect, is "less impartial" than is Homer. I do not believe, however, that the fact of the different characterizations of Aeneas and Turnus contradicts the statement that the poet sympathizes with both. The higher level of "humanity," the Roman manner and way of thinking, the inner discipline and mental superiority, the Roman feeling for the sanctity of law and treaty, all distinguish Aeneas from Turnus, and —according to the Roman concept of the laws of politics— Aeneas' victory is the necessary consequence of a higher morale. Still, this does not impair the poet's admiration of Turnus, who represents Italy in its original power—before any contact with a higher ideal. Roman grandeur springs from two elements, both of which are necessary and valuable: Aeneas' religious and moral mission, which is symbolic of the idea of Rome, and the primitive nature of Italy. Aeneas brings the Trojan gods to Italy (XII.192: *"sacra deosque dabo"*); he brings religion and ethics, the foundations of the Roman history to come. But Italy is worthy of receiving them. Italy possesses the noble strength of a nature meant for good and ready to blossom upon contact with a higher idea. Perhaps, then, Herder, Hegel, Mommsen, and others more recent were not entirely right in interpreting the Romans' unique historical success as the result of an instinctive inclination toward power politics. Perhaps there is some truth in the theory that healthy natural strength and a higher ideal are the real bases of true political and historical greatness.

Aeneas exists on a higher political plane than does Turnus and represents a more advanced form of armed conflict. All in all, he enters the battle only three times. First, when the Rutulians, in violation of the treaty made by Latinus,[60] resist the Trojans' landing (the attacker is Turnus: X.276 ff.); second, to avenge the death of Pallas; and finally, after much hesitation,[61] when the Latins violate the solemnly concluded compact. Aeneas actually names the latter as his reason for entering the battle (XII.496 f., 573). It is not he, but Turnus, who is the first to lift the sword in single combat. Like the Romans he fights *sui defendendi, ulciscendi,* and *iniuriae propulsandae causa.* This is to say that he personifies

the Roman idea of *bellum justum*. It should not be overlooked, however, that Turnus, too, is kept free of any sus-
picion of violation of the treaty. This is clearly the result of
Juturna's interference,[62] brought on by Tolumnius' being
deceived with a false *augurium*. It is another refutation of
the interpretation of Turnus as an "enemy of the state." Had
Vergil wanted him to be understood as such, he would obviously have charged him with violating the treaty.

A general battle precedes the meeting of the two heroes.
In a scene planned as a companion-piece to the siege of the
Trojan camp in the ninth book, Aeneas first turns to the walls
of the city (XII.554 ff.). The organized attack of the force
collected under his leadership is in contrast to Turnus' senseless, unplanned assault in the ninth book. *Disciplina Romana*
is contrasted with *vis consili expers:*

> When Aeneas had spoken, his troops adopted the wedge-
> formation, every spirit among them striving with equal
> ardor, and in a dense mass charged against the walls.

XII.574:
> Dixerat atque animis pariter certantibus omnes
> Dant cuneum densaque ad muros mole feruntur.

Thus, disciplined accord is confronted with growing *discordia* on the Latin side. Queen Amata hangs herself; [63]
Latinus covers his head with dust.

Meanwhile, protected by Juturna from clashing with
Aeneas, Turnus seems to win one contest after another (XII.
479). But, as usual, he is fighting in the wrong place for
the wrong goal. In contrast to Hector, who purposely avoids
Achilles upon the advice of Apollo (*Iliad* 20.379), he does
not know where the enemy is.[64] Not until he finally hears
the noise from the town does he realize what is happening
there. Differing from Homer, Vergil is at pains to avoid anything that might cast a bad light on the hostile hero. But
Turnus' joy in battle gradually diminishes and the noise from

the town further unsettles him. His words to his sister indicate that he no longer considers victory possible and expects to die:

> But who willed that you would descend from Olympus to endure our hearty toil? [65] Was it simply to allow you to look on your poor brother's death-agony? For what chances have I, now? What fortune can any longer promise me life? Myself have I seen, before my very eyes, Murranus, dearer than all whom I now have left to me, fall like a giant, vanquished by a giant's wound, and heard his own voice calling on my name as he died. The luckless Ufens has fallen, to be spared the sight of my dishonor, and Trojans hold his body and his arms.

XII.634:

Sed quis Olympo

Demissam tantos voluit te ferre labores
An fratris miseri letum ut crudele videres?
Nam quid ago aut quae iam spondet fortuna salutem?
Vidi oculos ante ipse meos me voce vocantem
Murranum quo non superat mihi carior alter
Oppetere ...
Occidit infelix, ne nostrum dedecus Ufens
Aspiceret, Teucri potiuntur corpore et armis.

These are the words of grief. They are also words expressing the sorrow and shame that beset a general who is unable to help his men. There is something here of the noble grief expressed in the delusion scene. He is wounded in a most vulnerable place. As Dido has been condemned to break her vow to her cruelly murdered and dearly beloved husband only to be deserted by the man for whose love she broke that faith, so it is the honor-covetous Turnus' bitter fate to lose his honor and bring ruin to his followers. It is no accident that the delusion scene recalls the *Ajax* of Sophocles— the great tragic model of such a fate. The hero is overcome by the suffocating awareness of desertion. He feels that he has been abandoned to dishonor by the gods. His defeat in battle is both predicted and intensified by his inner defeat. It is quite wrong to speak here of character weakness and not of the tragic dissolution of inner resources nor of how the growing realization of his predicament forces him to collapse. In fact, Turnus, like Dido, opposes inner pain and humiliation with a gradual acceptance of death and glory:

> Or shall I turn my back on the foe and let this land of Italy see Turnus in retreat? But is it then so very pitiable to die? O you Spirits below, be good to me, since the High Powers above have withdrawn their favor. I shall come down to you a guiltless soul with never a taint of the coward's sin, for never will I bring disgrace on my exalted forefathers.

XII.645:
> Terga dabo et Turnum fugientem haec terra videbit?
> Usque adeone mori miserum est? Vos o mihi manes
> Este boni, quoniam superis adversa voluntas.
> Sancta ad vos anima atque istius nescia culpae
> Descendam magnorum haud umquam indignus avorum.[66]

Turnus' tragic grandeur brings to mind Achilles. His misery at the thought of the shameful, helpless death of his comrades echoes the scene between Homer's hero and his mother. "Thetis answered, weeping, 'You have not long to live, my child, if you say that. Quick after Hector fate is ready for you.'"

Achilles bursts out in anger, "Quick let me die, since it seems my friend was killed and I not there to help him. He perished far from his native land, and I was not there to defend him. I brought no hope to Patroclos or my other comrades whom Hector killed, and how many there are" (*Iliad* 18.94 ff.).

Turnus' decision for death and glory (p. 112) is not unlike a reflection of the "tragic decision," the *prohairesis* of Achilles.

"Now I will go and find Hector, destroyer of that dear

life. Fate I will welcome whenever Zeus and all gods may choose to bring it. Not even the mighty Heracles escaped fate, and he was one that the Lord Zeus Cronion loved best of all. Yes, fate brought him low and the implacable anger of Hera. So with me; if a like fate has been ordained for me, there I shall lie when I am dead. But now may I win a glorious name" (*Iliad* 18.114 ff.).

"Why do you foretell death for me, Xanthos? You need not. I know well myself that it is my fate to die here, far from my father and my mother. Still, I will never cease driving the Trojans until they have had enough of war" (*Iliad* 19.420).

It is not Hector, then, who is the real model for Turnus as has always been assumed, but Achilles, just as the Sibyl said:

> A new Achilles, again a goddess's son, already breathes in Latium;

VI.89:

> Alius Latio iam partus Achilles
> Natus et ipse dea.

Thus, as stated before, everything significant comes from Achilles. The exterior points—the breach of the wall, the burning of the ships, the departure, the defeat in single combat—come from Hector. Even in these scenes, Achillean characteristics are present. As concerns the "tragic decision" this has been shown already. But his behavior in single combat is significantly different from Hector's, too. Facing death, when all hope is lost, Turnus reaches his full heroic stature. He decisively refuses Juturna's offer to save his life.[67] Aware like Achilles and greater than Hector, who before the battle considers more how to escape shame than how to acquire glory (*Iliad* 22.99 ff.),[68] Turnus chooses death for the sake of glory.[69] In the next scene his inner decision finds outer realization. On the foaming horse and with bleeding face,

Saces rushes in as the personification of the disaster that he comes to announce. His report of Aeneas' threat to raze the Italian castles, of Latinus' indecision, and of Amata's suicide is climaxed with a condemnation of the general's shameful laxity. His words are like a dagger in Turnus' heart:

> Messapus and the vigorous Atinas alone uphold our line of battle before the gates. About them on both sides stand enemies densely massed, whose naked swords stand bristling like a crop of iron corn. Yet you spend the time maneuvering your chariot out here on deserted grassland.

XII.661:

> Soli pro portis Messapus et acer Atinas
> Sustentant acies. Circum hos utrimque phalanges
> Stant densae strictisque seges mucronibus horret
> Ferrea: tu currum deserto in gramine versas.

Turnus is beside himself with grief:

> In that one heart together there surged a mighty tide of shame, madness, and misery blending, love tormented by passion for revenge, and valor which knew itself true.

XII.666:

> Aestuat ingens
> Uno in corde pudor mixtoque insania luctu
> Et furiis agitatus amor et conscia virtus.

Then when the darkness around him lifts and he sees the tower which he built collapse in smoke and flames, he interprets it as a symbol of the catastrophe of his life. But, like Dido, he momentarily frees himself from passion and rises, collected and resigned, to an attitude related in gesture and appearance to Stoicism:

> Sister, he said, at this very moment Fate is prevailing over us. Think not to cause delay. Let us follow where God and our own hard fortune call. I am resolved to meet Aeneas

hand to hand, and bear whatever bitterness death may hold
for me. Sister, never again shall you see me forget my
honor . . .

XII.676:

Iam iam fata, soror, superant, absiste morari,
Quo deus et quo dura vocat Fortuna, sequamur.
Stat conferre manum Aeneae, stat, quidquid acerbi est,
Morte pati; neque me indecorem, germana, videbis
Amplius.

Magnanimous resignation in the expectation of death—
glorified by philosophers since Plato—is united here with the
heroic decisiveness of the Homeric Achilles to produce one
grand effect. But giving in a last time to his demonic nature, he
ends with the unstoical: *"hunc sine me furere ante furorem."*

He pushes the last barrier aside. He leaves his sister, who
in trying to save him only increased his humiliation. His
courage does not stem from fear as does Hector's (*Iliad*
22.99 ff.), nor is he brave because he, like Hector,[70] has
been deceived by the gods (Allecto and Iris). Rather, he
voluntarily accepts the fate which he already knows.

Turnus' initial avoidance of death has an analogy in the
story of Dido, as does his sister's role and her absence when
death approaches. Like Dido, he again and again trusts in
false hopes only to have to turn to heroic death in order to
save his honor when the hopes collapse. Like the queen, he
cannot surrender his heart's desire—the salvation of his
country and his glory. The more he clings to it, the lower he
falls. Exactly like Dido, the more he tries to save his honor,
the more he loses it. For Turnus, though, the false hopes that
shield him from death (delusion, *aristeia* in the absence of
Aeneas) come from without, for Dido they are the creations
of her own heart. The same is true of the warnings and
premonitions. In both instances there is something like guilt
in this clinging to life, this refusal to come to the final decision.
Indeed, just as did Dido, he bears a two-fold guilt. There

is guilt in having started the war through demonic passion, and also guilt in refusing, through demonic passion, to end it. The realization of guilt contributes as much to Turnus' as to Dido's tragedy, even though, in accordance with his role as a fighting hero, his inner drama is only suggested. But the fact of guilt cannot be overlooked, and its existence in his inner drama proves the tragic conception of his fate.

After Juturna's departure, Turnus declares to the Rutulians that it is right that he "atone" [71] for the treaty in their place. This, too, proves his recognition of a guilt all the more pitiable in being, like Dido's, not a moral but a tragic one.

The heroes rush at each other with furious speed. The poet characterizes their natures in a pair of similes; Turnus plunges like a landslide toward the city wherein Aeneas rages:

> He came like a rock crashing headlong down from a mountain-crest, wrenched out perhaps by a wind after floods of rain have washed it free, or else time has crept beneath it with the years and worked it loose; sheer downwards the great crag charges with a mighty impulse, self-willed, bounding upwards off the ground, and rolling before it in its path forests, and herds, and men; so Turnus charged to the city's wall through shattered ranks where the ground was soaked deepest in streams of blood and the air whistled with the shafts of spears.

XII.684:

> Ac veluti montis saxum de vertice praeceps
> Cum ruit avolsum vento seu turbidus imber
> Proluit aut annis solvit sublapsa vetustas,
> Fertur in abruptum magno mons improbus actu
> Exultatque solo, silvas, armenta virosque
> Involvens secum: disiecta per agmina Turnus
> Sic urbis ruit ad muros, ubi plurima fuso
> Sanguine terra madet striduntque hastilibus aurae.

How different is Aeneas' approach:

> He . . . rejoiced exultantly, striking a dread thunder from his arms. He towered like Athos or like old Father Appen-

nine himself, with his rustle of shimmering holm-oak trees, joyously lifting his snow-covered head to the sky.

XII.700:

> Laetitia exultans horrendumque intonat armis
> Quantus Athos aut quantus Eryx aut ipse coruscis
> Cum fremit ilicibus quantus gaudetque nivali
> Vertice se attollens pater Appenninus ad auras.

Compare the plunging rock which leaves a downward path of destruction with the majestic power of the enduring mountains. Compare, too, darkness with light, falling with rising, the dark with the light tones. Besides the contrast of Turnus and Aeneas, these opposing symbols express the contrast between defeat and victory, demonic and divine forces, the barbarians and the Romans,[72] and between the temporary sway of wild violence and a power that endures. Vergil received the inspiration for all of this from just three of Homer's words—"like a snowy mountain" (*Iliad* 13.754)—which produce nothing but a visual impression.

The duel itself is emphasized by the presence and reactions of the spectators, including surrounding Nature. At Hector's death there is only frightening emptiness. The reaction is one of pity: "Earth sighs," "the whole world resounds with moaning," "a tremendous roar fills the aether." The word "aether" leads to Jupiter's weighing of the souls which, without being decided, leads to the sword's breaking in the hands of Turnus. This surprises the reader, for he is under the impression that Turnus wields the sword of Vulcan, as mentioned in the arming scene (XII.90 ff.). In his hurry, however, Turnus has forgotten it (*"vis consili expers"*) and has received another from his charioteer (735 ff.). The poet achieved two things with this invention: the tension is increased because both opponents seem equal in arms—the sword of Vulcan is a match for the shield of Vulcan—and it makes clear that although Turnus is inferior to Aeneas neither in courage nor fighting power, he *is* inferior in spirit, prudence, and luck. The blessing of the gods is not upon him. Aeneas (as Poseidon in the *Iliad* says of Achilles) is "dearer to the gods."

Even after the loss of the sword, tension does not diminish. It is true that Turnus flees, but not from fear or because he lacks a weapon with which to defend himself. He flees in order to find in some way the forgotten sword (758 ff.) so as to return to the fight with a better chance of winning.[73] He is not trying to escape. In this he differs from Hector, although not, as Heinze assumes, to his disadvantage (p. 135). Turnus flees only after losing his weapon, while Hector runs at the very sight of his opponent.

Turnus continues more praiseworthy than Hector. The situation is the reverse of its customary interpretation: Vergil is not more, but less "partial" than Homer; Turnus appears more heroic than Hector. Contrary to Heinze's interpretation, it is Hector and not Turnus who behaves miserably. It does not occur to Turnus to give up the fight. Hector seriously considers this course of action, although he decides against it. His reason for this decision is—significantly—not that it would be shameful, but that he cannot hope for mercy from his inexorable opponent. It is Hector, not Turnus (as Heinze assumes), who is bold in the absence [74] of his adversary and who loses courage when he approaches.[75]

Hector does not cover himself with glory in killing Patroclos. He attacks when the hero retreats after being hit in the back by the spear of Euphorbos. The dying Patroclos does not let him forget it (*Iliad* 16.846): "I could have killed twenty like you. Destructive Moira has killed me and the son of Leto, and among men, Euphorbos. You, who take my weapons, are the third." When Turnus does not succeed in getting his sword and Aeneas tries to pull the spear from the olive trunk (the Trojans had felled the holy tree of Faunus and incurred the wrath of that god), Turnus' prayer seems to have succeeded. Destiny hesitates for the last time when

Aeneas is unable to get possession of the spear. Then, when Juturna finally gives her brother his own sword and the fight might really threaten Aeneas, Venus interferes and pulls the spear from the tree. The goddess, not the man, brings the decision.

On the divine level Juno now restrains her wrath, but not without gaining the point that the Trojan name will be forever extinguished and that the Roman race will take its power from *"virtus Itala."* This victory does much to sweeten the death of Turnus. Jupiter sends one of the two Dirae (who as messengers of death keep watch at his throne) to separate Juturna from her brother. In the guise of a bird of death she flits around Turnus and brushes his shield with her wings [76] so that Aeneas can pierce it.

Thus, the cycle of Turnus' destiny returns unto itself, for it all began when he was possessed by Allecto, who, like the Dira, was a "daughter of night."

The demon's appearance paralyzes the hero just as Apollo paralyzes Patroclos (*Iliad* 16.805) and it causes Juturna's heart-breaking departure. Her misery parallels Anna's sorrow for Dido's death. Both would have preferred to follow their dead. Turnus cannot die in his sister's arms, but her mourning will alleviate his death.

When Turnus is finally confronted by Aeneas, he again expresses his feeling of having been deserted by the gods:

> Arrogant foe, it is not your heated words which affright me. I fear only gods, and especially the hostility of Jove.

XII.894:

> Non me tua fervida terrent
> Dicta, ferox: di me terrent et Iuppiter hostis.

Then, since his sword is powerless against the enemy's spear, he hurls a huge stone. That it is too heavy for him has been recognized by Heinze as a sign of his departing strength. When he throws it, he seems to be out of his mind (XII.903 ff.). The inner paralysis, inflicted upon him by the Dira, is expressed in a simile:

> As sometimes in our sleeping, when at night a languor of stillness lies heavy on our eyes, we dream that we strive desperately to run ever onward, and we fail, and sink down fainting at the very moment of our greatest effort; our tongue is strengthless, the body's powers will give no normal response, and neither words nor even voice will come: so was it with Turnus, for wherever he exerted his valor to find an opening, the weird goddess denied him progress. Through his mind flashed changing images. His eyes rested on the Rutulians, and on the city; he faltered in fear, and started to shudder at the spear-point's imminence. He could find no place of refuge, nor any strength to press home an attack on his foe; nor could he anywhere see his chariot or his sister at the reins.[77]

XII.908:
> Ac velut in somnis, oculos ubi languida pressit
> Nocte quies, nequiquam avidos extendere cursus
> Velle videmur et in mediis conatibus aegri
> Succidimus: non lingua valet, non corpore notae
> Sufficiunt vires nec vox aut verba sequuntur:
> Sic Turno, quacumque viam virtute petivit,
> Successum dea dira negat. Tum pectore sensus
> Vertuntur varii: Rutulos adspectat et urbem
> Cunctaturque metu telumque instare tremescit,
> Nec quo se eripiat nec qua vi tendat in hostem
> Nec currus usquam videt aurigamque sororem.

Here, the dream in the Homeric simile in which the pursuer cannot reach the pursued nor the pursued escape the pursuer (*Iliad* 22.199 ff.) has become a suffocating and paralyzing nightmare. Evidently, the purpose here is not only to prepare for the catastrophic moment when Aeneas will throw his spear and Turnus will fall.

To elicit tragic fear and tragic pity, Vergil also wants to show Turnus' god-willed weakness. When Turnus falls, the Rutulians rise with a single cry of grief echoed in all nature in much the same way that the whole of Carthage resounds with lamentation upon the death of Dido. The Trojans do not rejoice at Turnus' death and the Rutulians' grief. In the *Iliad* the Greeks intone the *paean* upon the death of Hector. This difference is again intended to arouse our compassion for Turnus. His last words should be understood with this in mind:

> Turnus, brought low, raised his eyes and an outstretched right hand in humble entreaty, and said: This is my own desert; I make no appeal. Enjoy the fortune which falls to you. And if a poor father's sorrow can affect you—and you yourself had in Anchises such a father as mine—I beg of you, take pity on Daunus in his old age, and restore me, or, if you so prefer it, my dead body despoiled of life, to my own people.

XII.930:
> Ille humilis supplexque oculos dextramque precantem
> Protendens: Equidem merui nec deprecor, inquit,
> Utere sorte tua. Miseri te si qua parentis
> Tangere cura potest, oro—fuit et tibi talis
> Anchises genitor—Dauni miserere senectae
> Et me seu corpus spoliatum lumine mavis
> Redde meis.

When Heinze [78] interprets Turnus' plea for mercy and his withdrawal as Lavinia's suitor as the result of unheroic character, he misconstrues the tragic situation. This behavior indicates only that he fulfills the stringent conditions of the treaty to the letter. The treaty stated that the outcome of the combat would determine who should be Lavinia's husband, and he had sworn to accept it. Therefore, his renunciation, far from being "miserable" is a legal consequence of the treaty. For a man like Turnus to acknowledge this situation

in plain words is a bitter penance. It is to his credit. Moreover, his words have a deeper meaning. When he says "I
deserve this," he confesses his guilt toward Aeneas for the
first and only time. In his last words to Juturna and the
Rutulians there is guilt only in terms of his own dignity. The
words of Latinus are borne out (VII.597 ff.): "Ah, Turnus,
the wrongfulness of your deed and its grim punishment will
overtake you, and when at last you offer vows to the gods in
veneration you will be too late." If Turnus is a failure, he is
a tragic failure, not a miserable one. There is something
deeply moving in the final confession of this unrestrained and
violent hero. His recognition of wrongdoing, alluded to in
the treaty scene, *"aram suppliciter venerans demisso voltu"*
(XII.220), reaches a climax in resignation. The mellowing
of Turnus is related to the "conversion" of the *"contemptor
deum,"* Mezentius, at the end of the tenth book, which is
itself one of the most moving inventions of the poet.

The confession of Turnus is necessary also as preparation
for the reconciliation of the Trojans and Italians, as required
in the treaty and as sanctioned on the highest level by Jupiter.
And if Turnus and Dido are compared, it is in the economy
of the whole that the reconciliation of Turnus forms the
counterpoint to the obdurateness of Dido. The queen changes
from love to irreconcilable hostility, while Turnus changes
from irreconcilable hostility to humble submission. Both Hector and Dido perish with a defiant threat of vengeance. Turnus at the end of the *Aeneid* is resigned to his fate, however
hard it may be.

Vergil has been criticized for having Turnus plead for
his life. But as a cue to Aeneas' indecisiveness this is necessary. Aeneas is quite prepared to spare the conquered (*"par-
cere subiectis"*), but he is obligated to Evander to avenge
Pallas' death. The conflict between Aeneas' heart and his
duty is once more shown to be basic to his character and
his tragedy. That Heinze was wrong in blaming Turnus for a

lack of nobility and for cowardice is proved by his proud-humble words:

> This is my own desert; I make no appeal.
> Enjoy the fortune which falls to you.

XII.931:

> Equidem merui nec deprecor, inquit
> Utere sorte tua

He then asks either that he or, as Hector also requested, that his corpse be returned to his aged father: *"me seu corpus spoliatum lumine mavis redde meis."* [79] These words abolish any doubt as to whether he cares about life or death. The worst for him is not dying but that the Ausonians "saw how he raised his hands, conquered." He pleads for his life, not for himself, but for his father's sake, for the love that binds him to Daunus:

> You yourself had in Anchises such a father as mine—
> I beg of you, take pity on Daunus in his old age.

XII.932:

> Fuit et tibi talis
> Anchises genitor, Dauni miserere senectae.

Aeneas is not deaf to this plea. Servius has remarked: "From *pietas* he wants to spare him and from *pietas* he has to kill him, and both enhance his glory." If the value which the poet places on *pietas* and filial love is considered, it cannot be assumed that his words disgrace Turnus. He dies a hero.[80]

Turnus and Dido are both tragic figures. Both have fallen into tragic guilt through divine interference; both are caught in a fatal passion [81] and both are filled with a love of glory that lends grandeur to their catastrophes. Yet Turnus does not quite equal the queen in dignity and tragic effect. He does not lack *magnitudo animi,* as is proven by his heroic willingness to face death, nor does he lack *pietas,* as is shown in his attitude toward gods, country, and his father. His *humanitas* is apparent in his compassion for his comrades and in his death. He, like Aeneas and Dido, personifies the three cardinal virtues in the *Aeneid*. What he lacks is the noble glow of Aeneas and Dido. Although he fights for honor and glory, he is too much possessed by the fury of Hell to arouse the same compassion that we feel for the magnanimous Dido. Moreover, he is Aeneas' antagonist and is vanquished by a representative of higher values. A balance is struck between Dido and Aeneas, and the inferiority of the queen can be traced to her femininity.[82] Nevertheless, a high measure of tragic effect is achieved through Turnus' grief over the defeat and loss of honor. There *is* something of the grandeur of Achilles in Turnus. It is the result of an astonishing number of preconceived notions that this fact has not been understood and that the tragic force of the last half of the *Aeneid* has not been recognized. The impact of this tragic force is insolubly connected with the figure of Turnus.

CHAPTER III

ARTISTIC PRINCIPLES

SYMBOLISM OF THE SEQUENCE OF MOOD

Concerning line 183 of the eleventh book of the *Aeneid,*
Servius writes: "Asinius Pollio says that in describing a day
Vergil always uses a particular phrase which befits the particular situation." Richard Heinze (p. 366 ff.) deserves the
credit for pointing out the truth of this remark, which had
utterly escaped both Ribbeck (*Prolegomena,* 116) and Georgii (*Aeneaskritik,* 145). I am convinced that it is possible
to exceed the limits set by Heinze's examples of a general
connection between the description of daybreak and the
epic situation, and to follow Servius to a higher plane from
which to observe the symbolic words in which daybreak
is described. Servius has attempted it, but the examples
which he quotes, either rightly or wrongly from Pollio, are
absurd.[1] It is less than pleasant to have *extulerat lucem*
(XI.183) connected with the *efferre* of the dead or *surgebat
Lucifer* (II.803) with *de patria discedere,* that is, *surgere*
of Aeneas. Better examples can be found, however. The
verses (X.256) relate to Aeneas as he relieves the Trojans'
troubles:

> Meanwhile the day had routed the darkness and,
> swiftly circling, returned with a light now full.

X.256:

> Et interea revoluta ruebat
> Matura iam luce dies *noctemque fugarat.*

The scene is reminiscent of Mozart's "the rays of the sun have chased the night." [2] The rise of Lucifer at the end of the second book, which is so oddly connected by Servius with the departure of Aeneas, has indeed a symbolic meaning; the star of Venus appears at the moment when Aeneas leaves Troy: *"Quem Venus ante alios astrorum diligit ignis"* (VIII. 590). The morning which breaks here is symbolic, just as is the morning of history in the beginning of the seventh book. The glorious history of the Gens Julia begins.[3]

As Pollio has significantly noticed, such an inner relation goes far beyond the description of daybreak. It affects the whole poem and all of its descriptions. It has been shown that the wounded deer (IV.68 ff.), the mortally injured lion (XII.4 ff.), and the Alpine oak (IV.441 ff.) are symbols of destiny as well as similes of situations. It could likewise be shown that most similes in the *Aeneid* are carried by the movement, not of the outer action, but of its inner accompaniment. The whole poem may be viewed as a sequence of moods, a series of changing sensations. I consider this to be the basic truth of Vergilian art, the appreciation of which is the *condicio sine qua non* for understanding. For example, the ant simile (IV.401 ff.), for which neither Homer nor Apollonius furnished the model, besides describing Aeneas' preparations for departure in the Homeric manner, symbolizes with somber coloring and dragging tempo Dido's state of mind as she sees what is happening. Just so the Diana simile describes Dido's entrance at the same time it illuminates Aeneas' reactions. Examples can easily be multiplied and because of the almost total blindness of the interpreters there is endless opportunity for new discoveries. The following remarks, far from being an attempt to exhaust a matter as large as it is beautiful, are invitations to further observation—to a more thorough inquiry into the form and poetic inspiration of the *Aeneid*.

The two first examples are meant to illustrate how the narrative conforms to the sequence of mood and how the poet manages to create subtle transitions and inner relations.

The Odyssean storm is followed by the landing in an Odyssean port, the "Phorcys port." Vergil used it because it is the most beautiful landing place described by Homer. In quiet contrast to the agitated sea, it is the goal and end of all wandering—*the* harbor. He excluded the olive tree under which Odysseus and Athene planned the death of the suitors and also the details of the nymph's cave where the Phaeacian gifts were stored. He added other things. The most striking difference is in the character of the landscape which, in Vergil, is much more threatening. Homer: "There are two bold headlands squatting at the cove's mouth to protect it from the heavy swell raised by rough weather in the open." Vergil:

> Here and there tremendous rocks, double cliffs threaten skyward.

I.162:

> Hinc atque hinc vastae rupes geminique minantur
> In caelum scopuli.

Their origin is not Homer's description of the port of Ithaca, but the eerie rocks of Scylla and Charybdis (*Ody.* 12.73): "Cliffs, the higher of which rears its sharp peak up to the very sky." [4] The next words were added for the same reason —to establish an inclination toward monumental pathos:

> A curtain of trees with quivering leaves, and behind them an over-hanging forest-clad mountainside, mysterious and dark.

I.164:

> Tum silvis scaena coruscis
> Desuper horrentique atrum nemus imminet umbra.

This preference for "grandeur," "pathos," and the "sublime" is a marked characteristic of Vergil's style. The first monologue of Aeneas (I.94) is a good example. Here, of course, the gloomy colors serve a definite purpose. The "black grove" with its "threatening, bristling, and quivering shadows," [5] emphasized by the "shimmering backdrop of the trees," [6] is not just a preparation for the saving of the ships (although this explanation would have satisfied the rationalistic school of philologists), but rather reinforces the wild and eerie impression [7] created by the tremendous rocks. The arrivals face an unknown country where danger may be lurking—as indeed it is.[8] With consummate artistry, Vergil has made the landscape fit the mood and character of the preceding and following action. Neither connection occurs in Homer. His description of the Phorcys harbor does not come after a storm but after the swift and untroubled fairy-tale voyage of the Phaeacian boat, and Carthage means for the Romans the opposite of what Ithaca is to Odysseus.

The order of the images reveals an artistic intention. First, the threatening rocks, the pointed, craggy *"hinc atque hinc,"* then, the groves, eerie but lit by *"silvis scaena coruscis,"* then the charming grotto of the nymphs, and finally, the gently rocking verses: [9]

> Here a tired ship will never need a cable or an anchor with a fluke to bite and make her fast.

I.168:

> Hic fessas non vincula navis
> Ulla tenent, unco non alligat ancora morsu.

The images are arranged as they appear to the travelers: the rocks, the grove, the grotto, the landing. They are also a continuum ranging from wild threats to alluring charms—

from the arrival out of the stormy sea to the gently subsiding movement both in nature and in the hearts of the Trojans. They reflect a modal curve which Homer's order of arrangement has been changed to produce.[10] Unlike Homer's, Vergil's landscape does not exist for its own sake. Nor is it all setting and background. Above all, it is symbolic of mood. It is a part and a reflection of the inner action. We are almost always watching a two-fold event—an inner and an outer drama. Vergil's main purpose is to express the inner event, not only directly, but through the artistic use of symbolism as well.

The arrival of the Trojans in Italy is the counterpart of their landing in Carthage. Their safe voyage from Caeta to the mouth of the Tiber complements the tempest:

> Favoring breezes blew onward into the night, and a radiant moon blessed their voyage; the sea sparkled under her quivering beam.

VII.8:

> Adspirant aurae in noctem nec candida cursus
> Luna negat, splendet tremulo sub lumine pontus.

Their arrival on that blessed morning follows:

> And now rays of light were beginning to redden the sea, and Aurora, saffron in her chariot of rose, was already shining forth from high heaven, when the winds dropped, and suddenly every breath of air was stilled, so that the oars strained in shining and languid water. Just then Aeneas, still far out from the land, saw a mighty forest, through which the Tiber flowed pleasantly, with rapid eddies and yellow from the quantities of sand, to burst forth into the sea. Birds of many kinds, whose home was the river's channel or the banks, caressed the air with their song around and above, as they flew about the forest. Aeneas signalled his comrades to change course and turn their prows to land. And happily he moved up into the shady river.

VII.25:

> Iamque rubescebat radiis mare et aethere ab alto
> Aurora in roseis fulgebat lutea bigis,
> Cum venti posuere omnisque repente resedit
> Flatus et in lento luctantur marmore tonsae.
> Atque hic Aeneas ingentem ex aequore lucum
> Prospicit. Hunc inter fluvio Tiberinus amoeno
> Verticibus rapidis et multa flavus harena
> In mare prorumpit. Variae circumque supraque
> Adsuetae ripis volucres et fluminis alveo
> Aethere mulcebant cantu lucoque volabant.
> Flectere iter sociis terraeque advertere proras
> Imperat et laetus fluvio succedit opaco.

The Tiber landscape is seen in the idyllic beauty of morning. Above it all, birds are singing. Only in the last word is there perhaps a slight premonition of danger. In any event, the word *opaco* diminishes the contrast with the following verses, which announce the violent conflicts to come. The bright, melodious verses symbolize the poet's love for the Roman landscape just as the bucolic poetry of Theocritus expresses the longing of the urban dweller for the countryside. The atmosphere of nature, unsullied as yet by history, is caught in the glowing image of morning on the river. In the *Eclogues,* Vergil had already used the idyll as a symbol of flight from time and history. His description of Mount Atlas in Mercury's visitation to Aeneas (IV.246) is another example of the way in which he symbolically relates landscape to narrative. Gislason,[10a] the Icelandic scholar, here and elsewhere may claim the credit for having questioned the inner connection of description with action, but his answer is unsatisfactory. He refers to the relation of Mercury to Atlas which Vergil himself mentions (IV.258: *"Materno veniens ab avo Cyllenia proles"*). He also notes the contrast between the image of Atlas and the splendidly arrayed Aeneas (IV.261 ff.). Both observations are correct, but he has missed the main point. The verses (IV.246–251) symbolize the grim fate awaiting the lovers. The monumental image of the harsh and suffering giant is like a motif of Mercury's message:

> And now as he flew he discerned the crest and steep flanks of Atlas the enduring, who supports the sky upon his head. His pine-clad crown is perpetually girt by blackest mist and beaten by wind and rain, his shoulders swathed in a mantle of snow, his aged chin a cascade of torrents, and his wild and shaggy beard frozen stiff with ice.

IV.248:

> Atlantis, cinctum adsidue cui nubibus atris
> Piniferum caput et vento pulsatur et imbri
> Nix umeros infusa tegit, tum flumina mento
> Praecipitant senis et glacie riget horrida barba.

Atlas symbolizes the cruelty of the gods and the harshness of destiny. He, too, exemplifies the fate which always overhangs mankind and now falls piteously on Dido. Mercury's journey is not interrupted by a "description of landscape" in the customary style of Homer; it is a concentrated symbol of the audience's feelings as they hear Jupiter's message. The somber tone of the description is heralded by Mercury's appearance, which contains the same *color tragicus* as the picture of Atlas, Homer's bringer of sleep (*Ody.* 5.47: "He picked up the wand which he can use at will to cast a spell upon our eyes or wake us from the soundest sleep") has become Hermes Psychopompos, the bringer of death. This is stressed twice:

> Then he took his wand; the wand with which he calls the pale souls forth from the Nether World and sends others down to grim Tartarus, gives sleep, and takes sleep away, and unseals eyes at death.

IV.242:

> Tum virgam capit, hac animas ille evocat Orco
> Pallentis, alias sub Tartara tristia mittit
> Dat somnos adimitque et lumina morte resignat.

The order is reversed. Homer puts the spell before the awakening. Vergil puts the darker note first three times: *"sub Tartara tristia mittit, adimitque, et lumina morte resignat."* Mercury comes as the bearer of death—in this case, Dido's death—and this is the secret meaning. To achieve this effect Vergil replaced Homer's sprightly god with the chthonic Hermes of the Orphic hymn.[11] This grave strain continues in the description of Atlas, where it is further intensified into a pitiless image of unfeeling fate. Although the subject matter may separate the description from the rest, there is still "unity of feeling" between it and the god's command which results in Dido's death. Logically and practically, there *is* separation, but artistically and aesthetically, there is a most intimate relation.

The passionately moving seventh book begins with an idyllic scene. The quiet eighth book starts with lively preparations for war and Aeneas' heartfelt sorrow. The poet makes the best use of contrasting backgrounds to emphasize light or dark movement, tranquillity, happiness, or sorrow.[12] Aeneas' inner tension is expressed in the simile of the shimmering sunbeams reflecting from a coffered ceiling. Apollonius Rhodius used this simile to picture the fluttering heart of the loving Medea (III.755). Vergil fits it into his plan with harmonious perfection, making it serve as a transition from the agitated beginning to the dream of helpful Tiber and the idyllic scenes that follow. The turbulent waves of sorrow in Aeneas' heart (VIII.19: *"Magno curarum fluctuat aestu"*) become less and less threatening until the god appears and Aeneas addresses him in prayer.

The mood of this simile is almost cheerfully contemplative and as such acts as an agent for reducing tension to tranquillity, thus creating a quiet movement. As such, it is also suitable for effecting transitions from darkness to light, from war to peace, and from history to idyll. A small seemingly unimportant touch, *"aut radiantis imagine lunae"* (V.23), is added by Vergil to Apollonius to make the simile even more appropriate to the character of peaceful night.[13] How different this is from Homer's description of Agamemnon's sorrows:

> As when the husband of Hera with the lovely tresses throws the lightning, sending unending rain or hail and snow or the horror of war, so Agamemnon often groaned from his innermost breast and his heart trembled.

Obviously, Vergil could not have used such a simile here. Nor, for that matter, has Apollonius given the simile a compositional function.

Many examples can be given to demonstrate Vergil's skill in making gentle transitions and careful connections. It has been already pointed out that the stallion simile is a preparatory image of the equestrian battle and that the two similes of Turnus' *aristeia* are fused together with the whole scene by means of the Thracian atmosphere and the mounting movement. The image of the Simois rolling over the Trojan corpses in Aeneas' monologue anticipates the loss of the ship in the storm. Turnus' inner fire is sustained in the outer conflagration and the swelling tide of beginning war falls into the movement of the similes. The description of the Trojan war reliefs in Juno's Carthaginian temple ends with Penthesilea (I.490 ff.): the Amazonian queen inwardly prepares the reader and Aeneas for the appearance of Dido which follows immediately.

The second catalogue of the Italians, the enumeration of Aeneas' allies ends with the image of Triton:

> The ship which carried him was the monstrous Triton, whose figure affrighted the blue channels with his horn of shell; as he swam, his hairy forepart down to his flanks displayed human shape but his belly ended in a beast of the sea. Beneath the breast of this hybrid monster the water murmured and foamed.

X.209:

> Hunc vehit immanis Triton et caerula concha
> Exterrens freta, cui laterum tenus hispida nanti
> Frons hominem praefert, in pristim desinit alvus:
> Spumea semifero sub pectore murmurat unda.

This, too, is pictorial preparation and leads to the related
scene of the sea nymphs who rise from the waves a few verses
later (X.219). The evil omens, auguring doom to Dido as
symptoms of her tragic ruin, continue into the description
of the witch's charms (IV.452 ff.), the magic of Dido, and
the witch's prayers to Erebus, Chaos, and the three-formed
Hecate (IV.504 ff.). A continuous line is formed of all
three. They are closely connected with each other, not rationally, but in feeling and form. They express Dido's turning
to the powers of death.

Vergil's presentations of works of art (including landscapes) are more symbolically meaningful than has been
heretofore recognized. Heinze's statement, "The content of
the presentation is everywhere related to the content of the
poem" (p. 400), is truer than he realized himself. And the
"content" of the poem must be understood as "inner" content rather than "outer" content. Aeneas' gifts to Dido are
listed:

> . . . a figured gown stiff with gold lace, and a mantle
> hemmed with a yellow thistle-pattern, both garments
> which had graced Argive Helen, fine gifts from her
> mother Leda which she had carried off from Mycenae
> when she first started for Troy and her wicked marriage.

I.648:

> Pallam signis auroque rigentem
> Et circumtextum croceo velamen acantho,
> Ornatus Argivae Helenae, quos illa Mycenis,
> Pergama cum peteret inconcessosque Hymenaeos,
> Extulerat.

Here is a premonition of the *inconcessi hymenaei* of Dido and Aeneas and of the doom which it means. The garments of the adulteress are an evil omen,[14] the fatal union of Paris and Helen will be repeated, and rulers and nations will suffer the consequences. The verses simultaneously prepare for the next scene, in which Venus has Amor deliver the gifts which will waken Dido's love and lead her to the "forbidden marriage." These symbolic gifts are mentioned several more times in the final verses of the book (I.657 ff.).

Gifts have symbolic meaning elsewhere, too. Mehmel (p. 50) remarks: "The presents, given by Helenus and Andromache at the departure, the weapons for Aeneas and his men, the horses, the warriors, rowers, and Andromache's gift to Ascanius, to the one who is now Hector's son 'Astyanax,' besides being tokens of friendship and hospitality, have a symbolic effect in transferring Trojan tradition to Aeneas and his followers." Similarly, the presentation of the royal insignia of Priam (scepter, crown, and *trabes,* as the commentaries explain) by Ilioneus to Latinus, indicates that Priam's rule over "the largest kingdom of the East" (VII.217) passes to Italy from whence the Dardanian clan originated in its ancestor, Dardanus.[15] The crime of the Danaids as pictured on Pallas' sword belt—the *nefas* and the *cruenti thalami*—is related to the "bloody marriage" which Turnus will celebrate. This is mentioned at the very moment when Turnus robs Pallas of his arms. Turnus collects his own death with the belt.

In his commentary on the sixth book, Eduard Norden has thoroughly analyzed the pictures on the temple of Daedalus (VI.114). He spared no effort in attempting to cleanse the poet of the charge that the matter has nothing to do with the action of the poem. He conceded, however, that the connection is unconvincing. He offers the excuse that this represents an interpretation of "a piece of early Italian history." But neither he nor Heinze, who essentially followed him, realized that the pictures symbolically mirror Aeneas' destiny, not literally, but in an aesthetically profound sense. Daedalus, like so many others in the poem, like Antenor, Diomedes, Andromache and Helenus, Dido and Evander, is an exile. This alone relates him to Aeneas and connects his fate most intimately with the main theme of the poem—the search for a new home. But there is more to it than that. It is already clear that the first verse of the episode recalls the other dangerous kingdom from which Aeneas escaped: [16] *"Daedalus, ut fama est, fugiens Minoia regna"* (VI.14). And who can miss the echo of Aeneas' love for Dido [17] in the beautiful reference to Ariadne: *"Magnum reginae sed enim miseratus amorem."* This is reminiscent of *"Multa gemens magnoque animum labefactus amore,"* and of the later:

> Aeneas was shocked by her unjust fate; and as she went gazed long after her with tearful eyes and pity for her in his heart.

VI.475:

> Nec minus Aeneas casu concussus iniquo
> Prosequitur lacrimis longe et miseratur euntem.

The heartbreaking love of Daedalus for Icarus reflects Aeneas' longing to meet Anchises. Both are examples of the deep *pietas,* that binds together those who are separated. That *pietas,* in its several forms, is the concealed but central motif of the sixth book. The "obvious parallel" of the connection with the pictures on Juno's Carthaginian temple in the first book is far more important than has been assumed. Aeneas finds his own story in both places; once, quite directly, then, symbolically disguised in the mysterious sixth book. Both times Aeneas is depicted as engrossed in sorrowful memories and interrupted by the entrance of a third person, the Sibyl in the second book and Dido in the first.

In a larger sense, Iopas' song at the Carthaginian banquet

(I.740–746) may also be considered as a work of art. Georgii, influenced by Servius for better or for worse, remarks in *Aeneiskritik* (p. 99): "Ancient criticism of Vergil would have been very blunt indeed—as blunt as it was sharp, not to attack the boring song of Iopas." Macrobius (*Saturnalia* 7. 1, 14) preserves a memory of this criticism, albeit incredibly distorted (as if Vergil had done the opposite): *"Nonne, si quis aut inter Phaeacas aut apud Poenos sermones de sapientia erutos convivalibus fabulis miscuisset, et gratiam illis coetibus aptam perderet et in se risum iustum moveret?"* [18]

After this, who could misunderstand a defense against the same criticism in the *Scholion* of Servius of the same passage: *"Bene philosophica introducitur cantilena in convivio reginae adhuc castae; contra inter nymphas (ubi solae feminae erant, Servius Danielis) ait, Vulcani Martisque dolos et dulcia furtia"* [19] (*Georgics* IV.346). We are not interested in the foggy argumentation and aberrations of Georgii, but is it correct that Iopas' song is boring? Why did not Vergil use some myth or other? Certainly, a frivolous story in the style of Demodokos (*Ody.* 8.266) would have been out of place—but why not another one, perhaps from the Phoenician past? Why should Vergil, perhaps inspired by the song of Orpheus in Apollonius (I.496), prefer the philosophical theme from cosmogony? In answer, I believe that the presentation was chosen that would most suitably accompany the inner action as it affects Dido. Let us study the lines. Note how consistent they are with both the spell cast over the queen by the god of love and the atmosphere of tragedy which this night introduces. Note also that these lines have the same alluring and melancholy quality and the same sadness as the story into which they are inserted. This is especially true at the beginning and the end:

> He sang now of the wandering moon and the laboring sun.
> Hic canit errantem lunam solisque labores

> His song told why on each winter day the sun so
> hastens to dip into the ocean, and told of the cause
> which then retards the nights.
>
> Oceano properent se tinguere soles
> Hiberni vel quae tardis mora noctibus obstet.

Is it wrong to connect the moon's wandering and the sun's
labors with the fate of Dido and Aeneas and with their past
and future wanderings in the true sense of a symbol? [20] The
book ends with the *"errores"* of Aeneas:

> Tell me the trap which the Greeks set, the calamity
> which befell your people, and your own wanderings;
> for it is now the seventh summer of your roaming over
> land and sea throughout the world.

I.754:

> Insidias, inquit, Danaum casusque tuorum
> Erroresque tuos: nam te iam septuma portat
> Omnibus errantem terris et fluctibus aestas.

For a moment, Sol and Luna appear as symbols of the lovers,[21] just as they are otherwise seen in the likenesses of Apollo
and Diana, sun god and moon goddess (cf. p. 67, the meeting of the pair). The relation of Luna to Dido returns again
by way of simile in the underworld meeting:

> Like one who early in the month sees or thinks that he
> sees the moon rising through the clouds

VI.453:

> Quam Troius heros
> Obscurus qualem primo qui surgere mense
> Aut videt aut vidisse putat per nubila Lunam.[22]

When Dido appears for the first time, she is, by means of the
simile, Diana. When she disappears forever, she is Luna.
When her destiny is shown in a simile, she is the deer which

also belongs to Diana's world. Such delicate connections are the hallmark of Vergil's art.

And just as the melancholy of Iopas' song relates to the destiny of Aeneas and Dido, so the "sun's hurry to throw itself into the ocean" belongs with the mood of "blessed longing" awakening in Dido's heart. And the *"mora quae tardis noctibus obstat"* is mysteriously related to the "dead of night" that Dido desires. The lovers' wish "let this night never end," may be heard in Iopas' song; it is one of those long winter nights of which he sings.[23] In the verse after the next (it is hard to mistake the relation, once it is recognized) the feeling and longing of the lovers are described:

> And the doomed Dido herself spent the whole night in talk of many kinds, drinking deep of her love.

I.748:

> Nec non et vario *noctem* sermone *trahebat*
> Infelix Dido longumque bibebat amorem.

This is an unforgettable night for Dido—one she wants to repeat again and again:

> At day's decline she would want the banqueting to begin again as before; she would insist beyond all reason on hearing yet once more the tale of Troy's anguish, and again she would hang breathless on the speaker's words.

IV.77:

> Nunc eadem labente die convivia quaerit
> Iliacosque iterum demens audire labores
> Exposcit pendetque iterum narrantis ab ore.

If an outer support is needed for the inner evidence of this interpretation, it may be found in the congruence with Vergil's model, the song of Orpheus in Apollonius in which the cosmological theme is also connected with the action. There too, the song's beginning, the conflict of the cosmic elements, is connected with the situation. The song is supposed to quiet minds eager for battle. This is, of course, an indication that the art of congruent relation of which Vergil is a master, must be considered a development of "Hellenistic" artistry. But what is purely exterior with Apollonius, has become atmosphere and mood in Vergil.

The song of Iopas is thus steeped in the mood that dominates the end of the first book. It is not a rationalistic allegory, but an element of poetic mood. The *labores* and *errores* of the king and the queen are symbolically reflected and repeated in the cosmic events described in Iopas' song. The winter sun's longing for the ocean and the endless nights symbolize Dido's feelings, particularly the secret awakening of her desire. This example makes the nature of poetic symbolism very clear: all that Iopas sings of is complete and meaningful in itself and does not require allegorical explanation. Nevertheless, there is something else mysteriously indicated in the song. The song becomes a metaphor of feeling. The words float in the light of the nocturnal banquet. They are tinged with the spell taking possession of the queen's heart. This is all the more true in that the only time in the *Aeneid* when music is heard is when it comes from Iopas' lyre. In the metaphorical sense, there is, of course, music everywhere in the poem. The song of Iopas is only an example. Beyond what is rationally sensory there exist units of poetically musical mood, held together through rhythm and melody and the language of their images.

The element of pure poetry and of art in general is the realm of the soul which nothing fills and shapes as completely as does music. Therefore, every art strives to become "pure art" or "music." Walter Pater, the English critic, has dealt with this in an essay on Giorgione—one of the most useful discussions on the principles of aesthetic criticism: "The ideal examples of poetry and painting being those in which the con-

stituent elements of the composition are so welded together,
that the material or subject no longer strikes the intellect only;
nor the form, the eye or the ear only; but form and matter,
in their union or identity, present one single effect to the 'imaginative reason,' that complex faculty for which every thought
and feeling is twin-born with its sensible analogue or symbol.
It is the art of music which most completely realizes this artistic ideal, this perfect identification of matter and form. In its
consummate moments, the end is not distinct from the means,
the form from the matter, the subject from the expression;
they inhere in and completely saturate each other; and to it,
therefore, to the condition of its perfect moments, all the arts
may be supposed constantly to tend and aspire. In music,
then, rather than in poetry, is to be found the true type or
measure of perfected art. Therefore, although each art has its
incommunicable element, its untranslatable order of impres-
sions, its unique mode of reaching the 'imaginative reason,'
yet the arts may be represented as continually struggling after
the law or principle of music, to a condition which music alone
completely realizes; and one of the chief functions of aesthetic
criticism, dealing with the products of art, new or old, is to es-
timate the degree in which each of these products approaches,
in this sense, to musical law."

It is Vergil's creative achievement to have conquered this
realm of the soul [24] for poetry. Here for the first time in Western poetry one can isolate the unity of poetically musical
mood from the unity of subject matter, which is open to rational comprehension, and the unity of structure, which is
similarly comprehensible. It is Vergil who has introduced this
kind of unity into poetry. He has used the new principle to
mold his matter first in pastorals, then in didactic poetry, and
finally in the epic.[25] His discovery is comparable to the discovery of those painters who discovered light as a pictorial
principle and in doing so launched a new epoch in the history

of painting. Ortega y Gasset has described it in an essay, "Sobre el punto de vista en las artes" (*Obras completas,* IV, p. 451): "Among the elements of the picture, a new object appears whose magic potentiality allows, nay obligates it to be everywhere and to fill the whole picture without thereby crowding out the remaining objects. The painter has to see the totality of his work immersed in the overwhelming object, 'light.' This holds for Ribera, Caravaggio, and the young Velásquez. In accordance with the inherited code, the body is still the object, but the interest is no longer concentrated primarily on it. The physical object itself begins to lose importance and accepts the function of serving as subject for the light falling upon it. The result is a magical solidarity and unification of all light parts in contrast to the dark ones."

Since Vergil, "mood" has become to poetry what "light" is to painting. "Mood changes the poetic object just as light clings to the objects of painting and changes and transcends them." To continue the comparison, Homer belongs to the older painters who paint the objects with their "hands" or with the "tactile" density of the "eye," as *Nahbild.* He strives to present the objects and situations in clear separation so that they may be touched and held. Vergil sees them as *Fernbild.* Light floods them and music enfolds them. They are embedded in a stream of feeling and movement. His poetry is an expression of the musical and imaginative side of the Latin people, especially of Italy, and not of their rational spirit, with whose French distortion he has been more or less equated in Germany for a long time. Vergil's poem is a stream of moods and feelings blended delicately together and which move the heart with melody and lead from one emotional quality to another. Light, painting, and music are only analogies, however, only helpful images with which we may try to make the basic nature of Vergil's poetry more intelligible. We should not forget that the movement of poetic mood is a phenomenon *sui generis.* The main task of Vergilian criticism is to draw this movement in detail. There is a lasting challenge for the reader in feeling and understanding the symbolism of its fine and subtle vibrations.

FORMS OF SEQUENCE OF MOOD

In order to reach a more profound understanding of Vergil's art it is important to outline, as it were, the sequence of mood which is the core of the narrative. Viewed as a whole, it proceeds in a swelling and ebbing motion or in recurring waves.[1] Heinze has already recognized "a basic law of Vergilian technique" in the "gradual heightening" and has proven the principle of undulation in the arrangement of the ninth–twelfth books and in the composition of the *Iliupersis* and the description of the games in the fifth book. I have shown the same thing for the Allecto scenes, for Turnus' *aristeia,* and for the composition of certain similes. Other examples, such as the organization of the sea storm (where it differs from Homer) or the eruption of Mount Etna (III.570 ff., where it differs from Vergil's model, Pindar), can be easily added to this. However, it is more constructive to state the nature of these waves, including their rhythm, shape, and distribution, more exactly.

The proem, on which, as on every other exposed passage, the poet has clearly lavished his most careful attention, is characteristic in this respect. Although it begins with vivid density, it still rises in a continuous movement from the hero's fortunes at sea, land, and war to the verse: *"Vi superum, saevae memorem Iunonis ob iram.* It ends strongly and significantly with the fruit of his sufferings: *"Dum conderet urbem inferretque deos Latio* [2] and, *"Genus unde Latinum Albanique patres atque altae moenia Romae."* This verse demonstrates a skillfully rising progression—one that is more than chronological —the Latin race, the Alban fathers (a hint of *senatus* and

ordo), and the "walls of high Rome." An emphatic crescendo
and accelerando and a solemn, glowing conclusion are like a
wave rolling in upon the beach and ending in foam. The form
of the proem is determined by these two movements. They
also determine the basic form of the Vergilian sequence of
mood. The high point comes exactly in the middle: *"Vi superum, saevae memorem Iunonis ob iram."* The next part,
"Urbs antiqua fuit" through *"Tantae molis erat,"* shows a
similar architecture. After the quiet epical start, the narrative
rises, growing rhythmically and musically more dynamic in
both its profundity of thought and pathos of imagery to *"Sic
volvere Parcas,"* the middle of the passage and the climax of
the climb which emphasizes the real cause of Juno's wrath.
The curve falls gently to the dark, grave final verses, where
the conclusion is drawn. The movement grows slower and
denser:

> And still she kept them far from Latium, wandering
> for years at the mercy of fate from sea to sea about
> the world. Such was the cost in heavy toil of beginning
> the life of Rome.

I.31:
> Arcebat longe Latio multosque per annos
> Errabant acti fatis maria omnia circum:
> Tantae molis erat Romanam condere gentem.

There are two pairs of eleven verses each. First comes Juno's
Carthaginian plan, which is wrecked by the decision of the
Parcae, followed by the interference by that goddess as a re-
sult of the decision.

A third repetition of this form is made in Juno's speech.
Beginning with the Trojan's calm and happy journey (contrast for heightening), it swells to Juno's thought of the revenge of Pallas as she hurled the lightning bolt upon the hated
fleet of the Argives:

> And when Ajax, pierced through the breast by the
> lightning-flame, was breathing his last, she caught him
> up in a tornado and impaled him on a pointed rock.

I.44:

> Illum exspirantem transfixo pectore flammas
> Turbine corripuit scopuloque infixit acuto.

It comes to an end with the still angry, but less violent words
(I.46–49) comprising both the mood sequence and the goddess's grief on suffering such an injury to her honor and her
will for power.

As the most forceful wave, the sea storm follows, framed
in the gloomy scene of Juno and Aeolus and the brighter
one of Neptune and the winds.[3] Next is the landing, in a falling movement, with Aeneas' speech of hope as the climax,
followed by the scene between Venus and Jupiter. These
speeches also rise in the middle [4] and drop at the end.[5] The
individual waves are united in one powerful movement of the
same character, rising (storm and Trojan catastrophe) and
falling to a sublime conclusion in the scene between the
divinities.

The lucid construction of the first group of scenes must not
raise expectations that all books of the *Aeneid* can be so divided, that is, be organizable among themselves according to
the same rhythm. Without a doubt there is some such tendency, but it is not always clear. It should not be assumed that
every scene and every speech must fit a scheme in the stipulated basic form. In every place, however, in which a closed
sequence of moods exists, this form may be seen. The concept
of a "closed" sequence of scene is relative, because openness
of form and unending series are characteristic of the epic. The
unity of such a sequence can best be called a "unit of mood,"
or, to use an expression of Schiller's, a "unit of sentiment"
(*Empfindungseinheit*). "We distinguish in all poetry," he says
in a review of Mattison's poems, "units of thought from 'units

of sentiment'—the musical from the logical attitude. We demand that each poetic composition, besides expressing content, be an imitation and expression of moods and feelings and affect us as music does."

If one considers the individual examples of these "units of sentiment" whose basic form I have described, one will find that special attention had been given to the final phrase, the "unrolling of the wave." This has to be true in a form of poetry where the mood sequence is the essence, because in the endings the aroused emotions flow into chords in which the memory of the complete inner movement is reflected. Much of the poetic effect depends on achieving the "right" form for the conclusion, for this form is the synthesis of the whole. For example, Aeneas' first speech accurately follows the stipulated plan, rising passionately to:

> Why did your arm not strike me down and give my spirit freedom in death on the battlefields of Ilium.

I.97:

> Mene Iliacis occumbere campis
> Non potuisse tuaque animam hanc effundere dextra.

It concludes with the majestic image of the Simois rolling along, "the shields and helmets of the heroes and their huge bodies" (increase in size). The wave rolls out in foaming movement. An image ends the mood sequence.

A beautiful image at the end of a mood unit is a characteristic of most similes. This principle is made most visible by contrast with Homer. The stallion simile ends with the magnificent *"Luduntque iubae per colla per armos"* (XI.497), to which there is nothing analogous in the *Iliad* (6.506).

> The bee simile: *Fervet opus redolentque thymo fragrantia mella* (I.436);
>
> the simile of Mars-Turnus' stormy ride: *Spargit rapida ungula rores*
> *Sanguineos mixtaque cruor calcatur harena;* (XII.339)

Mezentius' lion simile (X.727): *Lavit improba taeter*
Ora cruor;

the mountain slide simile (XII.688):
Exsultatque solo silvas armenta virosque
Involvens secum;

the mountain simile (XII.703):
Vertice se attollens pater Appenninus ad auras;

the simile of the Thracian winds (XII.455):
Sonitumque ferunt ad litora venti;

the bull fight (XII.722): *Gemitu nemus omne remugit.*

Homer usually concludes his similes with a concrete detail which adds nothing material to what precedes it. Vergil concludes his similes with an image that satisfies the musical requirement for a beautiful final chord. This brings the passage to a kind of solution, either in the direction of intensification and emphasis or of an eventual light and vivid disappearance.

Occasionally, the final phrase may best be termed a peak. The Diana simile rises to the dactylic verse which describes the divine appearance:

> She is taller than all other goddesses, as with her quiver slung from her shoulder she steps on her way.

I.500:

> Illa pharetram
> Fert umero gradiensque deas supereminet omnes.

However, the quieter conclusion contains the secret peak:

> Latonae tacitum pertemptant gaudia pectus.

The deer simile enhances the motion of flight which then slows and steadies in dark and heavy words, *"Haeret lateri letalis harundo."*

As a condensed symbol of impending destruction, an image of black smoke concludes the cauldron simile. *"Volat vapor ater ad auras"* (VII.466). In these and similar cases, a new and larger horizon opens at the end of the simile. Homer's individual unit of the single present matter is broken by Vergil and an "infinite perspective" opens up such as is revealed, as Goethe says, "by the symbolic object."

Like the similes, some scenes and groups of scenes and a number of enumerations tend to conclude with a particularly impressive picture. For instance, the first unit of the Dido book ends with the deserted walls outlined against the sky. This stark image, foretells the failure of the queen's work. It spotlights the dark destiny of Carthage:

> Work hung suspended on gigantic, menacing walls, and the sky-high cranes were still.

IV.88:

> Minaeque
> Murorum ingentes aequataque machina caelo.

Elsewhere, too, these symbolic points serve to emphasize the impression of a broken or doomed destiny by means of a final image. For example, at the low point of the second book, there is the tragically majestic image of Priam's death:

> His tall body was left lying headless on the shore, and by it the head hacked from the shoulders: a corpse without a name.

II.557:

> Iacet ingens litore truncus
> Avolsumque umeris caput et sine nomine corpus.

Or there is the image of Turnus' broken sword:

> And now its fragments gleamed back at him from the yellow sand.

XII.741:

> Fulva resplendent fragmina harena,

or the image symbolizing the fall of Troy at the end of the dream in which Hector appears to Aeneas:

Thus he spoke and he carried out in his hands from the innermost temple mighty Vesta and her headbands and the everlasting fire.

II.296:

Sic ait et manibus vittas Vestamque potentem
Aeternumque adytis effert penetralibus ignem,

where the eternal fire of Vesta is the symbol of Trojan power as it leaves its erstwhile home viewed in the later, Roman sense.

The catalogue of the bringers of misery in the antechamber of Orcus ends with the figure of Discordia surpassing all others. This emphasis on Discordia reflects the fact that she is by far the most dangerous power in the realm of politics. She relates directly to a main theme of the poem: the taming of *furor impius*.

The enumeration of the signs of doom frightening Dido (IV.450–472) close with the sinister sights of the furies, dark messengers of the nether world waiting, as it were, for their victim: *". . . ultricesque sedent in limine dirae."*

The Trojan war reliefs in the Carthaginian temple of Juno increase in tragic intensity, culminating in Hector's death (I.485–487). But they end with the brilliant figure of Penthesilea, "splendid among thousands," thus leading to Dido's appearance.

The enumeration of the Etruscan allies of Aeneas ends with the figure of Triton, resplendent in movement and in the music of the verses (X.209–212).

Venus' first words to Aeneas conclude with baroque pathos:

or shouting hard on the track of some foam-flecked boar.

I.324:

Aut spumantis apri cursum clamore prementem.

The hunt of Aeneas and Dido reaches a climax in Ascanius' longing for a boar and a lion (IV.158 ff.). The last word of the description is *leonem,* as *Romae* is the last word of the proem.

These passages are distinguished by splendid, powerful conclusions. There are also other possibilities for a "musical" end effect. The speech in which Dido tries for the first time to dissuade Aeneas from leaving, ends, after a series of passionate appeals, with the sweet wish for a child in the likeness of Aeneas. Logically, this seems the most touching and effective appeal, but musically it constitutes a calming and soothing element after the powerful preceding images. And its calm is not sublime or pathetic as elsewhere, but tender and delicately intimate. The rapid melody has changed into a sweeter, more subdued tune. Here, then, the final stage of the mood movement is characterized not by more but by less pathos and less sound.

The same softening and calming effect occurs in the fourth book, when the queen's pathetic catastrophe with its wild waves resolves in the loving gesture of the sister, in the queen's searching gaze for the light of heaven, and in Iris' soothing appearance; [6] in the sixth book, where the two "waves" of the historic preview climaxing in Augustus and in the famous verses about the mission of the Roman people are followed by the tones of tenderest melancholy for the doomed youth Marcellus; and in the fifth book, where the serene cavalcade of Neptune precedes the soft witchcraft of the god of sleep, under whose spell faithful Palinurus, with the rudder held tightly, slides overboard. The magic mood at the conclusion of the first book is another example of the same kind of ending. The most intimate secrets of existence, death, and love dominate the ends of Books I and II (Creusa), III (Anchises), IV (Dido), V (Palinurus), VI (Marcellus), X (Lausus-Mezentius), XI (Camilla), and XII (Turnus). If the musical analogy were replaced with a pictorial one, one kind of conclusion might be compared with the brilliant light of day and the other with the soft glow of the sinking sun or the soothing light of the moon; the evening lights in Dido's hall, the nightly peace of the sea, the purple tone of Elysium also determine the atmosphere at the end of the first, fifth, and sixth books.

It is not enough to determine the intensity of the mood; it is necessary to identify its color, its nuance, and quality. All of the sequences examined so far may be understood in terms of shades of light and darkness, and if so understood, we have another gauge for the interpretation of mood sequences. The stream of the Vergilian narrative resembles not only a dynamically undulating movement but an immense illumination as well. Throughout the whole poem there is a rhythmic pattern of light and shadow. The examples cited in the previous chapter may be interpreted in the sense of light and color development, and their artistic meaning is completely discernible only when they *are* thus interpreted. The amount of light and the shade of color reflect the place of the sequence within the larger context.

An analysis of the *Aeneid* from this point of view would supply a complement to the valuable results of Conway and Stadler concerning the composition of the poem. Although such analysis is impossible within the framework of this book, a survey of Books I, VII, and VIII will point out the direction that an inquiry should take. Darker and darker waves lead to the storm at sea in the first book and to the landing of the shipwrecked Trojans on the hostile beach. These are followed by lighter waves, the brightest being Jupiter's speech, in which this sublimely majestic god foretells the future grandeur of Rome. On earth there is a new crescendo of light waves, breaking more and more strongly against the dark. Aeneas' encounters with Venus and Dido and the splendid banquet are clearly a progression of increasing illumination, followed by the hero's gloomy complaint about his fate and Venus' words on Dido's black future. The relation of both destinies is established at this early stage. Venus' speech ends in happy annunciation, and the scene ends with a fragrantly splendid picture of the goddess as she disappears to return to Paphos and happily "visits the place where her temple stands and where a hundred altars breathe Sabaic incense and fresh flowers."

The Dido narrative begins with Aeneas' painful contemplation of the Trojan reliefs. The queen's glittering entrance in the likeness of Diana follows. Then comes godlike Aeneas, clothed by Venus in "the purple light of youth." The scene ends triumphantly with sacrifice to the gods, the mission to the beach (I.633), and the preparations for a grand banquet. There are purple and silver and golden dishes ornamented with "the brave deeds of the fathers, the long series of events with so many heroes succeeding each other since the early origins of the nation." The banquet, as the final pageant, is not without a tender motif. Aeneas sends for the boy Ascanius that he might bring Ilioneus' scepter and the gift that Helen received from Leda upon her wedding with Paris—a premonition of things to come. Instead, as arranged with Juno, Venus substitutes Amor for Ascanius.[7] The ill-starred queen lifts the great god onto her lap:

> She could not know, poor Dido, how mighty a god was entering her.

I.718:

> Inscia Dido
> Insideat quantus miserae deus.

The movement gains momentum. The symposium succeeds the banquet; the lights reflect from the golden ceilings; the torches shine; there is light everywhere in halls once dark (I.725 ff.). The tumult dies and Dido addresses herself to Bacchus and *"bona Juno,"* the protectoress of marriage: *"cui vincla jugalia curae . . ."* (as Vergil says elsewhere). The song of Iopas (analyzed earlier) stirs their hearts and the spell grows deeper. Dido drinks "longlasting love" and is eager to

hear Aeneas' story. Thus, the book ends in a return to darkness—to the fall of Troy and the hero's seven years' wandering. The end is mysteriously grave; dim, ominous shadows
rear behind the light. There are presentiments of sufferings
ahead for Dido and Aeneas. The light is truly *chiaroscuro*
and becomes so again and again, especially in the last parts
of the books. In this, too, shading and light represent a synthesis of preceding sentiments, including memory and premonition.

At the end of the bright books there are shadows, and,
conversely, there are bright images at the end of the dark
books. This is demonstrated in the seventh book, in which
the action of the powers of Hell and the triumph of the war
fury are followed by a lighter end. The star of Venus rises
at the end of the second book to announce salvation. It is
also seen in the fourth book, when Iris eases Dido's death.
And the ninth book concludes with the friendly Tiber washing
away Turnus' blood after the battle. Thus, a gentle conclusion
ends the cruel fighting (IX.816 ff.).

The development of mood in the seventh book antitheti-
cally parallels that of the first: while the first moves from
dark to light but concludes on a dark note, the seventh moves
in the opposite direction. There is light in the first third of
the book. The initial scene ends with the happy landing at
the mouth of the Tiber. The second scene ends with the
forecast of Latin world rule (VII.96 ff.). The third ends
with the sign of Jupiter in the clouds, which confirms the
dish oracle and with it the fact that the Trojans have reached
their destination (141 ff.). The fourth scenes concludes with
the treaty and marriage plan for Lavinia and Aeneas, whose
progeny is destined to bring about the forecast of the second
scene (259 ff.). These are manifest steps of a development
which moves quickly toward a happy and seemingly im-
minent fulfillment in the verse (VII.285): *"Sublimes in equis*
redeunt pacemque reportant"—a glowing conclusion.

The tragic countermovement—beginning with the three Allecto scenes, whose mounting curve has already been analyzed—is followed in the last third by the rousing pageantry of the Italian armies. This splendid finale sublimates the rising passion. The threat of horrible war is supplanted by a glorious image of the heroic strength of ancient Italy:

> Muses, the time has come for you to throw Helicon wide open and inspire me to tell who were the kings who were then rallied for war, what manner of soldiers followed each of them in their ranks to throng the plains, who were the men who even in those far days were the flower of Italy's fertile land, and what arms expressed her spirit's fire.

VII.641:

> Pandite nunc Helicona deae cantusque movete,
> Qui bello exciti reges, quae quemque secutae
> Complerint campos acies, quibus Itala iam tum
> Floruerit terra alma viris, quibus arserit armis.

The arrangement of the catalogue clearly demonstrates an ascent from turgid darkness to bright clarity, from gloomy threats to heroic glamor. Beginning with the evil Mezentius a series of Italian princes follows: Aventinus, the uncouth descendant of Heracles; Catillus and Coras, the huge brothers of Tiburtus, descending "like two centaurs, sons of clouds of the mountain tops"; Caeculus leading the Praenestians in their wolf helmets into battle; and the Faliscans under Mesapus. The movement gains force with their battle songs. The gloom begins to lift. After the entrance of the people of Clausus the throng of names keeps mounting. The soaring image is well expressed in the simile of the waves of the Libyan Sea and the wheatfields of the Valley of Hermes and the Lycian plains. We are here riding the dynamic climax of the wave. Now it unrolls in splendor with the list of the tribes of Halaesus, Oebalus, Ufens, and Umbro and culminates with the three young heroes, Virbius, son of Hippolytus, Turnus, and Camilla. The glittering figure of the Volscian queen represents the entire splendor and strength of Italy. She is queen and warrior, pure child of nature and servant of Diana. Her nature is symbolized by purple cloak and golden clip, quiver and pastoral myrtle. The catalogue and the book as a simile of the Italian shepherds rising to battle are concluded in the spear-tipped myrtle: *"et pastoralem praefixa cuspide myrtum."*

The dark fate which forces Aeneas into war is almost counterbalanced and canceled in Camilla and the apotheosis of Italian heroism. Yet, even this conclusion is *chiaroscuro,* for behind the glamor lies a definite threat to Aeneas.

The movement of light is perhaps not so clear in the other books. In the eighth, for example, whose "unity of composition" has always proved a headache for interpreters, it is possible to discern wave and light movements, although the order is different. Small waves succeed each other chiastically. This book begins with Turnus as he raises the ensign of war on the city of the Latins and with the raucous sound of horns. Hence the "flood of sorrows" in Aeneas' heart. This is followed by the light simile as a transition to the beauty of the Tiber at night and the profound peace of the ancient Roman countryside.

The characteristic charm of this book lies in the combination of these two moods—idyllic nature and the flare of primitive force, peace, and war. The gratifying journey and reception by Evander is followed by the dark wave of his story of Cacus and Heracles. Heracles' brilliant victory over the fire-breathing monster constitutes a mythical model for Aeneas' and Augustus' triumphs. After the praise of Heracles, the narrative twice rises; once, to Evander's history of Italy, which is climaxed in the wars of the "Ausonian tribe and the Sicanian people" (VIII.328), and then in the stroll through the Roman countryside which leads to a description of the

Capitol, with the farmers acknowledging the *dira religio* of the place and watching Jupiter brandish the black *aegis*. Then, at the site of the Forum, with calm restored, we see the herds of oxen lowing and the heroes enter the simple house of Evander. There the heroes sleep. "Night embraces earth with dark wings" (*"Nox ruit et fuscis tellurem amplectitur alis"*).

How beautifully this tender maternal gesture introduces the enchanting love scene between Vulcan and Venus. Vulcan grants Venus' request for arms for Aeneas, and from the night of love the story rises to Vulcan's forge over the simile of a housewife rising in the middle of the night to supervise the spinners. In its sustained stillness, the simile is suited to the quietest moment of the narrative. The old Roman [8] coloring fits the old Roman patriarchal quality of the book to perfection. Next, Vulcan's forge abounds with primitive strength. The book's "second" character crowds out the first. The demonic power of the Cyclopean race, once represented by Cacus, son of Vulcan, is here represented by Brontes, Steropes, and Pyracmon. The labors are arranged with such skill that the coloring grows darker and darker. Beginning with Zeus's lightning, the list includes Mars's chariot and the *aegis* of "embittered" Pallas Athena. Eventually, our thought is directed to the arms of Aeneas and the coming war. Then comes the forging of the hero's armor. The narrative gains momentum in the following scene until Aeneas is declared the leader of the Italians. In the grievous sorrow of war (VII.520 ff.) and the premonition of Pallas' awful fate, darkness comes again.

The apparently ominous celestial phenomenon still contributes light, since it is interpreted as a promise of arms and consequent victory. The leave-taking forms the conclusion, and the dark stream of sorrow swells. The climax is composed of Evander's touching farewell and the tender glances that the mothers give their departing sons. This is one of Vergil's unforgettable soul-baring gestures:

> Mothers stood on the city-walls in fear, following with their eyes the flash of bronze from the squadrons and the cloud of dust.

VIII.592:
> Stant pavidae in muris matres oculisque sequuntur
> Pulveream nubem et fulgentis aere catervas.

Venus gives Aeneas his armor and the description of the shield embossed with Rome's triumph is a splendid final picture. Depicted there are the she-wolf and the twins—a delicate touch inspired by the idyllic quality of the eighth book. Dark waves surround gold-gleaming Actium:

> All Leucate, in a ferment of moving martial array, came into view; the waves shone out with gold.

VIII.676:
> Totumque instructo Marte videres
> Fervere Leucaten auroque effulgere fluctus.

The battle is the high point of the description and the dramatic climax. It is followed by the rousing finale of Augustus' triumph. The rivers Nile, Euphrates, Rhine, and Araxes correspond to the Tiber of the beginning. In symbolic representation of the Roman people, the dark last verse emphasizes again the heavy responsibility of Aeneas' historical mission as the fulfillment of Roman destiny and as the symbolic representative of the Roman people: *"Attolens umero famamque et fata nepotum."* The great conflict throughout the whole poem between light and darkness should be recognized. The dark first third (I–IV), of which the storm at sea and the death of Dido are the high points, contains the most bitter blows for the hero—the fall of Troy, the loss of his wife, his father, and his beloved. Beginning with the races, the middle of the poem is bathed in light (V–VIII). The races are a symbolic glorification of Roman youth, as is the more significant and important story of *Ludus Troianus*. The sixth book contains the prophecy of Roman glory. The final scene of the eighth book pays tribute to the triumph of Augustus as the climax of Roman history. In this third of the *Aeneid* are amassed the brightest and most luminous scenes of the whole poem, including the Trojans' arrival at the Tiber's mouth, the journey upstream by night, the moon-lit voyage from Sicily to Italy, and the Elysian Fields.

The last third of the poem (IX–XII) is swathed again in dark colors as its main concern is the tragedy of war, with its everchanging situations and shadings from dark to light in the chiaroscurotic rhythm which governs the whole epic. Here, however, light is always overlaid with a darkness out of which bright rays erupt again and again. Joy and sorrow, victory and defeat, rampant passion and triumphant spirit are not only interwoven but penetrate each other. It is characteristic of the works of classical art to emphasize each individual part through contrast. This demonstrates the poet's sense of harmony and balance. One is constantly re-directed from the part to the whole, that is, to the entire world and the destinies of man and nations. In a very deep sense, all of these moods and degrees of light and shadow are scored as chords composed of minor and major tones. They are mingled because it is appropriate to Vergil's art of mood development that earlier phases be contained in later ones.

He strives to make the whole plan present in every moment. He succeeds when he emphasizes pain through a reference to joy, darkness through light, and failure through final triumph. Indeed, this is the goal of every work of art, for as Goethe has said in his review of *Des Knaben Wunderhorn:* "The work of art in whole and in part is a symbol of the universe." Moreover, Vergil expresses a religious feeling which precludes the isolation of any one part of life, any one individual or national destiny, any one life force or sensation. Beside and behind the individual aspect there is always the obverse. Behind joy there is pain, behind love there is death and behind death, love. Every single thing has a place in a divine world where glory and gloom, reason and emotion, demonic and divine are restricted and reinforced through their opposites.

Thus, Vergil's aesthetic concept, like all Classical concepts, postulates the harmonious balance of opposites. It is profoundly bound up with the poet's view of the world. He assumes a cosmic and historical continuity in which neither darkness nor light is dominant, but where the contrasts are united in a higher entity. This entity is given as a balance which, though it may be lost, is time and again regained.

NOTES

INTRODUCTION

1. Julius Stenzel ("Die Gefahren des modernen Denkens und der Humanismus," *Die Antike* 4, 1928) observed that only very late had the Greeks produced a somewhat adequate description of the aesthetic phenomenon.
2. The German Classical period had already basically discarded the rationalistic treatment of works of verbal art. Humboldt (in his essay on Schiller) observed: "No nation equals the Germans in their ability to look at art as it should be looked at."
3. Karl Vossler ("Benedetto Croces Sprachphilosophie," *Deutsche Vierteljahresschrift fuer Literatur und Geistesgeschichte*, 1941, 126) noted that there is nothing wrong with a philological analysis of a poem's metrical, rhythmical, syntactical, morphological, and phonetic forms as long as it is understood that they do not constitute part of the poetic atmosphere. But it is not analysis *per se* that is alien to poetry. Aesthetic analysis can be a key to the work of art.
4. Cartault's *L'Art de Virgile dans l'Éneide* (Paris, 1926) did not quite fulfill the expectations aroused by its title.
5. *Das neue Bild der Antike* (Berlin, 1942).
6. They are mostly published in a collection entitled *Roemische Geisteswelt* (Leipzig, 1943).
7. I wish to thank Mr. Harald Fuchs in Basel who supplied me with a number of extensive excerpts.
8. Has it been observed that poetry is not mentioned among the things in which the Greeks excel the Romans in the famous

lines of the sixth book? Sainte-Beuve notes Homer's absence and remarks that the chronological difficulty would not have been unsurmountable. See Macrobius (VI.1, 5) on the fact that Vergil has preserved earlier poetry in his work.

9. "2000 Jahre Virgil," *Neue schweizer Rundschau* (1930).

10. *Französischer Geist im neuen Europa*, p. 209.

11. For Vergil is the classical poet of Europe in the deep sense of T. S. Eliot, *What Is a Classic? Address Delivered before the Vergil Society on the 16th of October 1944* (London 1945).

CHAPTER ONE

1. Statius has imitated the motif in the beginning of the *Thebais* in the night storm which drives Tydeus and Polyneices into Adrastus' house. It would be interesting to follow the history of "storms" as an element in tragedy and as an opening symbol in Shakespeare and the moderns. It is very important in opera.

2. Vergil often makes one think of opera because of the great sweep and pathos, the skillful arrangement of the proceeding action, and the striving for impressive images and gestures. Modern, especially German, criticism too often tends to take a negative view of this necessary "theater." Vergil directly as well as indirectly exercised considerable influence on the evolution of opera in Italy. See *Romain Rolland,* "L'origine de l'Opéra," in *Musiciens d'autrefois.*

3. I am indebted to Richard Meister for pointing out these quotations from Goethe. A further discussion of the symbol occurs in Goethe's essay on "Philostratus' Painting" (Weimar ed., 1889 f.), v, 49, 141.

3a. *Iubiläumsausgabe,* 35, p. 326.

4. Wjatscheslaw Iwanow, *Vergil, Aufsaetze zur Geschichte der Antike und des Christentums* (Berlin, 1937), p. 66, notes the coincidence with *quoniam dilexit multum* in the gospel of Luke 7:47.

5. For this formal reason alone—a formal criterion always has *primum gradum certitudinis* in a classical work—Friedrich,

"Exkurse zur Aeneis," *Philologus,* 1940, is wrong when he suggests that Vergil had planned to discard Jupiter's speech in the final draft and to introduce Jupiter himself for the first time in the assembly of the gods in Book X. The reconciliation in Book XII.791 ff. demands their presence in the first. This does not diminish the correctness of Friedrich's suggestions on the temporary prop character of the verses introducing and ending the conversation.

6. The Stoics had the idea of a lord of the universe. See Cleanthes' hymn to Zeus: "And the universe obeys trembling, where it is hit by the force of the lightning" (Wilamowitz).

7. Zeus, too, has sublime traits. But Vergil's Jupiter would never argue from physical strength, as the primitive god of the *Iliad* does (especially 8.5 ff.).

8. The image itself is Greek. I mention the painting of Apelles, showing Alexander with the lightning, the Dioscuri, and Nike on a triumphal chariot, followed by War with hands tied behind his back. Servius says that there was such a representation of Furor Bound in the forum of Augustus.

9. I.126:   graviter commotus et alto
        Prospiciens summa placidum caput extulit unda.

Also 154 ff. On the "contradiction" between *graviter commotus* and *placidum caput extulit unda* Sainte-Beuve remarks: "Il n'y a pas là de contradiction pas plus que dans le *mens immota manet, lacrimae volvuntur inanes.* Si un homme ferme et qui a pris un parti pénible, peut verser des larmes sans que son coeur soit ébranlé, un dieu peut bien être ému au dedans, sans que cette émotion ôte le charactère de haute placidité à son front." One might go further and say that Aeneas, Neptune, and Jupiter all represent the taming of passion. Man does this with much pain, God with sublime serenity. Winckelmann in the famous passage on "noble simplicity and quiet grandeur as outstanding characteristics of the Greek masterworks" quotes the lines:

tum pietate gravem ac meritis si forte virum quem
conspexere, silent arrectisque auribus adstant

to illustrate the placid quiet of the majestic figures in Raphael's "Attila and Leo the Great."

9a. R. S. Conway, "Poesia ed impero," *Conference Virgiliane* (Milano, 1931).

10. Cp. Pöschl, *Grundwerte roemischer Staatsgesinnung in den Geschichtswerken des Sallust* (Berlin, 1940), p. 10.

11. As in Horace, it can be no more than a vague memory. *Pietas,* although it may be ascribed to Cato, is not the first virtue by which he is distinguished.

12. Translator's note: There is no English counterpart for the German *Allegorie,* which by definition admits of only one meaning, something in the nature of a large parable.

13. Cp. also Friedrich Gundolf, *Shakespeare und der deutsche Geist* (Bonn, 1911), p. 1: "Symbol is essence, coincides with the thing, represents its being. Allegorie points to something which it is not."

14. This shows the way in which the results of Conway and of D. L. Drew, *The Allegory of the Aeneid* (Oxford, 1927), have to be modified.

15. Cp. Klingner, "Rom als Idee," *Die Antike,* 3 (1927), 3, and *Das neue Bild der Antike,* 234.

16. "The field of the epopic, if it is worthy of its name, claims so to speak the co-operation of the whole nature, a complete view of the world between heaven and earth." Herder, *Adrastea,* X. Stueck, v.24.281 Suphan.

17. Details will be discussed in the sections on Aeneas and Dido and in the final chapter.

18. Cicero's *Somnium Scipionis* is another variation of the same form, as remarked by Norden.

19. Richard Heinze, *Virgil's epische Technik* (3d ed.; Leipzig, 1915), p. 82.

20. On *Vergil and Ennius,* Norden (Berlin, 1915) and S. Wiemer, *Ennianischer Einfluss auf Vergil's Aeneis VII–XII,* Greifswalder Beitraege zur Literatur-und Stilforschung (Greifswald, 1933).

21. The intensification is mentioned more than once: VII.354 ff. 374.

385: Quin etiam in silvas simulato numine Bacchi majus
adorta nefas majoremque orsa furorem evolat.

This would explain that, as Heinze says, we hear at first of
"simulated" madness (*"simulato numine Bacchi"*), and then
of the real thing (*"reginam Allecto, stimulis agit undique
Bacchi"*). There would then not necessarily be a contradiction. But *"simulato numine Bacchi"* does not signify
"simulated" madness. *Numen* here, as in I.8: *"quo numine
laeso"* and VII.583: *"bellum perverso numine poscunt,"* is
the will of the goddess. The phrase means that she pretends
the will of the gods, as if Dionysos had ordered her to go
to the woods, but not that her madness itself is pretended.

22. Heinze, *op. cit.,* p. 187. The connection with the beginning
of the war is sufficiently clearly stated through the verses:

VII.580 ff.: Tum, quorum attonitae Baccho nemora avia
matres
Insultant thiasis neque enim leve nomen Amatae
Undique collecti coeunt Martemque fatigant.

The mothers who belong to Amata's *thiasos,* take Turnus'
side against Aeneas; they are for war and they, of course,
influence their sons.

23. For the war was sufficiently motivated by the success of the
new suitor who upsets the queen's and Turnus' plans and the
hunting crime against the stag of Silvia.

24. The raging of the Sybil (VI.77), is connected with the war
prophecy through the motive of "divine madness."

25. IV.68:   Totaque vagatur urbe furens compared with
VII.376:   Ingentibus excita monstris
immensam sine more furit lymphata per urbem.

IV.300:   Saevit inops animi totamque incensa per urbem
Bacchatur, qualis commotis excita sacris
Thyias, ubi audito stimulant trieterica Baccho
Orgia nocturnusque vocat clamore Cithaeron.

26. It would have been impossible to achieve a movement of

similar force through the Turnus scene (VII.406 ff.) or the hunting scene (476 ff.) alone.

27. VII.461: scelerata insania belli
    VII.583: Ilicet infandum cuncti contra omina bellum
            contra fata deum perverso numine poscunt.

    Latinus calls the war a crime that must be expiated:

    VII.595: Ipsi has sacrilego pendetis sanguine poenas
            O miseri. Te, Turne, nefas, te triste manebit
            Supplicium votisque deos venerabere seris
    Latinus XII.31: arma impia sumpsi
        XI.305: bellum importunum, cives, cum gente de-
                orum
                invictisque viris gerimus.

    The Vergilian Diomede (XI.255 ff.) also considers the Tro-
    jan war a crime.

28. Meant also symbolically in reference to the dark end of the war.

29. Hermann Fränkel, *Die Homerischen Gleichnisse* (Goettin-
    gen, 1921), explains φρίξ as "shimmering blinking" (*blink-
    endes Flimmern*).

30. Sainte-Beuve has stressed this principle: "Cette qualité sou-
    veraine qui embrasse en elle et unit toutes les autres et que
    de nos jours on est trop tenté d'oublier et de méconnaître:
    je veux parler de l'unité de ton et de couleur, de l'harmonie
    et de la convenance des parties entre elles, de la proportion
    de ce goût soutenu, qui est ici un des signes du génie, parce
    qu'il tient au fond comme à la fleur de l'âme et qu'on me
    laissera appeler une suprême délicatesse."

31. But this boundary is fluid. Homer shows the beginning of
    unifying "dramatic" presentation and Aristotle demands
    drama from the epic (*Poetics* c. 23).

32. As proved especially by Schadewaldt, *Iliasstudien* (1938).
    Emil Staiger, *Grundbegriffe der Poetik* (Zurich 1946),
    points out that in Homer the stress is on the episode, not
    on the unity (p. 124 f.).

33. The poet intentionally put the word *pacem* at the end of the

first passage of the seventh book. Juno's interference which leads to war, follows immediately.

34. The scene opens with the serene verses I.314 ff., and it closes with the bright glamor of Paphos (I.415 f.), but the tragic tone is not absent. It is heard in Aeneas' speech (I.371) in *crudelis tu quoque mater* and in the tale of Dido's life.

CHAPTER II: 1. AENEAS

1. Besides the Odyssey passage see also *Iliad* 21.279 ff.
2. Friedrich Klingner's interpretation is as persuasive as it is touching (*Roemische Geisteswelt,* Leipzig, 1943).
3. Vergil, on the other hand, here as elsewhere strives to conclude a sense unit with a crowning image. The image of the river carrying off the corpses as the expression of the horror of war returns in the words of the Sibyl (VI.87) and in Aeneas' speech to Evander (VIII.538).
4. Both are already named in the *Iliad* as the leaders of the Trojans (6.77 ff.).

5. I.485: Tum vero ingentem gemitum dat pectore ab imo
   Ut spolia, ut currus atque ipsum corpus amici
   Tendentemque manus Priamum conspexit inermis.

6. As shown especially by Stadler, *Vergils Aeneis* (Einsiedeln, 1942), tripartition is the basic principle of arrangement next to bipartition. Books II and VIII only prepare the fight. The "Iliad" proper begins in IX.
7. About the proem of the *Aeneid:* H. Fuchs, *Museum Helveticum* v.4 (1947), 191.n.114.
8. He may not stay even if he wants to.

   III.190: hanc quoque deserimus sedem.
   III.493: Vivite felices quibus est fortuna peracta
   Jam sua, nos alia ex aliis in fata vocamur.
   Vobis parta quies, nullum maris aequor arandum
   Arva neque Ausoniae semper cedentia retro
   Quaerenda.

The "driver" Mercury:

IV.272: Quid struis aut qua spe Libycis teris otia terris?
   569: Heia age rumpe moras.
   574: Deus aethere missus ab alto
       Festinare fugam tortosque incidere funis
       Ecce iterum stimulat.

Nautes V.709: Nate dea, quo fata trahunt retrahuntque sequamur
The Sibyl VI.36: Non hoc ista sibi tempus spectacula poscit
        539: Nox ruit, Aeneas, nos flendo ducimus horas.

9. While the Carthaginian queen and the Rutulian prince violate or misjudge their duty, Aeneas remains faithful to it, even if he forgets it temporarily. He does not act from violence or passion but from obedience. He lives in valid bonds which he serves. In this as in some other traits which will be dealt with later, he is more closely related to the Christian heroes than to those of Homer. Schadewaldt, "Sinn und Werden der Vergilischen Dichtung," *Das Erbe der Alten,* Heft 20 (1931), 94, has called him a saint more than a hero.

10. Cp. Nietzsche *Menschliches, Allzumenschliches,* 2d division, nr. 216: "There is no denying that from the end of the eighteenth century a current of moral awakening flowed through Europe.... If we look for the sources of this current, we come upon Rousseau... The other origin lies in the resurrection of the Stoical side of Rome's greatness, whereby the French so nobly carried on the task of the Renaissance. With striking success they proceeded from the reproduction of antique forms to the reproduction of antique characters. Thus they may always claim a title to the highest honors, as the nation which has hitherto given the modern world its best books and its best men... Whence comes the moralism of Kant? He is continually reminding us: from Rousseau and the revival of Stoic Rome. The moralism of Schiller has the same source and the same glorification of the source. The moralism of Beethoven in notes is a continual song in

praise of Rousseau, the antique French, and Schiller. 'Young Germany' was the first to forget its gratitude."

11. The catastrophe takes place *ipsius ante oculos ad majorem dolorem,* as has been stressed by Servius.

12. Cf. 12.411 ff. The seeming coolness with which the dreadful details are given would have offended the Roman poet. Vergil discards Homer's realistic details and has Orontes washed overboard by the sea and the boat sucked down by eddies (I.113 ff.). The impression is more picturesque and musical than detailed and plastic.

13. Aeneas appears as the incarnation of that Roman constancy and grandeur for which Polybius praises the Romans after Cannae (6.58).

14. *Ody.* 5.151. A quite similar image occurs in the *Iliad* I.348, in which Achilles gazes weeping at the unceasingly rolling sea. This is the transition to the appearance of Thetis surfacing from the water. But here also the "unending" sea is felt as resonance for human feelings, as nature elsewhere in Homer answers, receives, and elevates human events. This expresses the unity of man and nature which we meet everywhere in Homer. Vergil, sensitive to such gestures of the soul, imitates this passage when he—albeit in a different sense—writes the wonderful verses about the Trojan women gazing out on the sea (V.613):

> At procul in sola secretae Troades acta
> Amissum Anchisen flebant cunctaeque profundum
> Pontum adspectabant flentes, heu tot vada fessis
> Et tantum superesse maris.

Note the artful adaptation of the Odyssean motif, so full of art that most readers forget that it is a literal translation from Homer. Albini, also, in his fine essay on Vergil's poetic art, *Conference Vergiliane* (Milano, 1931), has praised the Vergilian passage without noticing the imitation. The words of the first monologue of Goethe's *Iphigeneia* symbolizing the German longing for the "inner south," are also inspired by the verses from the *Odyssey* (209):

> Denn ach mich trennt das Land von den Geliebten
> Und an dem Ufer steh' ich lange Tage
> Das Land der Griechen mit der Seele suchend.

See also Lesky, *Thalatta* (Wien, 1947), 185 ff. on the Homeric passages.

15. *Cura* is found countless times in the meaning "love sorrow" or "love" since Plautus. It is characteristic of the tenderness of Roman feeling and simultaneously of Roman practical moralism that "love" in Latin has the connotation of "sorrow, care, worry." *Cura* does not originally signal passion or (as, e.g., ἔρως or *cupido*) desire, but sympathy with the beloved object. On *cura* as one of the concepts through which the Romans may be understood, see H. Fuchs, *Museum Helveticum*, 4 (1947), 103.

16. "Love" in the ethical more than in the erotic sense. Aeneas weeps for her bitter fate even in the underworld (VI.475).

17. Palinurus shows the same attitude (VI.352):

> Non ullum pro me tantum cepisse timorem
> Quam tua ne spoliata armis, excussa magistro
> Deficeret tantis navis surgentibus undis

Turnus, too, suffers most from the disgrace of having deserted his comrades (X.672 ff.) and of being unable to help them (XII.638 ff.).

18. There is a symbolic meaning in the adjective.

19. *Dialog* I.4: "Non est arbor solida nec fortis nisi in quam frequens ventus incursat. Ipsa enim vexatione constringitur et radices altius fingit." Homer lacks any simile expressing Man's attitude in an inner conflict in this manner. It would be interesting to write a history of tree metaphors up to Hölderlin's oaks, Hebbel's tree in the desert sand, Nietzsche's tree on the hill, and Valéry's palm.

20. The image is transferred from Homer's Olympus to the oak. The tree and through him Aeneas receives thus an almost superhuman grandeur.

21. *Magno pectore* is the equivalent of *magno animo*. He feels the grief of love with magnanimity, as a μεγαλόψυχος. He

feels all its tremendous weight, but his great soul enables him to bear and conquer it.

22. Conington-Nettleship, Forbiger, Cartault, Heyne-Wagner, K. H. Schelkle, *Virgil in der Deutung Augustins* (Stuttgart-Berlin 1939), think of Anna or of Anna and Dido. Henry in his unjustly neglected commentary is right, so is Pease who quotes Gross's excellent treatment in *Kritisches und Exegetisches zu Vergil's Aeneis*, 1883, 34–38. See Glover, *Vergil* (2d ed.), 195 nr. 5 and Rand, *The Magical Art of Vergil* (1931), 361–62.

23. Augustine in *De Civitate Dei* 9.4 explains that there is no essential difference between the academic-peripatetic doctrine of affects and that of the Stoics. He concludes: "ambo sane (sc. Peripatetici et Stoici), si bonorum istorum seu commodorum periculis ad flagitium vel facinus urgeantur, ut aliter ea retinere non possint, malle se dicunt haec amittere, quibus natura corporis salva et incolumis habetur quam illa committere quibus justitia violatur. Ita mens, ubi fixa est ista sententia, nullas perturbationes, etiamsi accident inferioribus animi partibus, in se contra rationem praevalere permittit, immo eis ipsa dominatur eisque non consentiendo et potius resistendo regnum virtutis exercet. Talem describit etiam Vergilius Aenean, ubi ait: *Mens immota manet, lacrimae volvuntur inanes.*" Augustine is completely right in understanding the words as expressing Aeneas' heroic, philosophical attitude. Servius explains correctly: *"lacrimae inanes, quia mens immota."* On the other hand Servius Danielis adds: *"lacrimae Aeneae vel Didonis vel Annae vel omnium,"* and so misleads the interpreters. A third testimonial that the ancient commentaries were based on correct understanding is a scholion to Juvenal (13.133), which calls Aeneas' tears hypocritical.

24. Thus, Pease in his commentary to Book IV: "The figure of Aeneas, as one in whom love and duty clash, is a far greater psychological and dramatic creation and one more in accord with the rest of his character than a portraiture which depicts him as an insensate brute."

25. Probably influence of *Ody.* 19.210:

Θυμῷ μὲν γοόωσαν ἐὴν ἐλέαιρε γυναῖκα,
ὀφθαλμοὶ δ'ὡς εἰ κερα ἕστασαν ἠὲ σίδηρος
ἀτρέμας ἐν βλεφάροισι· δόλῳ δ' ὅ γε δάκρυα κεῦθεν.

Here we have a similar "trias": the sympathetic heart
("*magno persentit pectore curas*"), the immobility of the
eyes ("*mens immota manet*") and the tears. The eyes were
mentioned in the two previous passages which describe a
similar attitude of Aeneas and recall the same *Odyssey* passage (IV.331 and 369). Here they are replaced by the
"*mens immota manet*" as the situation demands.

26. *Stridor, stridere*, cf., e.g., II.418: "*stridunt silvae*." I.87:
insequitur clamorque virum *stridor*que rudentum. VII.613:
reserat *stridentia* limina consul (at the opening of the temple of Janus).

VI.573: Tum demum horrisono *stridentes* cardine sacrae
Panduntur portae (the gates of hell)
VI.558: tum *stridor* ferri tractaeque catenae
IV.689: infixum *stridit* sub pectore volnus.

Statius *Thebais* I.32: *Stridentes* gemitus.

Ibid. about hell, in imitation of Vergil, II.51: "*stridor* ibi et
gemitus poenarum*."
In all of these cases the word serves to strengthen the impression of something uncanny, suffering, tragic.

27. Hermann Fränkel has shown in his book on the Homeric
similes, *Die Homerischen Gleichnisse* (Goettingen, 1921),
that in Homer, too, they are rarer than one has assumed.
Nevertheless, the difference between Homer and Vergil is
considerable.

28. The word *inanis* in Vergil often serves to stress the tragedy
of existence:

VI.884: Purpureos spargam flores animamque nepotis
His saltem adcumulem donis et fungar inani
Munere.
X.758: Di Jovis in tectis iram miserantur inanem
Amborum.

In both passages the word is emphasized through the en-
jambement.

29. Wagner: "certus hic non aliter dicitur ac certa hasta, certa sagitta, i.e. ad certum locum tendens. Itaque certus dicitur Aeneas recto non erratico itinere cursum intendens. Similiter certa pompa apud Tibullum III.1, 3. Ad consilium non potest certus hic referri cum jam in medio sit itinere Aeneas."

30. In the famous final words of Dido life is called a sea journey and destiny its wind: *"Vixi et quem dederat cursum fortuna peregi."* Likewise, in Latinus' words (VII.598): *"Omnisque in limine portus funere felici spolior."* It would be a worthwhile task to follow the history of this image through the ages. One of the most impressive renewals of the antique symbol is found in Petrarch, *Canzoniere* 189:

> Passa la nave mia calma d'obblio per aspro mare a mezza notte il verno. . . . al governo siede'l signore mio

and especially in Goethe's sea journey which concludes with these words:

Doch er stehet maennlich an dem Steuer,
Mit dem Schiffe spielen Wind und Wellen
Wind und Wellen nicht mit seinem Herzen.
Herrschend blickt er auf die grimme Tiefe,
Und vertrauet, scheiternd oder landend, seinen Goettern.

III.9: Et pater Anchises dare fatis vela jubebat.

V.20: Consurgunt venti atque in nubem cogitur aer
Nec nos obniti contra nec tendere tantum
Sufficimus. Superat quoniam fortuna, sequamur
Quoque vocat vertamus iter.

VII.594: (Latinus): Frangimur heu fatis, inquit, ferimurque procella.

31. The significance of the sea storm in the first book as a symbol of destiny is also connected with this metaphor.

32. V and XI, the last but one books of the "Aeneid" halves, correspond inasmuch as they begin and end with the appearance of Aeneas.

33. This regret returns in the Aeneid, significantly, in the case of the suicides:

> VI.436: Quam vellent aethere in alto
> Nunc et pauperiem et duros perferre labores!

34. Also Dido's famous verse: *"Non ignara mali miseris suc-currere disco"* refers to this never-ending school of suffering. *Disco,* not *didici,* as noted by Albini, *Conference Virgiliane* (Milano, 1931). Also the queen's utterance has Stoic color-ing:

> IV.419: Hunc ego si potui tantum sperare dolorem
> Et perferre, soror, potero.

That is the same inner preparedness for grief of which Aeneas speaks to the Sibyl. But it does not reflect her true feelings. In the tragic tumult of her passion she is far re-moved from such Stoic resignation. Her self-restraint is only exterior. Her state is more tragic through the contrast with the simulated Stoic attitude.

35. That the resolution of Aeneas contrasts with his harsh *fortuna* is the meaning of the famous verses:

> VI.95: Tu ne cede malis, sed contra audentior ito
> Quam tua te fortuna sinet.

Norden in the third edition of his commentary with the ap-proval of Wilamowitz accepted the reading *"qua tua te fortuna sinet."* This weakens the expression of Aeneas' *"magnitudo animi"* and leaves *audentior* without point of refer-ence. The conquest of Fortuna is a Stoic idea presented by Seneca in ever-renewed images as the task of human life.

36. Hermann Glockner, "Ueber Dichtung und Philosophie, Ty-pen ihrer Wechselwirkung von den Griechen bis auf Hegel," *Zeitschrift für Aesthetik,* 15 (1921), 187 ff.

37. Lessing had already rejected everything Stoic as object of art because it could only rouse cold admiration.

38. Max Pohlenz, *Antikes Fuehrertum, Ciceros De Officiis und das Lebensideal des Panaitios* (Leipzig, 1936), deserves credit for having shown this in detail. Panaitios explicitly rejects the Stoics' demand for complete absence of emotion. (Gellius *NA* 12.5).

39. IV.261: Atque illi stellatus jaspide fulva
Ensis erat Tyrioque ardebat murice laena
Demissa ex umeris, dives quae munera Dido
Fecerat et tenui telas discreverat auro

This may be an echo of Antony and Cleopatra. Otherwise Dido has nothing in common with the Egyptian queen. The recent interpretation of Dido as an *Allegorie* for Cleopatra is untenable. It is more important that Aeneas' sojourn in Carthage symbolizes the peril threatening the Roman spirit. The peril is of falling prey to Oriental softness and limitless luxury. All genuine Romans from the old Cato to Tacitus battled against this tendency in vain, and to do so was common in the Augustan period.

40. The contrast between the wealth of Carthage (banquet, hunt) and the poor early Rome of Evander is one of the most striking and significant features in the pictorialization of their antitheses.

41. The lions of the Magna Mater decorate his ship upon his return from Evander. This is an indication of the Roman world dominion and its eternity. The goddess' cult image which was brought to Rome in 192 B.C. belonged to the *"pignora imperi,"* with the holy fire of Vesta and the shields of Mars. The shield of Vulcan is the center of the scene where he appears to the Trojans and Rutulians as the bringer of salvation or doom (X.260 ff.). In the chapter on Turnus, I shall discuss his "Roman" appearance in the treaty scene and in the Apennines simile, where he is compared with the majesty of the Italian mountains.

CHAPTER II: 2. DIDO

1. Perhaps *dea* should be read with irrational lengthening as in P and R and perhaps originally in M. Conington-Nettleship (4th ed.) decide for *deas,* but remark correctly: *dea* would have a force of its own. A comparable lengthening: III.464.

2. Cf. Heinze, p. 328 f. Heinrich Wölfflin, *Die klassische Kunst* (1901), and *Gedanken zur Kunstgeschichte* (1940), Kurt

Riezler, *Parmenides* and *Traktat vom Schönen* (Frankfurt, 1935). Also Riezler, "Homer und die Anfänge der Philosophie," in *Die Antike* (1936).

3. Cf. Karl Reinhardt, *Sophocles* (Frankfurt, 1933), on the tragic reversal in Sophocles. Also Heinze's remarks on peripateia in the structure of the action.

4. In the fifth chapter of his poetics he demolished Probus' criticism. Falling into the opposite error himself he comments: *"Vergilianos versus a magistro, Homericos vero a discipulo confectos."* At the start he says with some pride: *"Hujusce modi judicatio tametsi est a doctis explosa atque ab omnibus excussa, nobis tamen, quae diceremus, non pauca eaque optima reliquere."* However, he too *non pauca reliquit.* Heinze (p. 120, n. 1) confronts Vergil's unlucky adaptation with Apollonius' success (III.175). But this does not hold upon close examination.

5. Hermann Fränkel has shown this for Homer in his beautiful book *Die Homerischen Gleichnisse* (Gottingen, 1921). See Riezler above. Bowra, *Tradition and Design in the Iliad,* 115 f. Friedrich Müller, "Das Homerische Gleichniss," *Neue Jahrbucher für antike und deutsche Bildung* (1941), 175 f. W. Schadewaldt, *Von Homers Welt und Werken* (Leipzig, 1944), 234 f. Emil Staiger, *Grundbegriffe der Poetik* (Zurich, 1946), 123 f., stresses the *tertium comparationis* in justified reaction against modern interpretationese and shows how the similes in Homer become independent.

6. The queen of the Amazons functions as an inner preparation for Dido's appearance and appears as such at the end of the Trojan picture sequence (I.490). She forms as it were the transition to the heroic queen: Penthesilea and Dido (*dux femina facti*) belong to related areas of myth. Considerations of this kind are characteristic for the "finesse" of Vergil's art. They are overlooked by the commentators because they transcend the usual problems of interpretation. More about this in my last chapter.

7. Scaliger stressed that there is no real hunt in Homer.

8. Scaliger has correctly said: "If one complains that Dido's mode of procedure is rather different from Diana's, one

obviously imagines a Diana who is conducting a Bacchanal!"

9. Servius' remark is not quite correct: *"Exercet Diana choros: hoc non ad comparationem pertinet, sed est poeticae descriptionis evagatio."*

10. Cf. I.455: Artificumque manus inter se operumque laborem Miratur.

The work at the temple is not described further because that would detract from the peaceful unity of the scene. For the interpretation of *inter se*, see Madvig, *Opuscula academica*, I.

11. I.454: *reginam opperiens.* The same is stated:

    I.494:   Haec dum Dardanio Aeneae miranda videntur
             Dum stupet obtutuque haeret defixus in uno,
             Regina ad templum. . . . incessit.

    Dido enters while Aeneas is wholly concentrated on the reliefs. Heinze (p. 319 f.) has observed that Vergil's principle is to open a sequence of action with a sudden strong jolt: e.g., the entrance of the Sibyl interrupts Aeneas' contemplation of the temple of Daedalus in Book VI.

12. Venus' words (I.535 f.), which awaken sympathy with Dido, both in the reader and Aeneas, have already paved the way for love. It might be said that Venus favored this love from the very beginning. See pp. 67–68.

13. The important statements are p. 362 f. "Vergil puts more emphasis on what his persons feel and want than on what they do. He prefers to evoke in the audience the illusion of sympathetic feeling rather than of physical sensation."—"The sentiments of the acting persons are suggested by the story without being spoken of in so many words. Vergil never tells anything without directing our attention to these sentiments through tone and color if not by more direct means. He has put himself into the soul of his persons and tells the story accordingly."

14. Cf. Donatus' description *sermone tardissimus* and his remark that Vergil had written only a few verses a day.

15. *Tacitum* is Vergil's own significant addition. Scaliger on *"pertemptant: Metaphora sumpta a citharoedis."* In *per-*

temptant we have a light, quick touch. Probus' irony is completely unjustified. Cerda's keen Spanish nose has noted an erotic nuance: *"Eodem verbo significari titillationem istam amoris blandam, quo in Georgicis titillatio equi appetentis coitum":*

Nonne vides, ut tota tremor pertemptet equorum corpora?

Quo satis apparet huic verbo hanc esse amoris et blanditi-arum potestatem.

His explanation is not so far-fetched after all.

16. Sainte-Beuve is wrong when he remarks reprovingly that in contrast to Nausicaa, Dido had no mother to rejoice in her daughter's glamor.

17. The moment of Dido's first meeting with Aeneas is elevated by a simile stressing his beauty (I.588 after *Ody.* 6.229).

18. The manner in which the meeting with the goddess of love is presented suggests the erotic sphere, preparing the meeting with Dido. Especially:

> I.318: Namque umeris de more habilem suspenderat arcum
> Venatrix dederatque comam diffundere ventis
> Nuda genu nodoque sinus collecta fluentis.

This, too, is an echo of Nausicaa.

19. One may recall the view of Macrobius (*Sat.* VI.1.6): "Judicio transferendi et imitandi consecutus est, ut quod apud illum legerimus alienum melius hic quam ubi natum est sonare miremur."

20. There are some fine remarks on the secrets of composition in Hugo von Hofmannsthal's essay "Gärten," in *Die Berüh-rung der Sphären* (1931). He says: "We gradually return to where our grandfathers were; to feel the harmony of the things of which a garden is composed; that they are harmonious and have something to say to each other; that there is a soul in their life together, just as the words of the poem and the colors of the picture glow at each other, make each other live. . . . The gardener does the same with his shrubs and plants that the poet does with words: he puts them to-

gether in such a way that they seem new and strange and at the same time mean themselves for the first time. The composition or separation is all; for a shrub or a plant is by itself neither high nor low, neither noble nor ignoble, neither ample nor slim: only its surroundings make it so. The wall which it overshadows, the bed from which it rises give it form and mien. All of this is ABC, but I fear it might nevertheless seem that I am talking of sophisticated things."

21. *foribus divae* refers to the door of the adyton, see Turnebus *Adv.* 10.11. Servius quotes Varro *De lingua Latina:*

In aedibus locus patulus relinquebatur sub divo, qui si non erat relictus, set contectus, appellabatur testudo.

22. This is stressed by the poet himself:

Musa mihi causas memora, quo numine laeso
Quidve dolens regina deum tot volvere casus
Insignem pietate virum, tot adire labores
Impulerit. Tantaene animis caelestibus irae?

23. I.462:   Sunt hic etiam sua praemia laudi
Sunt lacrimae rerum et mentem mortalia tangunt.

This, too, prepares Aeneas for love.
24. Misunderstood by Heinze, p. 138, n. 2. Apollonius' *Hypsipyle* (I.730) and his *Medea* (III.1008) may be Vergil's models, but the meaning of the gesture has changed.
25. Her love, too, springs from her humanity in Terence's sense: "*Homo sum, nihil humani a me alienum puto.*" Quintilian (IX.2,64) remarks to IV.550: "*Quamquam enim de matrimonio queritur Dido, tamen huc erumpit ejus affectus, ut sine thalamis vitam non hominum putet sed ferarum.*"
26. Heinze, p. 140 f.
27. Heinze, p. 141.
28. See p. 150 f.

29. IV.3:   Multa viri virtus animo multusque recursat
gentis honos, haerent infixi pectore voltus.
   11:   Quem sese ore ferens, quam forti pectore et armis,
Credo equidem nec vana fides genus esse deorum.

Degeneres animos timor arguit. Heu quibus ille
Iactatus fatis, quae bella exhausta canebat.

30. *Die Prosaischen Schriften gesammelt,* Erster Band (Berlin, 1917), p. 89.
31. In the words *"aut antiqua Tyros,"* Vergil characteristically expresses his own feelings through those of the Carthaginians. They remember Tyre as he remembers Troy.
32. See Callimachus' hymn on the death of Arsinoe.
33. Already emphasized in Venus' words to Aeneas:

    I.344: Huic conjunx Sychaeus erat . . . magno miserae dilectus amore.

34. Not as Servius, Heinze, and Pease understand *ignarae sc. amoris reginae.* The 'imitations' of Silius (VIII.100): *Heu sacri vatum errores,* and Apuleius (*Met.* X.2): *heu medicorum ignarae mentes,* only go to prove that the words were already misunderstood in antiquity. *Vatum* must be *Genetivus objectivus.* See VIII.626. Henry points out that *ignarus* never appears in Vergil with a *Genetivus subjectivus.* See also XI.501 for Turnus' tragic blindness.
35. Quintilian says that nothing that offends the anteroom of the ear is admitted to the audience of feeling and reason.
36. Gundolf, *Shakespeare und der deutsche Geist* (Bonn, 1911), p. 238.
37. Servius remarks: *"Satis perite loquitur; nam secundum Etruscam disciplinam nihil tam incongruum nubentibus quam terrae motus vel caeli."*
38. Cf. IV.490 f., for the priestess of the Hesperides and VI.255 f., for Hecate. In contrast, Apollonius III.1218 f.
39. It is perhaps no accident that after Dido's suicide Fama rages through the city like a Menad, glorying in her victory.
40. When this befalls her, permanent grief for her lost pride settles on her, especially after Aeneas' decision to leave. In deep sorrow she looks back on the image of her lost self:

                          Te propter eundem
    Exstinctus pudor et qua sola sidera adibam
    Fama prior.

41. When Allecto hits Turnus with the torch, "the torch smoking in black light" appears as the attribute of a fury.

42. See William Bedell Stanford, *Ambiguity in Greek Literature* (Oxford 1939).

43. This was considered a *locus indissolubilis* in antiquity and still remains unexplained. I tend to agree with Henry's interpretation: *morte Abl. temp. = in morte.*

44. She knows this very well herself:

> Per ego has lacrimas dextramque tuam te
> Quando aliud mihi jam miserae nihil ipsa reliqui (314)

45. The soul of the dead finds peace only through vengeance.

46. On the subject of the retarding moment as a necessary element of tragedy see also p. 95. The magic executed by Dido on the advice of the priestess (478) belongs here as well as the magic rites (512–516). See pp. 124 ff. for the duel between Aeneas and Turnus. For a different explanation of lines 512–516 see Heinze, p. 142 n.1.

47. The point is emphasized by a symbolic gesture taken from Odysseus' adventure with the Lestrygonians.

48. The mention of the priestess also has a symbolic relation: she is not only a witch but an intermediary between the lands of the living and the dead.

49. Goethe applied this ancient notion in his biography of Winckelmann when speaking of Winckelmann's end.

50. The event itself is not described, only its effect. Similarly, in *Georgics* IV, in the case of the death of Eurydice the serpent's bite is omitted and in *Aeneid* II the end of Laocoon is not described.

51. Goethe to Schiller, April 8, 1797.

52. Especially Aeneas' guilt concerning Dido. I wonder whether Conway is right when he understands the curses which come true for Aeneas as a proof of Vergil's chivalrous thinking. Heinze assents (p. 274 n. 1 and p. 136 n. 2). It is possible that Vergil thinks differently from modern men on this point. VI.463–464: *"nec credere quivi/hunc tantum tibi me discessu ferre dolorem"* would support this. Aeneas' main

guilt is that he forgets his task and makes no effort for his glory: *"nec super ipse sua molitur laude laborem."*

CHAPTER II: 3. TURNUS

1. Not only from lack of faith in the words of the priestess as Heinze suggests (p. 189).
2. It would be interesting to undertake a study on this type of triple scenes. An early example is Helena's conversation with Aphrodite in the third book of the *Iliad*. The same scheme appears in Palinurus' conquest by Somnus. The dialogue between Dido and Aeneas in Book IV also belongs here. This type is the natural expression of a climax characteristic of the drama.
3. *Iliad* 21.326.
4. Cp. the use of *fervere, fervidus, fervor*. So IX.66: *"ignescunt irae."* IX.736: *"mens exaestuat ira."* Both passages refer to Turnus. Also *Iliad* 18.108 "his anger increases like smoke."
5. In Homer similes are rarely used in this manner.
6. Rightly pointed out by Heinze.
7. Overlooked by Heinze (p. 189), who therefore maintains that Turnus' first resistance is not wholly justified. See above ch. II, note 1.
8. See W. Ehlers, *RE*, s, v, Turnus: Vergil's meaning was unmistakable for his contemporaries; modern interpretation only could succumb to the danger of misunderstanding the peculiar national tendency and see in Turnus the image of a tragic hero.
9. Heinze bases his view on Nettleship, *Lectures and Essays*, p. 108 f.
10. The wording is taken from Friedrich, *Cato, Caesar und Fortuna bei Lucan, Hermes*, 1938, p. 402.
11. For the Sallust passage see Lämmli, "Sallusts Stellung zu Cato, Caesar, Cicero," *Museum Helveticum*, 1946, p. 105.
12. This feeling, alien to modern man, explains passages such as:

    I.378: Sum pius Aeneas.... fama super aethera notus
    VIII.131: Sed mea me virtus et sancta oracula divum conjunxere tibi;

X.829 (Aeneas to Lausus): Hoc tamen infelix miseram
solabere mortem,/Aeneae magni dextra cadis.

XI.688 (Camilla to Ornytus): Nomen tamen haud leve
patrum/Manibus hoc referes telo cecidisse Camillae.

XII.435 (Aeneas to Ascanius): Disce puer virtutem ex
me.

I have discussed above the importance of this quality for
Dido's fate. The often blamed vanity in Cicero's speeches
is connected with this basic attitude of antiquity. Heinze, on
the other hand, speaks of "sick ambition."

13. Jupiter upon his death:
X.468: Famam extendere factis hoc virtutis opus.
Sallust clearly gives expression to this attitude.

14. The tragedy of Turnus is stressed by another means. Allecto
says to him: *"Bella manu letumque gero."* This is tragic
ambiguity in so far as she is bringing death to Turnus himself. This is underscored by his violent start from the nightmare, described in stronger terms than in similar situations,
e.g., III.175 (Aeneas, after the Penates dream) or IV.280
(Aeneas, after the appearance of Mercury).

15. Cf. Latinus' words of warning at the beginning of the war.

VII.596: Te Turne nefas te triste manebit
Supplicium votisque deos venerabere seris,

the warnings in the assembly (XI.305) and the symbol of
tragic development following. In similar manner Dido's suffering is accompanied by bad omens. This relationship is
another proof that Turnus' fate is meant to be tragic.

16. For this see, e.g., VII.470: Se satis ambobus Teucrisque
venire Latinisque.

IX.148: Non armis mihi Volcani, non mille carinis
Est opus in Teucros.

When Turnus robs Pallas of his swordbelt, the poet declares:

X.501: Nescia mens hominum fati sortisque futurae
Et servare modum rebus sublata secundis.

The divided being of Turnus is expressed:

XII.667: Uno in corde pudor mixtoque insania luctu
Et furiis agitatus amor et conscia virtus.

Drances accuses him of *"Mores sinistros"* (XI.347), Venus calls him *"tumidus Marte secundo"* (X.21).

17. Heyne mistook the connection with Turnus' daemonic character, which constitutes the difference from Homer, when he criticized the passage: *"Ornatus sane verbis, sed ut rei miraculo fidem parum faciat."*

18. Elsewhere, too, Vergil's presentation borders on the fantastic and the miraculous, e.g., when he describes the legendary speed of Camilla (VII.808 f.), or the effect of Aeneas' spear surpassing even the thunderbolt in force (XII.921 f.) or the rock hurled by Turnus which twelve men could not lift.

19. The Chimaera has its place among the mythical monsters of Vergil's hell (VI.288).

20. In accordance with the poet's sense of symmetry and balance the book ends with Turnus' return to the purifying power of the friendly river which cleanses him of murder (IX.816 f.). For more examples of *framing* by related motifs, cf. Franz Bömer, *Rhein. Museum,* 92 (1944), 333 f.

21. Gislason, *Die Naturschilderungen und Naturgleichnisse in Virgils Aeneis* (diss. Münster, 1937), p. 89, already stressed the frequency of wild beast similes as characteristic of the description of Turnus.

22. Wild beast similes for the Trojans and their allies are rare. Pallas: morning star, VIII.589; violet or hyacinth, XI.67. Pandarus and Bitias: oaks, IX.679. Ascanius: gem and ivory, X.134. Only Tarchon, who kidnaps a horseman, is compared to an eagle carrying off a serpent, Arruns who treacherously kills Camilla, to a wolf who ignominiously retreats to the mountains, and Nisus in the drunkenness of murder, which later will cause the death of the heroic pair (through the helmet of Messapus), to a lion.

23. Homer has some beginning of the use of similes for the internalization of the story. Cp. Riezler, *Die Antike,* 12 (1936). But plastic reality comes first with him.

24. It is significant that Goethe banished this sphere from the *Achilleis.* There were to be no fights. For the *Achilleis* see

Otto Regenbogen, *Griechische Gegenwart* (Leipzig, 1942) and Karl Reinhardt, *Von Werken und Formen* (Godesberg, 1948), p. 311 f.

25. In the *aristeia* of Pallas, the bloodiest moment is the high point of the whole scene. When the hero cuts off the arm of Larides and the head of his twin, the admiration of the Arcadians rises to inspired fighting pitch. The *aristeia* of Nisus and Euryalus likewise culminates in wild murder.

26. Only one of the wounds listed by Heinze (p. 206) is from this book—XI.689. Book II also lacks such scenes. The fact that everything is grouped around Aeneas (and perhaps consideration for Dido) caused the poet to repress pictures of horror. The only death described in detail is Priam's and that is important as a transition for the fate of Anchises. Cf. Heinze, p. 208, n. 1 for the poet's reluctance to spell out horror. He didn't avoid it altogether though, as the death of Laocoon shows. Goethe considered this disgusting.

27. After Iliad 22.308. The simile fits Vergil's situation better: Turnus really darts upon his victim like an eagle, while Hector, far from reaching Achilles, is himself killed. Vergil characteristically adds the *lupus Martius*. A second wolf simile follows the first (IX.59) in order to intensify the impression of bloodthirstiness. To unify the tone of the book the images are again related.

28. I also regret the interruption after IX.76. In the midst of a dramatic development the prehistory of the ships is broadly related. The interruption of Aeneas' and Turnus' duel by the scene between Jupiter and Juno is more bearable, since it is more narrowly connected with the action. The object of the interruptions is, of course, to heighten the interest, a means employed by countless epic writers ever since.

29. Cf. X.758: Di Jovis in tectis iram miserantur inanem
Amborum et tantos mortalibus esse labores
and XII.503: Tanton placuit concurrere motu,
Juppiter, aeterna gentis in pace futuras?

30. They are the "pathetic" books in contrast to the less pathetic ones. See R. S. Conway, "The Architecture of the Epic,"

Harvard Lectures on the Vergilian Age (Cambridge, 1928), as quoted by Stadler, *Vergils Äneis* (Einsiedeln, 1942).

31. The external model is the scene in the *Iliad* where Menelaos lifts Patroclos' corpse (17.587 f.). See B. Schweizer, *Die Antike*, 14 (1938), 43 f.

32. The model is not Aeneas' rescue (*Iliad* 5.445), but Agenor's (*Iliad* 21.595).

33. 10.31, 13: "Imperatorem clarissimum gentis suae amiserant, socios belli.... in eadem fortuna videbant qua ipsi erant, nec suis nec externis viribus jam stare poterant, tamen bello non abstinebant: adeo ne infeliciter quidem defensae libertatis taedebat et vinci quam non temptare victoriam malebant."

34. A gesture more majestic than Homer's lashing tail.

35. Or may one think of the inner wound, the grief over Patroclos' death?

36. The argument that a motif has originated where it fits best, is erroneous. Again and again Vergil with his poetic tact does more with a motif than the poet whom he imitates. This error is connected with the misunderstanding of the "imitator," who in Roman literature is identical with the great poet. In many cases one could almost reverse the argument. See Reinhardt, *Sophocles*, p. 68.

37. Line of Furius Antias, selected by Nietzsche as his motto.

38. Just as for Achilles and Hector in the *Iliad* one may here recognize a counterpointed parallelism of the course of destiny (Schadewaldt).

39. IX.21: Sequar omina tanta.

   Juno stresses his piety:
   X.619: Tua larga
         saepe manu multisque oneravit limina donis.

40. Vergil's tendency to use even quiet moments for developing the action is clearly visible: the resistance to war begins with mourning at the tombs and in the city.

41. XI.411–418, 443: Nec Drances potius sive est haec ira deorum, Morte luat.

42. This is one of the similes where Vergil deviates least from Homer (*Iliad* 6.506 f.). There is perhaps more weight in *tandem* and *campoque potitus aperto*. Perhaps the thought that the stallion heads for the mares is also an addition, unless Homer's μετ' ἤθεα καὶ νόμον ἵππων means the same. This is also true of *luxurians*. Vergil has added it to stress the blind passion of the hero. Vergil characteristically closes with a splendid picture (*luduntque jubae per colla, per armos*) while Homer's simile ends less brilliantly.

43. Lavinia's charm, doubled by her grief (XII.64 f.) is one more reason for Turnus to fight. His love for Lavinia is treated with the same restraint as that of Aeneas for Dido. Love, unless hallowed through *pietas* into marriage and family, is less glorious than reprehensible for a Roman.

44. Cf. *Iliad* 19.16 also 1.200 and Hector 15.605: "Hector was mad as spear-shaking Ares, mad as a conflagration in some thick forest upon the mountains. There was foam on Hector's lips, his eyes blazed under the shaggy brows, the helmet shook violently on his temples." These verses stand nearer to the Vergil passage than those of Achilles' armament do. Also Daunus' sword, forged in the Stygian wave (XII.90) points to the hellish sphere.

45. *Georgics* III.224. Heyne compares Euripides, *Bacchae* 724 ταῦροι εἰς κέρας θυμούμενοι for *irasci in cornua*. Voss explains correctly: *Iram quasi colligere in cornua*.

46. The effect of the scene is lessened by the next six verses dealing with Aeneas' preparation for fighting. It may have been necessary to mention Aeneas because of the consent to the treaty. I, for one, cannot believe that this is the final formulation. The lines are perhaps *tibicines*, temporary props or later additions of Varius and Tucca. Especially suspect are the lines XII.107 f.:

> nec minus interea maternis saevus in armis,
> Aeneas acuit Martem et se suscitat ira.

These are inconsistent with his manner. While he is subject to passion and anger during the fight, it seems odd that he would talk himself into fury on the eve of the fight, all, as it were, for the sake of a parallel with Turnus.

47. Cf. XII.9,10,19,45,101. Hector's presumptuousness is stressed elsewhere. See Schadewaldt, *Iliasstudien* (1938), p. 106 f.; H. Gundert, *Neue Jahrbuecher* (1940), p. 225 f.

48. Aeneas concludes a treaty with his opponent, in contrast to Achilles who violently refuses to do so, *Iliad* 22.262: "Lions and men make no truce, wolves and lambs have no friendship. So there can be no love between you and me and there shall be no truce for us."

49. Overlooked by the commentators. The verse already occurs I.313, where it fits the cautious exploration of the unknown country. Here it also contrasts with the mighty line describing Aeneas' armament:

Sidereo flagrans clipeo et caelestibus armis.

50. Heinze (p. 212) praises the "fine observation" and wrongly, I feel, quotes Aristotle, *Nicomachean Ethics* III.10, 1116a 7.

51. *Demisso lumine.* I.561: *voltum demissa* has the same meaning of "shame" (cf. above p. 70). Similar words in the description of Marcellus show the sorrow of the doomed youth:
VI.862: Sed frons laeta parum et dejecto lumina voltu.
Like Dido, Turnus is marked for death:

IV.499: Haec effata silet, pallor simul occupat ora.
      644: Pallida morte futura.

And this is said about Cleopatra:

VIII.709: Illam inter caedes pallentem morte futura.

52. The simile as such is not Homeric, although shaped after Achilles' and Hector's rides into the fight (*Iliad* 20.499 and 11.534. The "bloody" dew might be a characteristic contamination of 11.53). Homer compares his heroes with Ares when the situation warrants it, Vergil does it to characterize them. Turnus in his splendor is compared to a god. Nobody else is given this honor except Aeneas and Dido. This marks Turnus as one of the three main persons.

53. It would be worthwhile to investigate the stylistic and compositional functions of the horse in Vergil as compared to that in Homer. Cf. the death of Mezentius (X.892 f.), where the prancing and rearing horse reminds one of the Amazon sarcophagus.

54. Examples can be found for such "interlocking" movement. *Aut radiantis imagine lunae* (VIII.23) follows the mood of the Tiber night scene. For the simile in VII.525 see above p. 31 f.

55. Perhaps there is influence of *Iliad* 5.87, where Diomedes' raging is described in the image of a winter river destroying bridges and fences round "fertile fields."

56. The development goes from this *abruptum agmen* and *abrupto sidere nimbus* to Aeneas' spear bringing doom to Turnus *atri turbinis instar* (XII.923).

57. The death of Aeneas' enemies is also less cruel elsewhere, e.g., X.313,317,322,326. On the other hand, Turnus, e.g., IX.698,749,770. XII.356,380.

58. This follows from the context. Turnus had been named immediately before IX.462.

59. Achilles wastes himself in longing for battle and war *Iliad* 1.491; 19.213; 13.746. Yet Schadewaldt is right when he remarks that Achilles' cruelty is an expression of his determination to have revenge.

60. Latinus' consent to Ilioneus (VII.259 f.) is considered a *foedus*.

   Cf. VIII.540: Poscant acies et foedera rumpant!
   XII.582: Bis jam Italos hostis, haec altera foedera rumpi.
   VII.595: Ipsi has sacrilego pendetis sanguine poenas.

61. XII.465: Nec pede congressos aequo nec tela ferentis
   Insequitur, solum densa in caligine Turnum
   Vestigat lustrans, solum in certamina poscit,

   according to the treaty. Rage seizes him only when Messapus' spear scrapes his crest.

62. Juno had no part in it (XII.134 f.).

63. This *letum informe* is a mark of the queen's unallayed evil,

not merely, as Heyne suggests, a mode of death usual in tragedy.

64. Heinze is mistaken (p. 212): "He allows himself to be separated from Aeneas half-knowingly until the old feeling of honor slowly reawakens in the face of his suffering men."

65. Related to the words in which Aeneas expresses his sense of life's tragedy. VI.721: Quae miseris lucis tam dira cupido? It is also an echo of the scene in the *Iliad* in which the same feeling finds moving expression in Zeus' words to the immortal horses of Achilles (*Iliad* 17.443): "Ah, poor things! Why did we give you to a mortal man like Peleus, when you are immortal and never grow old? To share the sorrows of miserable mankind? For I think there is no more miserable thing than man, of all creatures that breathe and move on the earth."

66. The words are related in pathos and function to Dido's *"et magna mei sub terras ibit imago."*

67. Juturna, in sisterly love, only thinks of her brother's life. Cf. Venus (X.42–46), whose words are not to be taken seriously, however.

68. Shame and glory as Hector's motives in the leave-taking from Andromache (6.441 f.).

69. Heinze suggests that only Saces "stirs up the old ambition in him."

70. 18.310: "Thus spoke Hector and the Trojans cheered his speech, in their folly, for Pallas Athene stole their sense away."

71. XII.694:   me verius unam
    Pro vobis foedus luere et decernere ferro.

72. The idea of Rome is expressed in the symbol of the immovable rock, IX.448:

    Dum domus Aeneae Capitoli immobile saxum
    Accolet imperiumque pater Romanus habebit.

73. His chance for success is improved because Aeneas is impeded by his wound.

74. Hector, 18.306 "I at least will never turn my back on battle!

I will stand up to meet him." 20.371: "I will meet him face to face, even if his hands are like fire, and his spirit like flashing steel."

75. Hector assumes a heroic attitude only after all hope is lost.

76. XII.865 f. Dido, too, sees a bird of death (IV.462).

77. This recalls Hector's vain watch for Deiphobos. He has been deceived by the goddess, while Juturna retreats on Jupiter's command.

78. P. 212. He seems to think that the contrast between Hector and Turnus favors the former, but the opposite is true.

79. In the words *seu corpus spoliatum lumine mavis* there is also the thought that the enemy will not want to be so cruel.

80. The last verse of the *Aeneid* seems to contain the idea of Turnus' restless, agonizing fate. This is not contradicted by the fact that the verse is a translation from Homer, perhaps used before Vergil. The poet intends to produce new effects from old forms. The same verse is used at Camilla's death to denote the end of a life that was restless fight.

81. The passion for fighting and the love for Lavinia are obliterated.

82. "The tragic conflict is all the more significant, the deeper and more alike the conflicting powers are," says Kierkegaard, *Der Reflex des antik Tragischen im modern Tragischen.*

CHAPTER III: 1: SYMBOLISM OF THE SEQUENCE OF MOOD.

1. With the exception of Servius Danielis' remark on XII.114: *Quia res perturbatae secuturae sunt, diem quoque cum fervore oriri facit.* Examples are collected by Ribbeck and Georgii.

2. The rescue from danger is reiterated symbolically when in the simile the cranes flee from the rain storms *sub nubibus atris* (X.264).

3. The morning star in the *Odyssey* rises when Odysseus reaches his island (13.93 f.).

4. The way in which Vergil handles Homer's poetry presupposes not only deep study, but the continuous presence of

all of Homer. As Dante knew Vergil, so Vergil knew
Homer. *Minantur* surpasses even these Homeric rocks.
"Threatening" rocks as symbol of the eerie are also found
in the Tartarus of the shield.

VIII.668:   Te Catilina minaci
                pendentem scopulo.

In the Dido book the skyscraping constructions and the
"threat" of the walls paint a sinister state:

IV.88:   Pendent opera interrupta minaeque
            Murorum ingentes aequataque machina caelo.

5. Robert Seymour Conway, *P. Vergili Maronis Aeneidos liber
   primus* (Cambridge, 1935) explains *horrenti:* "bristling and
   quivering," a typical example of the Vergilian economy of
   saying one thing by a word which is itself suggestive of
   another thing also. Note here the effect upon the spectator,
   who cannot help trembling too.
6. Sainte-Beuve: "Un beau et vaste mouvement de lumière
   dans le paysage, et qu'Homere lui-même a bien connu quand
   d'un mot il a peint le mont Pelion agitateur des feuilles." It
   is not, however, quite correct to say that Vergil made a
   whole forest out of Homer's one olive tree. The forest is
   already present in the Ithaca landscape of which the
   Phorcys harbor is part: *Ody.* 13.196, 246 f.
7. The words in the Harpy scene,

   III.229: In secessu longo sub rupe cavata
              Arboribus clausi circum atque horrentibus umbris

   are part of the gloomy coloring of the scene. The same is
   true of the description of the Amsanctus Valley, where Allecto travels to hell.

   VII.565: Densis hunc frondibus atrum
              Urget utrimque latus nemoris

8. Might the reverse be true and the lovely cave of the nymphs
   point forward to the love temptations awaiting Aeneas? Such
   irrational connections are not impossible in Vergil.

9. Scaliger: "versus ipsis aquis dulcior."

10. Homer has this sequence: the two cliffs, the olive tree, the cave. There is no question of a gradual quieting and brightening.

10a. *Die Naturschilderungen und Naturgleichnisse in Vergils Aeneis* (diss. Münster, 1937).

11. Norden (VI.749) sees Vergil's probable immediate model in the Orphic Hymn 57. Should he be right, which must remain doubtful, Vergil has reversed the order to achieve the gloomy character of the scene.

12. The energetic books, II, VI, VII, IX, X, XI, begin quietly enough; the quiet ones, I, V, VIII, begin energetically. The tragic books, IV and XII, are continuously passionate and fast.

13. This is the reason for the addition of the moon, not *Ody.* 4.45 as suggested by Mehmel, *Virgil and Apollonius Rhodius, Hamburger Arbeiten zur Altertumswissenschaft*, I (1940). Difficulties arise only if one assumes the influence of Lucretius (IV.211 f.). *Radiantis imagine lunae* refers to the moon, not to her reflection.

14. The reference to Helen in the Sibyl prophecy is a premonition of doom, VI.93:

    Causa mali tanti conjunx iterum hospita Teucris
    Externique iterum thalami.

    The same is true of the wine that Bitias spills, I.738 f. Cf. Apollonius I.472, where this same gesture expresses fatal hybris.

15. The conversation between Latinus and Ilioneus begins with the mention of Dardanus VII.195 *Dicite Dardanidae* and 205 f., and ends with Priam and his insignia now returning to Italy.

16. This is even truer if one considers the Libyan journey as immediately preceding Book VI as Vergil seems to have done. This conclusion derives from VI.338: *qui Libyco nuper cursu . . . exciderat puppi* which contradicts the report in Book V; Cp. Norden's commentary; Heinze, p. 146, 1. If Book IV is recited immediately before Book VI the reference is unmistakable.

17. Even the choice of the word *regina* refers to Dido. Ariadne was not a queen.

18. "Wouldn't it destroy the charm that is connected with such gatherings and wouldn't he be ridiculous among the Phaeacians or the Carthaginians who would mix philosophical conversations with the stories that are usual at banquets?"

19. "At the banquet of the chaste queen a philosophical song is very much in place; among the nymphs (where there are only women present) he sings of the trickery of Vulcan and Mars and of sweet deceit."

20. Venus on Dido's life:

> I.341: Longa est injuria, longae ambages
> IV.211: Femina quae nostris errans in finibus urbem . . . posuit
> = I.628: Me quoque per multos similis fortuna labores Iactatam hac demum voluit consistere terra.

In the underworld she wanders in a great forest, VI.450, *labores* of Aeneas: I.10, 241, 373, etc.

21. It would be an attractive task to write the history of these metaphors of Man. Did "wise" Vergil think of the Phoenician myth of Baal and Astarte? Cp. Heinrich Heine's *Die Nordsee* and Goethe's "Die Sonne kommt ein Prachterscheinen" from the *Westoestlicher Divan?* I do not seem to be able to find examples for the love between sun and moon in folklore, but there must be many.

22. Cp. IV.80:   Post ubi digressi lumenque obscura vicissim
>   Luna premit suadentque cadentia sidera somnos,
>   Sola domo maeret vacua.

There is an irrational connection between the moon who loses her light and the deserted queen, as there is one between moon and death.

23. Mehmel above, and M. H. Potter, *Classical Journal* (1926), place Aeneas' arrival in Carthage in the summer. I prefer autumn. Orion arises late from Nov. 29 until Dec. 8. See A. Constans, *Revue des Études Latines*, 13 (1935), 398 f. *Adsurgens* always refers to an hostile act. See Conway above.

24. Among the Greeks Sappho is an important predecessor of Vergil in this respect.

25. The art of inner "musical" movement is not limited to poetry. It may be found in Livy, as Klingner has shown (*Die
Antike*, I (1925), 95 f.).

CHAPTER III: 2. FORMS OF SEQUENCES OF MOOD.

1. "In Vergil's world one cannot escape the ideas of sea, tide,
waves." Stadler.
2. This is not simply a hysteron proteron, as the commentaries
say, but heightened emphasis. To bring the gods to Latium
is more than to found a city.
3. Gislason above has described the growing of the storm.
4. The climax of Venus' speech is in the exact middle:
I.241: quem das finem, rex magne, laborum?
So is the climax of Jupiter's speech, the founding of Rome,
I.275–277.
5. Venus' speech ends with the happy fate of Antenor to whom
a new home in Italy is granted. His successful journey is
contrasted with the fatal trip of Ajax Oileus mentioned by
Juno. Jupiter's speech ends with the picture of "furor impius" chained by Augustus.
6. The serene, sublime world of the gods serves here as in
Homer to light up the gloomy events, to intersperse points
of rest, where the painful movement resolves into Olympian
peace and seriousness into cheerful play. Such points are—
besides Iris' appearance—Neptune's ride after the seastorm,
his even more splendid ride in Book V, Venus' brilliant appearance in Books I and VIII.
7. This conversation also ends on a sweet light tone, in accordance with the mood development of the book:

I.691:   At Venus Ascanio placidam per membra quietem
          Inrigat et fotum gremio dea tollit in altos
          Idaliae lucos, ubi mollis amaracus illum
          Floribus et dulci adspirans complectitur umbra.

8. VIII.408.

INDEX

Acca, 35
Achilles, 112, 115, 122, 126,
    200n.38
Aeneas
    —and Dido, 47
    —and Hector, 36 f.
    —and Turnus, 15, 99 f.,
        101 f., 111, 117, 122,
        198n.21
    Christian traits, 53 f.
    duty, 39 f., 122
    feeling for tragedy, 50 f.
    "Historical" attitude, 38 f.
    stoicism, 45, 53 f.
    symbol of Augustan spirit,
        37
    symbol of idea of Rome, 18,
        117, 123 f., 178n.13
    symbol of a new heroism, 99,
        115, 123 f.
    sympathy and love, 40, 43 f.,
        50, 54 f., 58, 106
Aeneid
    battlescenes, 100 f.
    classical work of art, 2, 16,
        32, 36, 70, 173
    composition
        Aeneas and Turnus in
            countermovement, 111
        Dido and Turnus in
            countermovement, 136
        bk. I and VII in counter-

movement, 33, 167
    concentration, 42, 116,
        200n.40
    contrast, 16–18, 47, 61,
        97 f., 116 f., 120, 146,
        158
    correspondence of Dido's
        and Turnus' books, 97,
        110–11, 113 f., 129,
        133, 136–37, 197n.15,
        204n.66
    dramatic and epic ele-
        ments, 24, 32 f., 67, 103
    expression of ordered
        thought, 16, 37 f.
    parts and the whole, 24,
        32 f., 81, 114, 157 f.,
        192n.20
    tripartition, 37, 172
    connected symbols, 32 f.,
        67, 81 f., 103, 118–
        19, 121 f., 147,
        203n.56
    sequence of mood
        assimilation of forms to
            the sequence of mood,
            53–55, 59 f., 109,
            128 f., 170, 173,
            190n.6, 199n.27,
            203n.54, 203n.56
        conclusions, 38, 47, 67,
            80, 158 f., 181n.3

Aeneid (*continued*)
continuum, 142 f., 170
high point of, 157 f.
illumination, 165 f.
images and pictures, 36,
103 f., 148, 170 f.,
190n.6
mounting progression, 29,
30 f., 33 f., 41, 102 f.,
110, 157 f., 167 f.
recurring waves, 157 f.
softening and calming, 35,
89, 164 f.
unit and unity of feeling,
146
similes, 23, 31 f., 45–
47, 60 f., 67 f., 77 f.,
91 f., 98 f., 103, 109 f.,
117 f., 146 f., 170
symbol and *Allegorie,* 21 f.
symbolic similes and images
animals, 98
Apollo, 67 f., 152
Atlas, 143 f.
bird of death, 133
cauldron, 91 f.
Daedalus, 149 f.
Danaids, 149
Diana, 62 f., 152
fire, 103
landscapes, 142 f.
Maenad, 30
matron at work, 170
mountain ash, 46
oak, 45
Paris-Helen, 148
princeps rei publicae, 20–
22
reflections of light, 146 f.,
203n.54

river with corpses, 147,
181n.3
ship, 48
stallion, 102, 147
stone avalanche, 130
sun and moon, 152 f.
wind and storm, 13, 31 f.,
33, 48 f., 119, 121 f.,
147, 203n.54
works of art, 148 f.
wounded deer, 79 f., 152
wounded lion, 109
symbolism
symbolic expressions and
ambiguities, 48 f., 154,
180n.28, 184n.18
symbolic figures, *see*
Aeneas, Antony, Au-
gustus, Cacus, Dido,
Juno, Jupiter, Turnus
symbolic gestures, 47, 107,
171, 195n.47
themes
civil War, 14, 95
conquest of the demonic,
18 f., 22, 90
interpretation of history,
1, 15
interpretation of life, 1,
24, 48
interpretation of politics,
15, 18, 73 f.
Odyssey and *Iliad,* 24 f.
Rome and Carthage, 14 f.
Rome and Italy, 14, 104,
123
tragic, 15, 24, 38–39, 59,
105, 125
Aeolus, 19, 177n.9
Aeschylus, 112

Ajax, 108, 125
Alexander, 177n.8
Allecto, 28 f., 91, 129
Amata, 15, 29, 112, 124,
    179n.22
Amphibology, 83, 85, 191n.14,
    195n.43
Anchises, 150
Andromache, 36, 42, 150
Antenor, 150
Antony, 18, 21–22, 188n.39
Apelles, 177n.8
Apollonius Rhodius, 7, 14, 77,
    113, 146, 153
Aristotle, 53, 82, 180n.31
Art, interpretation of, 4 ff.
Ascanius, 29, 94, 163
Atlas, 143
Auctoritas majorum, 8
Augustan Age, 9 f., 21, 37
Augustine, St., 18, 46 f., 54, 73
Augustus, 18, 21, 23, 86

Baudelaire, 73
Bergson, 5
Boecklin, 47
Burckhardt, 39, 73

Cacus, 22
Callimachus, 196n.2
Camilla, 35, 101 f., 117–18,
    169, 205n.80
Caravaggio, 156
Catiline, 21, 28
Cato Censorius, 189n.39
Cato Uticensis, 20
Christianity, 40, 53 f.
Cicero, 21, 23, 57, 178n.18
Cleanthes, 177n.6
Cleopatra, 35, 189n.39

Croce, 5
crispare, 202n.49
cura, 184n.15
Curtius, E. R., 11, 16

Dante, 7, 11, 28, 94, 205n.4
Daedalus, 149 f.
Dardanids, 30, 149
Dehmel, 94
Dido
    —and Aeneas, *see* Aeneas
    —and Cleopatra, 194n.39
    —and Medea, 77
    —and Turnus, *see* Turnus
    conscious of guilt, 85, 87
    duty, 39, 85, 87
    exile, 150
    humanity, 70, 85
    love of self, 53, 82 f.
    piety, 70
    symbol of Carthage, 74 f., 89
    symbol of the demonic, 18,
        99
    symbol of a loving woman,
        88 f.
    tension in the character of,
        57 f., 100
    tragedy of, 70 ff., 77, 80,
        82 f., 87 f., 90, 194n.34
Diomedes, 111, 150
Discordia, 29, 163
Donatus, 7, 191n.14
Drances, 109

Eliot, T. S., 176n.11
Ennius, 9, 29, 31, 103 f.
Eteocles, 112
Euripides, 30, 77
Euryalus, 15, 36, 93–94, 102
Evander, 15, 59, 86, 150

Fama, 194n.39
Furius Antias, 200n.37
furor impius, 18 f., 93, 95, 163

Gellius, 7, 62, 188n.38
Goethe, 4, 6, 15, 24, 32, 57, 80,
        90, 100, 162, 172,
        176n.3, 187n.30,
        195n.49, 199n.26,
        208n.21
Grillparzer, 57
Gundolf, 80, 178n.13

Hebbel, 2, 15
Hector, 36, 64, 107, 132 f., 184,
        200n.38
Hegel, 73, 123
Heine, 47, 208n.21
Helena, 196n.2
Helenus, 36, 150
Hoelderlin, 184n.19
Hofmannsthal, 7, 67, 73,
        192n.20
Homer
    —and Vergil, 1, 7, 25 f., 36,
        38–41, 46, 81–82, 92,
        141, 147, 156 f.,
        209n.6
    Iliad and *Odyssey,* 13, 39, 43
    Homeric and Vergilian
        similes, 46, 63, 81, 92,
        99, 119, 121 f., 161,
        199n.27
    preservation of Homer in
        the *Aeneid,* 7
Horace, 9, 21, 49
Humboldt, 175n.2

impotentia, 30
inanis, 186n.28
Iopas, 150 f., 166

Iris, 35, 89, 129
iustitia, 27
Iwanow, 176n.4

Juno
    symbol of Carthage, 15
    symbol of the demonic, 18
Jupiter
    symbol of the idea of Rome,
        17 f.
    symbol of *serenitas,* 17
    symbol of the ordering mind,
        16–17, 177n.9
Juturna, 124, 127

Kant, 40
Kierkegaard, 205n.82

Laocoön, 16, 199n.26
Latinus, 15, 33 f., 112, 124
Lausus, 15, 35, 93, 106
Lavinia, 112
Lessing, 188n.37
Livius, 109, 209n.25
Lucan, 101

Macrobius, 7, 151
Marcus Aurelius, 57
Menelaos, 200n.31
Mezentius, 15, 35, 95, 106,
        202n.53
Mommsen, 123
mos maiorum, 9

Naevius, 9
Neptune, 19
Nietzsche, 69, 182n.10,
        184n.19, 200n.37
Nisus, 35, 94, 102

Oedipus, 61
Opera, 176n.1, 176n.2

Orion, 208n.23
Orontes, 40
Ortega y Gasset, 156
ostentatio, 56

Palinurus, 184n.17
Pallas, 35, 49, 93–94, 106
Panaitios, 54, 57
Patroclus, 107, 133
Penthesilea, 147, 164, 190n.6
Petrarch, 187n.30
pietas, 40, 150, 178n.11
Pindar, 157
Plato and Platonism, 23, 129
Poetry and Philosophy, 24,
        57 f.
Pollio, 139
Probus, 62 f.

Quintilian, 194n.35

Raphael, 177n.9
Revenge, 86
Ribera, 156
Rolland, Romain, 176n.2
Roman duty, 39 f.
Roman feeling for time, 38 f.
Rome, idea of, 23, 123
Rousseau, 182n.10

Sainte-Beuve, 7, 19, 34, 62,
        175n.8, 177n.9,
        192n.16, 206n.6
Sallust, 21, 94
Sappho, 208n.24
Scaliger, 7, 63, 190n.8, 206n.9
Schelling, 57
Schiller, 15, 32, 40, 67, 159
Seneca, 45, 56, 101
serenitas, 17

Servius, 5, 25, 46 f., 83, 137,
        139, 151, 183n.11,
        194n.37
Sibyl, 179n.24
Silvia, 29
Sophocles, 61, 108, 125,
        190n.3
Staiger, 180n.32
Statius, 176n.1
Stoa, 45, 54 f., 128, 177n.6,
        182n.10
stridere, 186n.26

Tacitus, 189n.39
Taine, 9 f.
Theocritus, 7, 144
Tolumnius, 124
Turnebus, 193n.21
Turnus
   —and Aeneas, *see* Aeneas
   —and Dido, 97, 110–11,
        113 f., 129, 133, 136 f.,
        197n.15, 204n.66
   —and Hector, 107, 114 f.,
        124, 127, 129, 132
   conscious of guilt, 117, 130
   not Enemy of the State, 93 f.,
        124
   excess of passion, 112,
        197n.16
   fire as symbol of, 103
   gentleness, 107
   humanity, 184n.17
   love, 201n.43
   love of self, 53, 94 f.
   piety, 96, 111
   stoicism, 128
   symbol of the demonic, 18,
        93–96, 113
   symbol of Homeric heroism,
        92, 115

Turnus (*continued*)
  symbol of the Italians, 104,
    123
  tragedy of, 39, 91 f., 95, 107,
    114 f., 125, 136

Valéry, 184n.19
Velásquez, 156
Venus, 16, 204n.67
Vergil
  contrasts within, 100
  essence of, 50
  feeling for tragedy, 50
  interpreter of history, 123 f.

  mediator between antique
    and medieval world,
    53 f., 58
  religiosity, 72 f., 172
  significance for the history
    of poetry, 2 f., 155 f.
Vesta, 163
Vico, 5
Vossler, 175n.3

Winckelmann, 177n.9
Woelfflin, 32
Wolf, F. A., 32

Selected Ann Arbor Paperbacks
Works of enduring merit

AA 1   **THE WRITER AND HIS CRAFT**   Roy W. Cowden, ed.
AA 2   **ELIZABETHAN PLAYS AND PLAYERS**   G. B. Harrison
AA 3   **THE INTELLECTUAL MILIEU OF JOHN DRYDEN**   Louis I. Bredvold
AA 6   **RICHARD CRASHAW**   Austin Warren
AA 11   **LITERATURE AND PSYCHOLOGY**   F. L. Lucas
AA 12   **THIS WAS A POET: EMILY DICKINSON**   George Frisbie Whicher
AA 16   **SHAKESPEARE AT WORK, 1592-1603**   G. B. Harrison
AA 26   **RONSARD: PRINCE OF POETS**   Morris Bishop
AA 32   **THE SONG OF ROLAND**   Translated by C. K. Scott Moncrieff
AA 33   **RAGE FOR ORDER**   Austin Warren
AA 36   **NEW BEARINGS IN ENGLISH POETRY**   F. R. Leavis
AA 40   **THE SUBLIME**   Samuel H. Monk
AA 43   **LITERATURE AND REVOLUTION**   Leon Trotsky
AA 46   **THE ART OF LITERATURE**   Arthur Schopenhauer
AA 58   **SEBASTOPOL**   Leo Tolstoi
AA 63   **POEMS FROM THE GREEK ANTHOLOGY**   Translated by Kenneth Rexroth
AA 64   **THE SATYRICON—PETRONIUS**   Translated by William Arrowsmith
AA 68   **AUBREY'S BRIEF LIVES**   John Aubrey
AA 70   **SCENES FROM THE BATHHOUSE And Other Stories of Communist Russia**   M. Zoshchenko
AA 81   **THE LOYALTIES OF ROBINSON JEFFERS**   Radcliffe Squires
AA 82   **MILTON'S KNOWLEDGE OF MUSIC**   Sigmund Spaeth
AA 85   **THE COMPLETE POETRY**   Catullus
AA 87   **THE CLOUD MESSENGER**   Kalidasa
AA 89   **THE INTERIOR DISTANCE**   Georges Poulet
AA 91   **THE BOW AND THE LYRE: The Art of Robert Browning**   Roma A. King, Jr.
AA 101 **CONTEMPORARY FRENCH POETRY**   Alexander Aspel and Donald Justice, ed.
AA 102 **TO THE YOUNG WRITER**   A. L. Bader, ed.
AA 113 **CHEKHOV AND OTHER ESSAYS**   Leon Shestov
AA 116 **GREEK ORATIONS**   W. Robert Connor, ed.
AA 117 **THE STORY OF THE ILIAD**   E. T. Owen
AA 125 **THE STRUCTURE OF COMPLEX WORDS**   William Empson
AA 128 **CAN THESE BONES LIVE**   Edward Dahlberg
AA 132 **PARADISE LOST AND THE SEVENTEENTH CENTURY READER**   B. Rajan
AA 134 **THE WIFE OF HIS YOUTH**   Charles W. Chesnutt
AA 135 **THE SKALDS**   Lee M. Hollander
AA 138 **ELIZABETHAN POETRY**   Hallett Smith
AA 140 **THE RECOGNITION OF EMILY DICKINSON**   Caesar R. Blake and Carlton F. Wells, eds.
AA 141 **SOUND AND FORM IN MODERN POETRY**   Harvey Gross
AA 142 **THE ART OF F. SCOTT FITZGERALD**   Sergio Perosa
AA 143 **THE ULYSSES THEME**   W. B. Stanford
AA 144 **SIR THOMAS BROWNE**   Frank Livingstone Huntley
AA 145 **THE MASTERPIECE**   Emile Zola
AA 146 **STORY PATTERNS IN GREEK TRAGEDY**   Richmond Lattimore
AA 147 **THE MARROW OF TRADITION**   Charles W. Chesnutt
AA 149 **THE MAJOR THEMES OF ROBERT FROST**   Radcliffe Squires
AA 150 **YOUNG CHERRY TREES SECURED AGAINST HARES**   André Breton
AA 152 **FOUR COMEDIES—ARISTOPHANES**   William Arrowsmith, ed.
AA 153 **THREE COMEDIES—ARISTOPHANES**   William Arrowsmith, ed.
AA 154 **THE PHILOSOPHY OF SURREALISM**   Ferdinand Alquié
AA 156 **THE CONJURE WOMAN**   Charles W. Chesnutt
AA 159 **TRANSCENDENTALISM AND ITS LEGACY**   Myron Simon and Thornton H. Parsons, eds.
AA 161 **PARTIAL PORTRAITS**   Henry James
AA 163 **SELECTED WRITINGS**   Gérard de Nerval Translated by Geoffrey Wagner
AA 164 **THE RECOGNITION OF HERMAN MELVILLE**   Hershel Parker, ed.
AA 168 **THE RECOGNITION OF EDGAR ALLAN POE**   Eric W. Carlson, ed.
AA 170 **THE ART OF VERGIL**   Viktor Pöschl

For a complete list of Ann Arbor Paperback titles write:
THE UNIVERSITY OF MICHIGAN PRESS ANN ARBOR